Stalag Luft III, Colonel Fuller, a dual-national family, international travel and ghosts

By

Matthew L. Fuller

Introduction

This book briefly summarises the international and unusual lives of my Dad, Col. James Fuller, and mother, Jean and Family, across a broad spectrum of experience and vast cultural differences between Europe and America and beyond. War, authentic travel, strange/true crime/paranormal events, brushes with death and wartime characters, knowing movie stars, and even talking with kings fill these pages with echoes from the past and more, with some comedy thrown in.

James Fuller was a war veteran of World War II and Korea. He became a prisoner at the infamous Stalag Luft III, the German World War Two Prison Camp made famous by the daring escape of March 1944 and subsequent Hollywood film and won the Purple Heart. Dad and Mum met in the 1950s in England and had a happy but sometimes turbulent life together that spanned the decades. The first quarter of this book describing his early life and the war years is written by Dad posthumously through me, and I come in there with a discussion of past events and interjections from him and others throughout. This book is, in part, a war story and part of a family story. It also touches on some famous relatives' lives. Dad was probably one of the first men in Alaska to help decipher the facts of the attack on Pearl Harbour, and at first, he wasn't believed and reprimanded. These events would set up his involvement directly in WWII in the European theatre as a pilot and radio specialist and a harrowing account of his being shot down over Germany and spending time at Stalag Luft III, The Great Escape Camp. Throughout his military career, he met such diverse people as admirals and actors, plus an Indian professor with aristocratic connections and a family friend. He wasn't always a conventional person, with a sense of humour and manner that could get him into difficulties. Mum was smart and good-looking but put her career on hold to look after seven children in the United States and England. My uncles also served in the war, and I have written down a few stories heard from them directly here.

The family had adventures along the way that were fun and productive but also that could be serious and turbulent, as, with any family, one assumes! These pages also contain events in the lives of the extended Fuller and Holder family in the United States, Britain, and Europe and friends along the way. A trip down memory lane of England and the USA from the past and lost pockets of time unique to a mid-Atlantic family. It is also a travel document that includes a road trip to India via Afghanistan! It encompasses subjects such as the paranormal as mentioned that seems to follow us, as well as family life in the US and beyond and characters at home and abroad (wherever that is); ergo, it is also an account of an international group never knowing which country they were to settle in, but hopefully enjoying the ride.

I hope you find it interesting.

Contents

Chapter 1

A Fuller Tennessee History

James Allen Fuller was born in a small town in rural East Tennessee to a family involved in the road haulage industry in Maryville, just a little east of the Great Smoky Mountains National Park. He spent most of his boyhood on the outskirts of this town, attending school and doing most of the things a lad of his age would do, chatting up the local girls and exploring the mountains and the rich nature contained therein. Farming and logging were the primary industries, and time off for recreation was greatly appreciated; the work was hard.

Mum was born a world away, in the heart of one of the most populous and influential Western cities, London. Born in Shoreditch in what can be classified as the East End of London, to Elsie Holder, milliner and later landlady of a Public House-The Enterprise, and Thomas Holder, carpenter/cabinet maker, vintner and later Soldier in WWI. My Mother's early years would be happy, cycling on her bike around Central London. Still, later she was embroiled in the bombing of London in WWII and sent away for a short time to the country as one of the millions sent away as evacuees before quickly wanting to come home! After the war, Mum emigrated briefly to Canada to work as a psychiatric nurse before returning home for family commitments. My family and I have completed a short study of our ancestors in the United States. I shall first mention some of our history and characters, most notably in Eastern Tennessee and the Great Smoky Mountains.

One roguish ancestor in the USA includes William Allen Fuller, a Western & Atlantic Railroad conductor during the American Civil War era. He was noted for his role in the 1862 Great Locomotive Chase, a daring sabotage mission and raid conducted by soldiers of the Union in northern Georgia.

Fuller's determined pursuit prevented the Union agents from driving a captured train north to Tennessee and the Union lines. The unusual and 'fun' element of this was that he moved this train backwards through the chase!

My Dad's Great Uncle, Tom Sexton, was a famous late-nineteenth-century preacher. He moved around the South with his family and started drinking at an early age. This and other matters partially added to his desire to become a minister and help others later on in his life.

He finally moved to Maryville in Tennessee, set up a blacksmith shop in town, and settled down. But unfortunately, drinking was still a feature of his life. So he turned to the Bible and became an itinerant preacher, moving around Tennessee, Virginia, North Carolina and Kentucky to try and ween himself off the booze. On his 'journey of enlightenment,' he wrote 'From The Anvil To The Pulpit-an autobiography. The 'hell and brimstone preacher' still took to a nip occasionally, but it never impeded his lack of enthusiasm in religious matters. Sexton's sermons were similar to the modern stand-up comic because he liked to spice up his sermons with plenty of laughs. He is said to have a theory that if he could make his congregation laugh, he could persuade them to attend church more often. On one occasion, Sexton was walking down the street in Knoxville when he passed an intoxicated man. The man recognized Sexton and called to him-"I'll bet you don't remember me". "I don't believe I do", Sexton replied. "I am the one you saved at the meeting last night," the man said."It must have been me that saved you because it surely couldn't have been the lord", Sexton responded. Sexton died in the 1920s.

Summers in Tennessee were usually hot and humid; relief was granted by swimming and perhaps the odd bottle of Coca-Cola from the ice box after chores. In some ways, it was a Tom Sawyer life. Winters could often be cold with snow, especially in the higher elevations. The Fall is a time for beauty and the changing colour of the leaves, attracting many tourists nowadays searching for nature outside the big cities and suburban lifestyles. Recreation would include swimming, as mentioned, or just larking in the Little River that flows into the Mountains past Maryville and Walland on to Townsend and the Y Fork (known as the 'Y'), where it then 'gets in deep' to the mountains with rapids and on to Gatlinburg, which was a small and sleepy lumber town then. It was not the entertainment mecca it would become in the later 20th Century. If you were smart, you could find an old tyre and float it down as far as you wanted with you on top. Nowadays, it is called 'tubing', and you buy or hire rubber rings to do the same thing.

From an early age, Dad was interested in radio and communications to keep him away from monotonous chores and school work! There was a huge pecan tree in one of his boyhood homes in Maryville. Dad was always thinking about new ways to communicate with the world outside his house and far-off places. In an attempt to get better reception from the crystal radio, he devised and built it himself; he strung an antenna array from the tree to the house and nearly broke his neck. The local squirrel population must have thought of him as an alien, having not been party to this type of scene previously in the coming new age of technology. Nevertheless, the family and locals were thrilled, listening to the 'new sound' of old Hollywood radio programming of mystery, intrigue, crime, and horror.

The local General Store owner would give him extra sweets from the colossal glass jars on the still Edwardian shelves at no charge for his ingenuity and braveness in climbing that tree in the first place.

On one occasion, James Fuller, as a child, was run over by a Model T Ford in the early days of motoring in the United States. He could remember being in a semi-conscious state and the adults around him thinking he might not pull through, and he always remembered that. He did survive however, and the story continued.

Chapter 2

Tennessee Family, The Alcoa Aluminum Factory or the Military

Before the Fuller Meat Packing business became viable in later years, Dad had to choose between working at the famous Alcoa Aluminum Plant or having an adventure. He chose the adventure.

My Grandfather Ben Fuller had remarried, and half brothers and sisters were introduced.

Dad's birth mother had died, and there was some friction between his stepmother and family, as is very often the case when possible rivalry and differences occur between half sisters and brothers (which I guess could be said of natural brothers and sisters, but you lived with them since birth, and were more used to their foibles.) They were on reasonably friendly terms most of the time, but Dad had a wanderlust to leave and 'find his fortune' as they say. Dad also had a full sister, Gladys, who was quite a character and is mentioned in the upcoming stories. I never met many of the other family members, only a handful.

I would like to mention one here. Dad's half brother (Theodore) and his wife Nancy lived in an old Victorian House on the Little River in Townsend, Tennessee. You had to cross an old turn of the century iron bridge which spanned the river to get to the house, and it swung quite precariously and appeared rusty on the outside. However, it had stood the test of time thus far, and I guess it was safe! Ted was a schoolteacher at the local high school.

On one occasion in the mid-1960s, he had noticed a man sitting by the river and staring out in contemplation. He appeared well dressed, and as Ted was friendly and he asked how he was; "Bet this place is great for fishing," said the man, and Ted replied, "Sure is". "Would you like a pole to try out the waters"?'- "That would be lovely", replied the man. So Ted obliged, returned to the house, and brought the man a fishing pole. The gentleman was as happy as Larry and sat for hours eating lunch and fishing. Later, he returned the rod to the house, and Ted quickly thought to ask if he had anything to do with the 'film people' currently in town. "Yes, sorry I didn't introduce myself; my name is Anthony Perkins-call me Tony"! He was a famous movie star, most notably playing the lead in the 1960 Alfred Hitchcock film Psycho. Being more of a book reader and not visiting the cinema much, Ted had not recognized him. Perkins was in town filming the 1965 adventure/thriller 'The Fool Killers' about a young boy travelling in the post-civil war South with a philosophical axe murderer; a little bit of typecasting there, perhaps!? Later, Ted was chided at school by the students for not recognizing this famous movies star, and Ted was a little embarrassed but nonchalant about it; what was all the fuss! In subsequent years, the house became too much to maintain and was abandoned for the most part, and Ted and Nancy built a place higher up on their property. The river would flood occasionally as well, causing more problems. It still stood when I was last there and looks slightly like the Norman Bates house on misty, murky days, usually near Halloween.

In the Summer of 1936, Dad entered the CMTC (Civilian Military Training Corp) as a new recruit at Fort Oglethorpe, Georgia, in year 1 'Basic'. It was a Calvary unit, and he hoped later to obtain a reserve commission in the U.S. Army Cavalry. He repeated this training as a 'Red' in the second-year course in 1937 before enlisting in the U.S. Army Air Corps. (The classes were held each year in the Summer and were classified as Basic, Red, White, and Blue. Each applicant had to pass one of these courses each year for four years. Upon completing these courses, a high school diploma and a series of War Department courses passed successfully with recommendations typically qualified for a Reserve Officer Commission was the desirable outcome strived for.)

He liked the military and especially wanted to fly. So instead of waiting, he enlisted as a private at Fort Oglethorpe as soon as he finished the 'Red' course on September 1, 1937, for assignment in the U.S. Army Air Force Corps, Panama Canal Zone at Albrook Field. He had several 'close encounters' during his time stationed in Panama. The place was mysterious and new to him, almost like being on a lush tropical island and very different to Tennessee. Contact with the wildlife, including Capuchin and Spider monkeys, was a novelty and not uncommon, as with the exotic marine life! On a beautiful sunny day, he was one-day pleasure rafting about half a mile offshore in the Pacific and suddenly had an eerie feeling. Enjoying the warm weather, he was dangling his feet in the sea. Then, instinctually, he retracted his legs and turned around to see a large fin approaching the boat and about to go under-a shark! On reflection, he thought it was a tiger shark by the stripes on the side of its body as it glided underneath and came out the other side (Jaws comes to mind, but of course, this was pre-Jaws.) Maybe it was a premonition, like the feeling someone or something has their eye on you.

Certainly an exotic location, but this was a somewhat extreme initiation to the unknown.

Later, he was transferred to Fort McPherson in Atlanta, Georgia, where he first saw 'Major' George Patton (later to become famous). Here he began his basic military training in the regular army. About one month later, he boarded a troop train for Charleston, SC, and sailed with a troop ship back to Panama. Afterwards, he was assigned duties in the electric shop in an Air Base Squadron, which turned out to be dull. After struggling to transfer to an entire flying squadron unsuccessfully, he sneaked away from a weekly fatigue detail to talk to the Officer in charge in the Radio section of the flying Squadron near him on Base. The NCO (non-commissioned officer) was very receptive and said he would ask for a transfer tailored to my Dad. However, he was missed from the Fatigue detail, reported to the squadron commander, and nearly Court-Martialed! (The Squadron Commander was Captain Nathan B. Forrest III, great-grandson of the famous Civil War General. The later Brigadier General was killed in the ETO -' European

Theatre Of Operations' in a B17 over Kiel, Germany, on a bombing mission to destroy the submarine yards.)

To quote Dad: 'He told me that if I'd had six months in the military at the time, I would have certainly been court-martialled. I (on reflection) had taken an awful chance but was very happy that I did later on! The transfer to the 74th Attack Squadron came through a few days later. The Squadron flew the Northrop A-17 two-seater attack plane, the most modern aircraft on the Base'.

In this Squadron, I felt I had finally found my niche in the military. I increased my Morse code speed beyond my expectations, successfully passed an introductory radio course in airborne and ground communication, and later passed the Air Mechanic Exam for radio giving me the pay of a Staff Sergeant. I flew frequent air missions over the canal and the Panama countryside, later completing a few tasks with Maj. Gen Hugh Dargue (later killed in a B17 crash) and several missions with Brig. Gen George Brett who was later temporary commander of the 5th Air Force in Australia at the beginning of WW2. Further, I was on several air manoeuvres in Rio Hato and Pocree in Panama. I flew simulated air attacks on the Panama Canal during 1938-1939. The ground troops didn't like it when we dropped flour bombs on them in some episodes!

I was asked if I wanted to extend my tour for another year in Panama, but I waited until too late to make the decision. So I concluded my short two-year term by returning to Charleston. I was discharged from the Air Corps on September 5' 1939, at Fort Moultrie, SC, just two days after England declared war on Germany.

After applying for some dull jobs in my hometown, later that autumn, I investigated joining the RAF or RAFC as a volunteer for combat pilot training. However, after visiting Washington DC, authorities told me that I most likely would lose my U.S. citizenship (this was rescinded in July 1940, long after I had already re-enlisted in the Air Corps-what a shame!)

I then visited several military airfields in the southeastern U.S. for possible re-enlisting. At Bolling Field, Washington

DC, I ran into my buddies from Panama. They urged me to re-enlist there. Upon enquiring about this, the OIC (Officer In Charge) said I could immediately be assigned as a second airborne radio operator on the Secretary Of War's B-17. This was very scary, as I felt too young to accept this responsibility! So I returned to the nightlife of my hometown and surrounding urban nightclubs, but my savings were running low.
I was a free agent and unsure what to do at this time.

Chapter 3

Free to Roam

In March 1940, with an acquaintance from my home town -' Fuchet' (of French origins), set out to visit several airbases to see if we might enlist in the Air Corps. However, we didn't particularly like any of them since the military had begun a build-up and were quartering some troops in large hangers, as there weren't enough barracks to house them. So we eventually set out hitchhiking to California, which I always wanted to visit anyway and possibly this could be an interesting experience.

Somewhere near the town of Murfreesboro in Arkansaw we were let out by a local farmer as he had arrived at his home having visited Eastern Tennessee for a family reunion. He advised of a cheap local motel in town, and we pooled our monies together and got a room in a bungalow-style complex that was basic yet clean. We had a coffee pot and radio in the room and thought we were lucky with that. The manager was friendly and always had a pork roast on hand behind the counter that he would make sandwiches with and offered us some, and we readily accepted the few days we were there. Fuchet had got the idea that diamonds had been found in the area. A farmer had seen them on his land and then been bought out by a consortium or company later on. I didn't believe him at the time and, knowing what little of the gem, thought that they could only really be found in places like Africa and far away places like that.

A younger guy told us this was true upon asking around town and receiving some reluctance from the townspeople in general!

He gave us a rough guide to where the place was, and we decided that we would do a little prospecting. The property, however, most likely would be private, and we wanted to avoid getting in trouble. Moreover, we needed transport, so the hotel manager's wife gave us old rickety bicycles that we said we wanted to use to get into town whilst we stayed there. So starting in the early morning, we rode to the general vicinity after acquiring some shovels from the town hardware store, which was somewhat ridiculous as we needed more funds and couldn't afford all the trappings of the prospector on tour! It must have looked odd and evident what we were doing to some. We were in the right spot with no apparent signs or indications; we found a field about half a mile from a homestead and started digging in a place we thought was not private land with a creek and a small thicket close to our location.

That day we dug a hole about 5 feet deep and found zero! The next day we did the same thing next to the spot that we first searched and amazingly found an old coin that turned out to be from the Civil War. It must have been dropped by some anxious soldier or civilian going about their business all those years ago. We were feeling all excited by this, almost like pirates finding lost treasure. So, the following day, we decided to try one last time, dug a shallower hole, and found the sum total of rocks and dirt! We were drawing attention to ourselves, and it was amazing that someone did not run us off. Trying to be reasonably good citizens, we filled in the holes as best we could and returned to the motel to get ready to depart! We figured we would not get rich this way and didn't have a claim in any case. I have since been back to the area but could not find the exact spot that my friend and I were digging long ago. It is now The Crater of Diamonds State Park, and people can pay to dig! Most people find what we did or lesser gems, but some get lucky. However, from my research, I discovered that the Strawn-Wagner Diamond—one of the most flawless diamonds ever discovered—and the huge 40.23 carats Uncle Sam diamond was found in the Crater of Diamonds. We may have been only 100 feet from them or similar, I like to think(or not)!

Attitudes over rights of way and private property were a little more relaxed then, and anything west of the east coast was likely determined as being the 'frontier'. If we tried to do this now in most places, it would be much more difficult and we would likely be 'run off'.

Hitchhiking and looking for cheap hotels formed part of the rest of our trip to California. Many little towns, some thriving, some not. Most of these places have died or are very quiet with the arrival of the new interstate system.

After a long trip, we finally arrived in Ojai and Ventura in sunny southern California. We stayed at Fuchet's uncle's house, who had a young son and showed us the local area, as well as Los Angeles and the environs-movies stars and touching for a moment that life of glamour in Hollywood of old. We then stayed at his Aunt's house in Santa Barbara, listening to Johann Strauss' waltzes for several days! Then moved on up the coast toward San Francisco, and another relative who was comfortably off owning a sailboat, etc-we; we were glad of relatives!

Then reality dawned, and our original plan collapsed (at least, his did). I was running low on finances, too, and had to say goodbye to Fuchet and set out alone for San Francisco. I hitchhiked about halfway through the first day, and a little old lady let me stay in her tiny house in her backyard at night. The following day I got a ride with a rich man into town. As soon as I told him that I'd been in the Army Air Corps, he immediately assumed I was a pilot and offered me a job flying his private airplane. But, of course, I could never convince him otherwise,

as he thought everyone in The Air Corps was a pilot. So he
bought me lunch in a large hotel restaurant, and I departed.

Chapter 4

A Military Man Again

The next day I started looking for a job. I was initially enthusiastic, but I was getting very discouraged after three days of looking. Now I was practically broke. Previously, I had passed the army recruiting station and dropped in to see what the deal was if I re-enlisted. He gave me a big spiel as to my advantages, especially as I would be a re-enlistee! So finally, I decided this was the best avenue to take and went back and re-enlisted on April 27, 1940. After being offered the choice of Hamilton Field in Oakland or March Field in Southern California, I chose the latter. I was then sent to Fort McDowell, Angel Island (past Alcatraz Prison) in the bay to await transportation.

Looking at Alcatraz from the city of San Francisco was quite eerie and foreboding, especially in the mist that often prevails there. The prisoners were only a stone's throw from the glitz of downtown, but it would be many years before most could see it again or return to their homes all over the country. Moreover, any escape attempt would have been difficult as the water was so choppy and cold, with fast-moving currents, and I felt sorry for them.

I tried swimming on the beach at Fort Funston, and the water was freezing. I would have to wear a wet suit to stay in there for a prolonged time.

They assigned me to the Headquarters Squadron in the 19th Bombardment Group upon arrival at March Field—also the home of the 17th Bomb Group. Lt Col. Hap Arnold had just left the Base for assignment to Washington DC (He later became Gen. Hap Arnold and head of the Air Corps as Chief.) I was received as an old 'old timer' in the group of recruits arriving there at the time. I was given favorable status by the First

Sergeant of the Squadron and assigned as a radio operator on B-18s, which I later loved like no other airplane. After a few crashes in the outfit, limited personnel, and a good recommendation, I was promoted to Corporal and again received the Air Mechanic rating.

About two months later, they gave me a choice to go with the 19th to the Philippines or transfer to the 17th, which was moving to activate a new airfield, McChord Field, in Tacoma, Washington. To me, McChord sounded the better of the two! I flew many missions out of that Base. Besides many other missions back to California, I qualified as an aerial gunner at Galeta near Santa Barbara, off the Pacific Coast, in August 1940. Later, after the war started, I received extra pay for this. In those days, McChord was a wonderful place, and the natives didn't have signs stating, 'Dogs and soldiers, don't walk here'! But in a short time, we came to the status of the 'ground pounders' (soldiers) at nearby Fort Lewis.

Most of my flying was in the B-18, but some missions were in the old B-23 (Dragon). Very often on runs, we would pass over Mount Shasta so low that we blew the snow off the summit as we skimmed over; this was a mighty mountain indeed and filled me with awe and a sense of mystery.

Before Christmas 1940, I was assigned a mission to Minneapolis, Minnesota, to cover the two weeks we were given the airplane to go home for the Holidays. Unbeknownst to me at the time, this trip saved my life. In January 1941, I was scheduled for a mission to California again. I had the radio equipment all checked out and signed out the headphones for all on board, but at the last minute, the radio section chief came running out to the airplane and 'pulled' me off the flight. He stated that I had too much flying time compared to some of the other operators. Besides that, I had been to California more than anyone else in the section. The B-18 disappeared and was never heard from again. We searched for it for weeks from Washington to California. I have never had rougher air flights in the mountains than I did on those missions. We flew so close to the tops of the peaks that, again, we blew the snow off the tops of them, including Mt. St Helens. A sheepherder saw the glint of metal on a mountaintop in February or March; it was the tail section of that bomber. It hit the top of a mountain and left the tail on one side and the rest of the plane on the other side. Snow had covered most of it. I later thanked the chief who had pulled me off that flight, but before, we had never got on too well. He was an old-timer I'd known from my Panama days and had worked in the electric shop before my transfer there.

Later, my Squadron was alerted for transfer to Alaska in March 1941. We departed McChord making stops for refuelling in Prince George, BC, White Horse, Yukon Territory, and Fairbanks before arriving at our permanent Base in Elmendorf. There occurred some interesting incidents on this trip, but I will save those for another day. These included unusual lights and visual anomalies we thought that the Japanese or Russians might have been testing. I Flew on the Nome Patrol that Summer, aerial mapping the Aleutians part-time, and dropped papers in an attempt to draft the natives and others around Alaska, including Point Barrow that Summer, by parachute as we couldn't land. It was a piece of cake until December 7, 1941.

Chapter 5

Pearl Harbour and Beyond

On December 7, 1941, I was copying Morse code as I usually did every Sunday morning in the barracks. This particular Sunday, I was copying JAP in Tokyo (Japanese press wireless in English) as I often did. Some of my fellow radio operators were copying simultaneously, but they were slightly slower in Morse code. So my pulse quickened when I copied the words that Japan had declared war on the United States and had taken the life changing decision to bomb Pearl Harbor-and this while they were bombing Pearl at that exact time (Anchorage was in the same time zone as Hawaii). The other two fellows, Cooper and Stevens, were still determining if they got all the code right, but I was convinced I had. So I spread the word that we were at war. The first Sergeant got word that I had said this and prepared the following day to begin drawing up papers for my court-martial for spreading false rumours- in trouble again! It wasn't until late that day, December 8, that the official word came in that it was true. So far as I know, I was the first one in Alaska to learn that we were at war.

I returned to the U.S. by air transport early in 1942 to help crew the Martin (short wing) B-26 from Spokane, Washington, back to Alaska for combat duty. After three hours of transition from the B-18, my pilots were checked out in the B-26 to fly back. We came very close to crashing on take-off at Spokane because we had an overload in weight, and they forgot to use quarter flaps which they weren't used to doing in the B-18. Nevertheless, it was a much faster trip back to Alaska this time than when we went up there a year before in the B-18s.

After standing alert in B-26s at Elmendorf Field and no enemy attacks on the mainland, I was sent along with several other airmen to Cold Bay in the Aleutians on a former cattle boat. Here we lived in temporary 'thrown-up' buildings and tents. I was still assigned to flying and ground radio operations. Here, again I was lucky when a friend of mine was on a plane that sustained damage after encountering a Japanese ship, came back and refuelled, and went back out to hunt for more targets but crashed on the home approach trying to land in fog. I was supposed to have been the radio operator on the plane that day. I was thinking that I may have nine lives!

At Cold Bay, I decided to try out for an aviation cadet appointment in Summer. Several fellows had talked about it, and I thought it might be a good idea. I was flown back to Elmendorf, passed the physical exam, and was transported to Seattle, Washington. In November 1942 contracted pleurisy there and stayed two weeks in the hospital. After, I was released and took the train to southern California again. On January 15, 1943, I entered pre-flight and graduated from advanced flying school on November 3, 1943.

Chapter 6

A Real Pilot And A Brush With Hollywood

My next destination was Chico Army Air Field in California, where I was assigned for a time and was to experience a new atmosphere of learning.

There, I did basic flight training and transitioned to bombers, but the field was quite remote, with basic housing. In California, I met Robert Cummings, whom I was to be acquainted with for some time at the base, meeting occasionally during training for a drink with the other crew. He was a famous Hollywood movie actor who appeared in films like the Hitchcock thriller 'Dial M For Murder' and Saboteur, amongst many others.

He was among the first men to be classed as a flight instructor in the USA. Robert Cummings promoted flying and new innovations in plane concepts and general aviation. He was a generally friendly and affable guy.

And later helped establish a squadron in California involved in the Pacific Theatre of Operations and went on various reconnaissance missions. Once, he went on the lookout for a Japanese Submarine that had attacked a refinery in Santa Barbara County in California. Also, he was involved in search and rescue missions throughout California and forestry /fire watch duties.

Bob was a flight instructor throughout the war and had a successful film career through the 1950s and even into the 1980s. He even had his own show at one point.

All the time in flight school, I had requested to be a fighter pilot. Still, no one was receptive to this and recommended me for bombers (I suspect because they needed bomber pilots more than fighter pilots). So, even before graduation, I refused bomber transition training, still hoping to get fighters. Shortly after graduation, I was sent to the pilot pool at Salt Lake City and a short time later assigned to the 490th Bomb Group, which was already beginning the second phase of combat training in B-24s in Idaho. There was a need for Pilots in Britain to fight in the European Theatre, so In the early Spring of 1944, we departed for England via Nebraska, Florida, the Caribbean, South America and Africa, the South Atlantic route.

During our stopover in Libya, we were stuck for a few days because of weather issues and were told by a local we should visit the great Roman ruins of Leptis Magna. The guide told us it had been abandoned in the first millennium AD after the Muslim invasion. A local 'vendor' who was trying to sell his goods (possibly antiquities!) at the site. Quite a culture shock after living in the USA most of my life and the ruins of this old ancient city were quite something to behold. We piled back into the old army Jeep after sleeping in tents overnight and headed back to the airfield. Funny to see part of this city transported by the British in a place called Virginia Water (near Windsor) just outside of London years later when visiting with family.

Chapter 7

England And War 1944

The first sound I heard from St Mawgan in Cornwall was 'Hello Dark; this is Nebo'- these were landing instructions. We were based as part of the 8th Air Force USAAF 490th Bomb Group at RAF Eye in Suffolk, England, and for a short time at RAF Thorpe Abbots near Diss-'The Bloody Hundredth' moved here from Podington, flying 306 B-17 Flying Fortress combat missions. Known as the 'Bloody Hundredth' due to high combat losses, this unit lost no more than was average for its length of service. The local towns, which were quaint and rural, included Stowmarket and Bury St Edmunds. The surrounding countryside was relatively flat but pretty, and the locals, on the whole, were amiable.

My first mission was a bomb run to Noball, France, in the Summer of 1944, then moved to Germany.

Mission List:

1. Noball, France. 7th June 1944
2. Sully-Sur-Loire, France 17th July 1944
3. Recall, 27th August 1944
4. Recall, 1st September 1944
5. Frankfurt, Germany 8th September 1944
6. Monheim, Germany 9th September 1944
7. Nurenberg, Germany 10th September 1944
8. Magdeburg, Germany 12th September 1944
9. Ludwigshafen, Germany 13th September 1944
10. Bielefield, Germany 19th September 1944
11. Ludwigshafen, Germany 27th September 1944
12. Merseburg, Germany 7th October 1944
13. Hamburg, Germany 25th October 1944

14. Hamm, Germany 28th October 1944
15. Recall
16. Hamburg, Germany 4th November 1944
17. Ludwigshafen, Germany 5th November 1944 MIA also 5th November 1944

Chapter 8

Capture: Germany

The combat mission that fateful Sunday, November 5, 1944, included several 'fireworks'! I was downed over Germany and was initially scheduled to support General Patton's army in Eastern France. We were to bomb along the German front lines to allow Patton to accelerate into Germany. However, this was not to be on Guy Fawkes Day, November 5, 1944. Scattered clouds covered most of the area, and our orders were not to bomb should the clouds partially obscure the ground. (Reference the bombing of Gen. McNair's troops earlier, killing him and several of his soldiers in Western France because of cloud cover.)

We were then ordered to bomb our secondary target, the I.G. Farben Synthetic Rubber Plant on the Rhine at Ludwigshafen. Everything appeared normal while our group proceeded toward the initial point. We could see the flak ahead, and on our straight-in approach, we began to pick up heavy flak on our easterly course. We opened our bomb bay doors. We then dropped our bombs on the signal. I noticed the time- high noon, 1200 hours. I remember immediately trying to close the bomb bay doors; however, they would not close. I then remember seeing two bursts of red flak high on our port side and pointing them out to Bob Jackson in the left seat. We had begun our letdown, dropping altitude 2000 feet to pick up speed and make our turn to the west.

The red flak bursts were typically a German signal for the fighters to come in for an attack. A few seconds later, I glimpsed a B-17 on our port veer underneath us; however, I thought that it was far enough beneath to avoid contact. But how wrong I was! Immediately our B-17 shuddered violently, and so did I. The control columns crashed forward with such force that it appeared to break every glass on the instrument panel. We were still in a right turn and losing altitude. At this time, from the right seat, I saw a blur as our number four engine literally jumped out from the right wing and disappeared. I couldn't believe my eyes. The aircraft began banking toward the right; the rate increased rapidly. Lt Jackson and I immediately cut power on one and two engines and increased power on three while using the controls in an attempt to hold the aircraft level. There was little response. The bank kept getting steeper. At this time, I realized that we could no longer control the plane regardless of what we did.

My first thoughts had been that we might hold the aircraft level long enough to make a letdown and crash land, but now this thought was long gone! I looked up toward the engineer, who was still in the top gun turret and motioned for him to leave his position in a hurry. He responded without hesitation. Needless to say, these were very tense moments. I quickly tried to contact the rest of the crew, but the intercom had utterly failed. So then, since there was nothing else we could do, I knew we must abandon the plane as quickly as possible. I looked squarely at Jackson; his face was white, and he somehow appeared to be mesmerized in his seat. I grabbed his arm and motioned we should evacuate immediately, but he seemed frozen in the chair and didn't respond. We were losing altitude fast, and I estimate we had already lost perhaps more than 4000 feet from the 25,000 feet when the collision occurred. I then jumped from the cockpit down into the 'tunnel,' where I saw the bombardier and navigator tugging away each end of the same chest pack parachute. Their positions were filled with papers, litter, and debris beyond belief, and one of the parachutes had been covered underneath this mess. They quickly got this sorted out and clamped on their chutes; this really pleased me; at least I now had company to go to! The propellers of the other plane had cut through the nose of our aircraft squarely; it appeared between the navigator and bombardier and cut through their briefcases and maps. How lucky they were! From this vantage point through the nose, I could see the sky and ground go around and around; we were tumbling and rolling in the sky, thinking this was my last day on earth, alive! I turned and crawled, holding on to the fuselage ribs, toward the escape door. The door opened when I turned the handle escape door and waved in the breeze, but when I pushed the emergency release handle to jettison it, the cable would not move. I cut my silk gloves nearly to ribbons, still trying to eject the door, but it hung on and continued to wave in the wind. Meanwhile, the bombardier and the navigator jumped out and disappeared. Had any of us caught the parachute harness in the door handle, we would have hung there helpless and unable to get loose. Further, we might have blocked the opening for the others to escape-but, these were desperate moments and any way to get out for you could be paramount. It was about this time I pulled the red emergency strap to release my flak suit, but it broke in my hand. I didn't take the time to reach up and manually release it- no way! By this time, the number three engine had altogether quit because of the lack of fuel (the wing tank had long gone, and it had been running on fuel left in the lines), and the eerie sound of rushing air was horrifying, even though my ears were blocking like mad. I had been off oxygen for over a minute and was becoming quite groggy. The engineer, who was now at my side, yelled a message into my ear that I'll never forget-"Lt. if we don't get out of here now, we're dead"! And as he went out of the door, he grabbed my arm, pulled me along with him, and we both went out of the door together. As I left the plane, I passed dangerously close to the propellers, missed them, it seemed, by about less than an inch or so and could feel the heat and whoosh of the metal spinning on my face and shoulder. I still had on my flak suit and helmet! I hadn't spared the time to take off either one. Upon departing the plane, there had been a split second when it all seemed like a dream-ha! And I felt like I was going to pass out. But the cold air and lower altitude soon alerted me to the situation, and I was wide awake. I felt motionless in the sky and, at first, hesitated to pull my ripcord. Looking down, I could see that I was falling towards the middle of the big river and reached under my flak suit and jerked the ripcord. Immediately, the chute's opening pushed the flak helmet down over my face. I then pushed it back and looked up the see the chute fully blossom open with a big hole in the center and a small rip along the two seams of one panel. However, what a good feeling that was-at least now I had a chance to live. There were a few scattered low clouds beneath, but they didn't obscure the view below. I was still over the Rhine, but the wind gradually drifted me eastwards toward Mannheim. I could see some aircraft falling out of the sky, one with all four engines blazing, heading nearly straight down. Pieces of aircraft and, I suspect, flak were falling all around me. It was (as some said of the U.S. 8th Air Force bombing of Germany) "The greatest show on earth", and it was living up to its name today. Upon nearing the ground, I could hear gunfire while pieces of debris were still falling all around me. I had already taken off my flak helmet and was holding it along with my ripcord but decided to keep my flak suit on, as it might protect me from gunfire, not realizing it would add to my weight upon hitting the ground. The ground was beginning to come up fast, and I was falling towards a clearing in the woods; however, a large two-story house was directly in my path. I pulled the parachute shroud lines to try and avoid it but grazed the side of it with my leg, nearly collapsing the chute. I hit the ground with a heavy thud and felt my leg go limp, and then pain in that area. The ankle, as well as the knee joint, began to swell up. I was wearing the well-known fur-lined 'bunny boots', which did not support my feet and turning my foot at an angle when hitting the ground so hard. I believe that had not that ankle broken, my knee joint would have come out of the socket, and then I would have been in greater trouble. To add insult to injury, I'd landed in a new toilet pit near the house that had not yet been dug very deep. For a minute, I lay there on my back, watching the last of the bombers passing over. They were nearly invisible so high up in the sky. I felt very lonely and sad. I wouldn't be going home to England today and maybe would never see it again.

This was my 17th mission. No longer could I look forward to 25, 30 or even 35 missions and hope to receive the DFC? It was all over for me now in the ETC (European Theatre of Conflict), and I just felt lucky to be alive!

An older man and woman ran through the woods towards me within a few minutes. Behind them, a third figure, what seemed to be a tall crazed German waving a huge knife and motioning that he was going to cut my throat. The old man and woman stopped a few feet away from me and held back the younger man, and began talking to him in an attempt to calm him down; it appeared, I think to have worked. The lady then approached me and asked me in German if I was a German pilot. I shook my head-no. She then asked if I was a British pilot, and I again said no. Then she said, "You are Americanish!"-I nodded yes. They had got rid of the crazed guy somehow. Had he tried to cut my throat, he would have had a very rough time. Underneath my uniform and escape suit, I had a large pocket knife I'd bought at the American Military Exchange in London a few weeks before.

I would have used it had it been necessary to try and save my life. The old man left for a few minutes and returned, pulling a two-wheel cart. He and the lady helped me up onto the rear of the cart. They wheeled me through the woods, where 200 feet away sat my engineer with a sprained ankle. They also helped him onto the cart and pulled us to the edge of the woods where some Hitler Youth and possibly Brown Shirts were gathered in a circle. They had machine pistols and rifles, and it appeared they had been firing at the parachutes. An older fellow, well dressed in civilian clothes standing with the group, came over to me and spoke in perfect English. He stated that he had attended university in England (maybe Oxford) many years before. He was pretty pleasant and wished me well. Afterwards, we were pulled on the cart up a sloping hill to a Flak -Gunnery camp a few hundred feet away and turned over to the Luftwaffe. I thanked the old man and the woman and never saw them again. The Luftwaffe camp was in high spirits because they believed that they had shot us down, and in a way, they may have been correct because I think that the plane that hit us may have got a direct flak hit, possibly killing the pilots or damaging the aircraft. I heard from some sources that the Luftwaffe gunners claimed that sixteen bombers came down in the target area that day and thought they shot most of them down.

Also, they had said they had found a man slumped in a tree, and it was a hideous sight; he had appeared to be nearly cut jaggedly in half vertically, probably by a propeller blade. They say the man had red hair, and the build and features sounded very much like my pilot Jackson, who had hesitated at the controls, not quite believing what was happening. That whoosh of death I felt when exiting the plane had nearly got me too.

They put me in a tiny building on a canvas cot and covered me with a blanket. A young private was put in charge of me. During my very short stay there, he slipped me a couple of cigarettes but warned me not to tell the NCO, a Staff Sergeant (Feltswable).

On one wall was a larger-than-life picture of General Von Runsted and a small window above my head. In a short while, a man dressed as a cook stuck his head in the window and asked what part of the US I was from. I told him that I could not give him that information. He said that he had spent several years in Chicago and was drafted into the German military while on a vacation trip. He appeared disgusted when I again refused to tell him what part of the States I came from and walked away. He had said (from the sound of my speech) that I came from the mid-west somewhere.

In about two hours, I was helped into a military truck, my engineer, and four or five other POWs and driven out of the camp. Along the way, they stopped to pick up two or more POWs. We tried to talk to each other, but the guards warned us to remain silent. Finally, we passed through a section of a town where I saw a B-17 tail sticking out the top of a building. It had crashed into the structure on a near-vertical descent. It was most likely one of the planes I saw whilst coming down in my parachute.

We arrived a short time later at a compound that appeared to be a former concentration camp. Our wounded were first taken to a small clinic inside the fence. A medical technician examined our wounds. Seeing my leg, he asked if I would like morphine. I readily agreed as the pain was becoming worse. My engineer was offered the same but refused. He told me later that he had rejected the morphine because he had heard that the Germans used poison serum to kill many enemy prisoners! Just before leaving, the medic covered my leg with cheesecloth and asked if I wanted another shot; I gladly excepted. We were then taken to the main prison building and placed into small cells. My engineer and I were put into a cell together. It had very thick walls, two or three feet wide, and there was a tiny window at the very top at the rear, which you could not see out of. It very much reminded me of the dungeon cell in the story of the 'Prisoner of Zenda' many years before. There was only one wooden bed with a straw tick mattress and one blanket. I took the bed, and the engineer rolled up in the blanket and slept on the floor. I slept in my clothes with no cover. It was a cold night.

Early the following day, we heard a terrible commotion and loud voices in the hallway. The guards were bringing in more prisoners. One was our tail gunner, a boisterous little guy even in normal times. He was black and blue, scratched and a little bloody. Unknown to my engineer and me, the tail had broken off our aircraft in midair. He had been trapped inside most of the way down, cursing humanity and far away from where we had landed. (Too long of a story to relate in this account). He had been badly cut trying to extricate himself from the tail section and, upon landing, had fallen into the hands of angry civilians. There was another interesting chap too. He was, oddly enough, the tail gunner from the airplane that had collided with us! He stated that his plane had exploded after hitting and breaking away from us. He was forcefully blown out of the tail, except one foot got caught inside, leaving him hanging with the tail section. He said that if he had a knife at the time, he would have cut off his foot to break free, but at the last minute, it broke loose. He hit the ground with the chute, having fortunately just opened in time a few seconds later, having just enough air to make it to the ground.

A few days later, we left this prison, and my engineer and one of the gunners carried me to the truck, then to train later with wooden seats bound for Frankfurt. Strange, I had never been on a train before with wooden chairs! Upon arrival at the Bahnhof, they again carried me through the station to a streetcar, which took us to the Dulog interrogation center. The guards had given us tickets to ride the car – which was handy! A beautiful blond girl came to collect my ticket; she leaned over and whispered into my ear, "How are you doing," then ", Good luck"! She spoke to me in perfect English. I nearly fell off my seat in surprise. I wish I could have met her again. When we arrived at the center, I sat in freezing rain in line for about an hour before being allowed inside the building.

At first, they put ten or more of us in the same room. Everyone was talking about their outfit and experiences. I'm nearly positive that they had planted a spy in our midsts or had the room bugged with hidden microphones, so I tried to say minor and trivial things at that. Later, I was placed in a solitary room with a small bed. It felt good to rest my leg and foot. The next morning my breakfast consisted of ersatz coffee, supposedly made from acorns and a piece of black bread. It was lousy. The second day, a guard came and took me down a hallway to a small office. Inside was a Luftwaffe major at a large desk. He sympathetically noted my wounded leg. He offered me an American cigarette (He had two or three packs of Chesterfield or Camel cigarettes lying on his desk.)I gladly accepted and later took another one. After a short conversation, he handed me a questionnaire booklet with several pages pertaining to my life and military information. The way I accepted the booklet, he seemed confident that I would fill it out completely. I wrote down my name, rank, and serial number on the first page then thumbed down the rest of the pages. Then I went back and began making large 'Xs' across each page. He tried to stop me, pounded his fist on the desk, and stated: "You must fill out this information- you are under German orders now"! I said that I was very sorry about his position, but under the Geneva Convention, I was not required to answer any further questions.

After ranting on, he hinted that I might be tried and court-martialled and possibly shot. (Long before, back in England, the RAF had briefed us twice as to what might happen if we were captured and told us they might threaten a firing squad if we failed to give them information, but rarely ever carried out the threat.) Finally, after a few more bitter words, the major ordered the guard to take me back to my room. This time the guard didn't offer to assist me down the hallway. Instead, I hobbled along on my right foot, using my hands on the walls to make it back to the room.

The following day, I was put on a charcoal-burning bus with others and transported to a large hospital in the area. Here the doctors were supposed to examine me and admit me as a patient. However, more information was necessary before I could be admitted, including my age and home address in the United States. I refused, again stating my rights under the Geneva Convention. The German captain in charge of the group kept calling me "silly boy'. Finally, he told me; I could not stay in the hospital. The doctor explained that he needed to know my age to treat me and my home address to notify my parents if anything terrible happened. I suspected this was a lie. During my short stay at the hospital, I met a Lt Col., a POW whom I'd known in Panama and had flown with a few times. He advised me to stay at the hospital for medical treatment and felt the information they had asked for was innocent enough; however, I disagreed.

I was then ordered to get back on the bus, taking POWs to the train station and transferring to a Dulog at Wetzler, North of Frankfurt. I saw a pair of crutches in a corner and quickly grabbed them on the way out. No one appeared to notice, and I kept them. No one had to help me walk after this.

Another train ride on those wooden seats was in store for me. At Wetzler, a Plaster of Paris cast with an iron walker up to the knee was put on my leg. A very short time afterwards, the first one cracked. I requested another one, but the sergeant medical technician stated that I could not have another one as they were short of medical supplies, and besides, the soldiers on the front line needed them more than I did. However, a doctor (an old soldier) overheard the conversation and countermanded this. He was the CIC, a colonel, highly decorated, wearing the Iron Cross, Jewels, Saber decorations etc. He said, "I don't want to be branded as a war criminal after the war," and laughed! I am sure he must have also served in WWI. I met several British Paratroopers who had been taken as POWs at Arnhem. They told me of the foul-up when they were dropped with the wrong ammunition for their guns, etc. It was a genuine mix-up, and it also happened to the US Paratroopers.

They put me on a train bound for East Germany; however, I became very sick at Giessen, just south of Wetzler, after switching in the railroad yards all night. I believe this was due to my internal injuries in the parachute fall. Two men dressed as US officers, a major and a captain in the same compartment, who would not help me and said that they hoped I would die! I couldn't believe they were Americans, but Germans dressed as such. They were, at the time, requesting personnel that could speak English or English with an American accent for the 'Battle Of The Bulge' Offensive. This mission was intended to stop Allied use of the Belgian port of Antwerp and to split the Allied lines in the hope of allowing the Germans to encircle and destroy the four Allied forces and cause the Allies to negotiate a peace treaty in the Axis powers' favour. I wonder if it was these men in training for the Bulge push who were so malicious toward me. Had they been Americans and I had met them after the war I was so mad, I believe I may have killed them outright.

I was taken off the train at Giessen station and walked through the railroad yard guarded by a young German soldier, who was taking me to the large hospital on the hill above the town. Unfortunately, we had to walk through a bombed-out area, which was supposed to have delayed fuses in some of the bombs. The young guard tried to hurry me up to get me out of the site, but it was slow going on crutches; he was very annoyed and too, he was afraid that a bomb might explode at any minute.

We made it, and the hospital turned out to be a lovely place, and I was placed in a ward with five other Allied soldiers. Only two of us were not amputees. The rest of the hospital was filled primarily with amputees from the Afrika Corps. An ex-Afrika Corps army sergeant was in charge of our ward repatriated by the British. He brought each of us a stein of beer every night and said that the British had been good to him, and he would be good to us. He was a nice guy.

The medics examined me, took blood tests, and gave me medicine, but as far as I know, they did not come to any conclusion as far as my ailment. I suspected the hard parachute landing tore something loose internally, but it had never given me any noticeable pain at the time.

While in Geissen Hospital, there was an air raid. A group or two of B-17s bombed the Leika optical factory in the town just below the hospital. The patients were brought down from the top floors, and the high-ranking wounded were evacuated to the basement. It was, at that time, the first air raid I'd been in proximity to, except for the V-1s in England, and actually, it was pretty exciting. The hospital building shook a lot, and I could see debris out of the window flying high into the sky and lots of black smoke. But no bombs appeared to hit the hospital. Even knowing that I was an allied POW, many of the old German soldiers shook hands with me, those who still had hands. It was pitiful and sad to see humanity, even the enemy, under those conditions. I will never forget my stay there.

I was again back on the train to East Germany with the other POWs in less than a week.

Chapter 9

Stalag Luft III

Upon entering the camp at Sagan, a sergeant, who was a black man, helped and carried my cardboard Red Cross suitcase to the gate as I was still on crutches. The Luftwaffe captain who met us greeted me, thundering, "Lt Fuller, you have given all of us more trouble than the rest of the Air Corps combined"! Guess he wasn't kidding, and at this, I gave a slight smile, realizing that I had unintentionally caused them a lot of trouble, which was exactly what a POW was supposed to do!

The camp, at first glance, really surprised me. Although the buildings stood out as dull and drab, the grounds were spacious, and beyond the fence outside the perimeter bordering the North Compound were beautiful. The pines stood out like nothing else. Inside there was plenty of space to walk, play games and get outdoor exercise in the fresh country air. Now, this was my home-but for how long?

I began to wonder what my fate would be here deep inside Germany. Some of the American POWs I spoke to were ashamed that they were captured and stated that they would never tell anyone they were a POW if they ever got out of Germany. To me, it was undoubtedly humiliating, sad and painful to be captured; however, I'd done my duty, had thought I had little chance of escape, and was alive to fight another day if necessary.

One thing I had forgotten: as I remember, I had kept my escape kit through all my travels in Germany-until now. They scoured my body, found my escape kit, and took it. Before, I believe that they had searched me for a weapon and only taken my pocket knife at Mannheim, but left the kit.

I was given the one empty bunk in my assigned block. The room already housed nine or ten Krieges (Slang term for inmates of Stalag Luft III). I remember three Americans, then three Canadians and the rest British RAF. My bunk, which was quite important to me, was the third one up from the floor, at the highest level near the ceiling, even though I had a cast on and was clumsily climbing up. Later, one of the fellows traded places with me and gave me his bunk down lower. He said it was warmer at the top anyway. To me, it was always chilly in the room. We had a potbelly stove which was turned down at night. Yet some of the men (Canadians, I believe) wanted a window open at night, even though it was 20 degrees below zero at night outside and below freezing inside. I would spread my damp towel on top of my blanket in order to try and stay warm. A few days after I arrived, a board of Camp POW officers convened to interview new Krieges. They wanted to ascertain who we said we were and to be assured we were not a German plant. They asked me about my background and certain events in the US, such as sports and personal experiences. Finally, I suppose they were satisfied that we were genuine allied POWs.

The actual 'Great Escape' made famous by the 1960s film occurred after a previous ingenious escape made by two British Lieutenants who made it out of Germany and back to Britain via ship to Stockholm. The men constructed a 'wooden horse' for exercise and vaulting over. It was placed near the fence, and a tunnel was dug underneath whilst the men exercised above to cover the sound of shovelling. Also, the Germans had microphones buried underneath the ground, which was another hazard to a successful escape. A wooden horse, not to gain access, as in the Legend of Troy, but as a means to be free! In many ways, this was a more successful escape on a much smaller scale with minor sacrifice, time and energy and costs in terms of lives lost.

The 'main escape' occurred in March 1944, many months before I arrived on the scene. Most of the British were located in the North compound, where it was planned and executed.

Three tunnels were dug-Tom, Dick and Harry. Dick was used for storing items, i.e. escape materials for digging, shoring, and even clothes to be used outside the camp. Tom, I believe, was found by the Germans, leaving only Harry for the actual escape.

Squadron Leader Roger Bushell was the mastermind behind it all, with the idea of allowing 200 or so men to escape at one time. He was born in South Africa and had a glorious career in Britain as a defence attorney and accomplished skier before the war. I was told he was very recognizable by a gash near his eye caused by a skiing accident. The problems of hiding the soil from the excavated tunnels and shoring them up were the primary considerations of the plan, plus the security, of course.

The depiction in the film of men siphoning the very noticeable yellow sandy soil with the grey type through a 'mechanism' in their trousers was accurate. They mixed it in the garden and vegetable patch of the compound. Also, a space under the theatre was utilized, and the crawl space above the sleeping quarters. Bed slats from the beds of jailbirds were used for the framework and scaffold of the tunnels. Even mess cans were employed for another purpose in a rudimentary pump and ventilation system. The tailoring of suits by the men and even stealing or creating the so-called 'goon suits' (German uniforms) for this and other escape attempts were also made. However, the escapees received help from within and without this and the forging of documents. Some citizens did not like the regime and Adolf Hitler, especially towards the then-unknown closing stages of the war.

The escape occurred on March 24 1944, and of the 200 men that tried to get out, only 76 managed it. A German Guard spotted them. Snow was still on the ground, and their wriggling through this and creating a trail was part of the problem. Also, the tunnel was not as long as it should have been, and they came out in a thin and sparsely populated area of trees.

The first group spoke fluent or rudimentary German and had more experience in the art, thus their first-in-line status. After that, the rest of the 600 involved had to draw lots and take their chances that way. The American escapee was Johnnie Dodge.

His Grandfather had served in the American Civil War, and Johnnie had served in the First World War and had won the Distinguished Flying Cross and, in WW2, transferred to the British Army to attain the rank of Major. Captured by the Luftwaffe in the early stages of the war and papers altered, he managed to stay with the fliers. However, his feet were severely cut after his capture and march from France. He was eventually put on a barge. Again he tried to escape by jumping into the River Scheldt. Finally, he made it out of the camp in the escape but was captured at Hirschberg Railway Station the next day. He was sent to a concentration camp, and later on, amazingly, he became a peace envoy in Berlin and finally made it back to Britain in May. At that time in 1945, the peace offer made by the German High Command was not considered for acceptance by Churchill. He died, aged 66, of a heart attack when hailing a taxi near Hyde Park in London in November 1960.

Only three men of the 76 made it to freedom-two Norwegians, and a Dutchman managed to evade capture. The Norwegian pair made it by train to the port at Stettin. There they were smuggled onto a Swedish ship and taken to Gothenburg. The Dutchman made it across most of occupied Europe via rail, foot, and even riding a bike, aided along the way by various resistance movements. He would eventually end up in Gibraltar and be flown from there to England, where he would rejoin the RAF and fight during Operation Overload.

50 of the men were executed by the Gestapo, not all in one group, as depicted in the film, but in twos or threes by the side of the road. The mastermind-Roger Bushell was amongst the killed.

The Luftwaffe higher-ups were appalled by this, and it would not bode well for them in terms of reputation and was pointless. However, many realized in March 1944 that Germany had all but lost the war. So the next commander of the camp allowed the remaining prisoners to put up a memorial to the men who did not make it back. Anyway, back to my experiences after that famous breakout.

Most of the fellows in my combine were friendly and easy to get along with, all except one American. They made me feel at 'home' as best they could under the circumstances and accepted me for who I was. I took to them as well. It appeared that these guys were fine men who had served their country well and could be proud of themselves. I was never sure who was responsible for staying in my room during appell (lining up for Roll Call) for a couple of weeks while I still had my cast. I'm sure the German captain in charge had to approve, and the OIC of my block had requested that he do so. Anyway, while the rest of the krieges were out of the building standing appell, I stayed in the room. Then I became somewhat helpful in a way that I would not have suspected previously. I would hear the German 'Ferrets' (spies) crawling under the building to later listen to conversations when the boys returned. I would quietly warn them when they came in the door from appell by pointing to the floor and putting my finger on my lips. Also, the Germans were always trying to find the radios on which we listened to the BBC to find out about current events/news. The Guards always gave us the information several days later, especially if they were losing, and even then, they would not admit anything except to make themselves/the German military look good.

One young U.S. P-38 pilot in my room, with whom I certainly did not get along, bragged about how he made ground strafing attacks, machine-gunning German school children on their bicycles. I will never forget he was from Detroit, Michigan. His justification was that these children would grow up to be Nazis, fight for Germany, and be fair game. I most certainly disagreed with him and told him so. At this, he became outraged. He was a real bully, and I suspect a coward too.

An old-timer in our combine was from Boston, Massachusetts, and joined the RAF as a gunner during the early part of the war. He knew about our resentment towards each other and thought it might become physical. So he taught me a lot of tricks about boxing and how to defend myself if the P-38 pilot and myself did get into a fight. This was the closest I ever came to a physical conflict during my entire time as a POW.

After this, I spent more of my time punching the homemade punching bag in the gymnasium. It was interesting to note all the different physical training equipment that the men had improvised. It was something else!

Further, it was interesting to note that there were hundreds of packets of French Cigarettes behind the punching bag in the corner of the gym! It was an indication that they weren't liked very well and were thrown there some time ago. I tried smoking two or three for a change and thought they were alright.
However, the British and American cigarettes were not as strong but were the best for flavour in the long run.

I was surprised that the camp was kept so clean. The Russian POWs took care of the 'honey buckets' (rudimentary toilets) and were generally treated poorly.

Since Russia wasn't a member of the Geneva Convention, the captured military was the least respected. One story I heard was that several Russians were fighting over a piece of bread, and one lost his eye in the melee; they were that hungry. On the other hand, the camp administration appeared to be very good. The officers and guards did not exert their authority unless necessary. I had expected a lot worse upon my arrival there. Most of the time, all of the German personnel were even respectful of us to a great extent. But some of the old-timers in the RAF told me of the harsher regime earlier on in the war when the Germans expected to win; they were very strict and arrogant towards POWs.

There was one Luftwaffe Captain who I shall never forget. He always joked with the POWs, especially at appell, when he would go along the line counting in several different languages. I was told that he spoke five languages fluently. He was always smiling and joking with the POWs. I will never forget his gold teeth with that big smile. Strange, though, I cannot remember the names of my fellow inmates or the Germans. I often wish I had written down all those names to reinforce my memory. Since those days, I have realized just how important it is to remember personal names from the past and present. However, I can remember the names of crew members on my last mission and a few before and most of the pilots I flew with in my career.

My main hobby was reading. This pastime was mainly because of the reasonably fresh broken bones that did not allow me to sprint around the compound. I would have liked to have been enjoying amateur radio, flying a plane for the sheer enjoyment of it, or racing around in a car or motorcycle -only in my dreams for the moment. It was not too difficult to get to the library nearly every day with the cast and iron walker, and I enjoyed the books there, especially the technical ones. All of the books I read were in English, mainly from England, sent to the men who had been incarcerated at the camp for a long time, many from families of those in Stalag Luft III. I suppose I learned more of the theory of flying and aviation in general there than I did in flying school. As I have mentioned before in the book, jogging and even fast walking were out, but I could still get to the gym-lift weights and punch the bag.

The theatre was remarkable. The one big play/production rehearsed and presented on stage was very good. The actors were outstanding, the sound effects were authentic, and the decorations were exceptional. Yet now, I cannot remember the name of the play! I learned that the Germans shipped much of the stage decor and equipment from the bombed-out Berlin Opera and other places just for the camp. That was hard to believe. Still, one would think he was watching a professional drama in a ritzy London theatre instead of a remote POW camp.

In England in the 1960s, I saw a billboard for a British Comedy Film; it was a series called 'Carry On' which was not really my 'cup of tea', and I did not see any of them. But one guy's face stood out, and I thought I recognized that guy! A little older, but in my 'memory bank' nonetheless. His name was Peter Butterworth, and he was a player/organiser in the theatrical productions at the camp. Sure enough, I looked him up with the help of my daughters in England, and they recognised him well before me as being famous.

The actor was at the Stalag with the British contingent andwas flying with the British Navy Fleet Air Arm, but he was shot down earlier in the war and had been at the camp much longer than me. He also had been at other camps before Stalag Luft III. I also learned that Peter helped in the two escape attempts by organizing plays and singing to muffle the sounds of the diggers and escape preparations for the March 1944 'push'. Now he was a famous actor in Britain.'

You felt you weren't a prisoner if you just concentrated on the spectacle. The one big play was around Christmas time, and it was one of the last. I had been warned to seek shelter in case of an air raid warning while outside on the grounds. I believe they gave us three minutes; otherwise, you might get shot when failing to take cover in time. And when on the first occasion, I hurried into the nearest building, it was a stroke of luck. I happened to enter a block where several RAF types were all sitting around a large table. They welcomed me and motioned me to join them. These were all old-timers captured in the early forties, one I believe in 1939. They told me how rougher it was in the camps then, about the Great Escape, the tunnels and the fellow who was shot for being tardy during the air raid alert. But according to them, times had changed remarkably, and the Germans began to realize the war was lost for them. Well, at this time, I heard the phrase 'Alles Kooput' repeatedly from the guards nearly every day.

Chapter 10

Changing Camps and 'Light at the End of The Tunnel'!

Everything changed fast in late January 1945, and the Russians were on or near the Oder River defences. The orders were for all able-bodied POWs to pack up and march out of the camp to the South-West. At this time, I didn't know where they planned to go. I wanted to march out with them; however, the RAF Col (South African Lt. Col.) in charge of my block advised me not to try with my leg and foot in poor shape. He thought that perhaps the Germans might shoot me if I fell out on the march.

It was a sad and somewhat alarming night when most of the boys began marching out of the camp with only what they could carry. It was bitter cold with snow on the ground. As I saw the last ones leave, I wondered what would happen to us left behind. Four hundred of us called "sick, lame or lazy" stayed behind. Later, we were herded into the hospital and lined against the walls sitting down. I was near the front entrance. Suddenly the doors flew open, and a group of soldiers (S.S. I believe) with machine guns came tramping in. They all walked along the corridors giving us a grim look as they passed by. I must say they looked lean, mean and dirty and hung around too long. I had a bad feeling. Finally, it occurred to me that we were all to be shot, and I still believe that had the Russians broken through the East Wall defences of the Odor River, they might have shot us to keep us out of Russian hands.

After this, we were allowed to move back into the blocks of the North Compound and given somewhat free reign. Again, it was a sight to behold! There was clothing, cigarettes, books, keepsakes, and hundreds of other items left in every building. It was a wonderment to see so many things scattered about the place. And as we were allowed to wander into any of the buildings, I picked up all the British and American cigarettes I could carry, plus two perfectly new RAF Uxbridge Blue uniforms.

Several days later, we were herded into trucks, taken to the Bonhof, loaded on old French 40 and 8 rail cars, and told that we were headed for Nurnberg. The floors of the vehicles were covered with straw, and we were highly crowded in; I believe 60 to 80 in each one. We were so packed in that we had to put our legs across about three others just to stretch out. It was a miserable ride. I had carried all the cigarettes I possibly could in a red cross parcel box, as I knew these would be the ultimate trade items. Along the way, I threw out a few packs to two railway workers, who I believe were French POWs. They threw up their arms and waved in thanks. The guard sat at the door and left it halfway open most of the time. In this way, I could see some of the countryside in the daytime. There was an overhead air-raid warning while stopping at the marshalling yards at either Chemnitz or Leipzig. We sat in the cars whilst they uncoupled the engine and ran it out of the yard. Most of us thought this was it this time, but the bombers overflew the yard to another target. It appears they suspected we were there. At this stop, we were let out to go to the toilet. I remember a crowd gathering at the top of a bridge and laughing as we pulled down our pants. I couldn't believe it! I thought, what an odd sense of humour. It was a miserable trip.

Upon passing through the city of Nurnburg, I was shocked to see the appalling damage. It was the first time I had seen a sizeable bombed-out city. It was a shell of a once beautiful place—hulks of buildings, naked walls and twisted metal parts of nightmare proportions. I could hardly believe that anyone could mentally or physically survive such ruins.

The Nurnburg POW camp was nowhere like SLIII. It wasn't organized and had limited grounds around the rows of buildings. The food rations were scarce. We ate soup called the 'Green Death' that had white millet in it, and each one had a white worm inside. The millets, we were told, originally came from Ukraine in Russia when the Germans backed out. They were part of the German army's strategic food storage.

The green came from added vegetables; if you were lucky, there could be a piece of meat or two (about a one-half inches square) in your bowl.

Shortly after arriving there, the RAF "Nuisance Raiders" flying the Mosquito bomber dropped a "Blockbuster" bomb by mistake within a few hundred feet of the camp. I saw the RAF boys get awfully nervous after hearing the plane prowling around in the heavy overcast skies. Then, it went away for a few minutes and returned, the sound more powerful than ever. I heard the whistle, saw the flash silhouetted by pine trees in the wood just out of the camp, and had just turned halfway around to hit the deck (floor) of the back porch when the blast hit me and caught me in midair and pushed me hard to the floor. My ears went wild for a while. I was completely deaf from the concussion. The building walls came away from the floor by inches and stayed away from the floor by more than an inch permanently. You could see the ground outside the building.

Eventually, the Germans let us build (dig) slit trenches outside the buildings to jump into during the air raids. It took some long arguments by the ranking officers with the Germans to finally let us do this.

There were several raids on Nurnberg again. I saw RAF bombers go down in flames at night, and the B-17s explode in midair during their bombing missions. My thoughts-poor, guys- I know what some of you might be going through! The slit trenches were unnecessary, after all, but they could have saved us from a fiery building and burning parts that hit them.

Once, several of us were permitted out of the camp to collect firewood for the kriege burners. We were under heavy guard. It was the first time I had been out of the camp except to be transferred to another location. During this short trip outside, I noticed metal buttons and other small pieces resembling military insignia. I was told that this area was formerly a POW camp for French Officers captured earlier in the war and that an RAF bomber in trouble salvoed its bombs directly on top of the camp, killing two thousand of them. I don't know how accurate the story was.

As previously stated, we were always ravenous at Nurnberg. Some of the boys told me that the Germans regularly carted potatoes through the camp very early in the morning. From then on, I got up very early in the morning and made raids on the waggon as it passed. The guards attempted to ward us off, but we always came away with a few raw potatoes-potato pilferers!

One inspiring moment at Nurnberg was when two F-51 fighters flew low over the camp to give us a little show. It was an encouraging incident and gave us some hope. But we heard a short time later that at least one of them was shot down and wound up as a POW with us!

SL III was a country club to me compared to Nurnberg. We got a shower about every 30 days. At least, I believe that I had two showers the whole time there, which was about two months. There was no proper library as such and no homemade sports equipment. Little fuel for the fires, and we were down to about 800 calories a day in food. I was losing weight faster than ever. But it appeared the war would be over soon. That lifted my spirits more than anything. I only hoped I could be alive and in good condition (as well as I was, anyway) at that time.

Then came the day when we were alerted that we would be marching out the next day. The allied armies were moving fast toward us-Patton's Third Army. Our destination was south. I wasn't sure where we were going all the time. That day, I went to the temporary hospital, packing up to leave and asking for any food (especially powdered milk) and medicine that would help me with my lame foot and leg since I was determined to march. To my surprise, they gave me a few core items-more than I expected. That night, I put all these treasured supplies under my bed to safeguard them until the next morning. I thought I would awaken if anyone tried to take them. How wrong I was because I must have slept very soundly, for the following day, everything was gone! It was with a strange surprise to think my fellow krieges would do such a thing. But hunger does strange things to people?

The day we moved out, it would be hard to forget the sight of two young Luftwaffe pilots helping to make arrangements for the march. They looked smart in their uniforms and appeared quite efficient. Unfortunately for them, they had no planes to fly and were ordered to join the army. I really felt sorry for them.

The camp commander had offered all lame and wounded space on the hospital train, but I refused even though I knew I would be lucky to complete the march. Red crosses were painted on the top of each coach, but I figure some trigger-happy allied pilots would fire on the train anyway. I had lived through too much to be killed on a train at this stage of the war.

Sure enough, a short time after we marched out of the camp, it sounded like all hell had broken loose. I heard air and ground fire in all directions. There were what sounded like a lot of planes all over the sky. Several of us took shelter under a small bridge until most of the firing ceased. Many POWs ran behind buildings, trees, et al, which afforded little protection. However, no one was hurt in the raid, as far as I know.

On the march, I met one of my crew members from my bomb group who had been transferred to another crew. He was on the same raid I was on the day we collided with the bomber from our Squadron. He was pretty surprised to see me as he and all the members of the bomb group thought we were all killed in the collision. They had not seen any parachutes from either aircraft and presumed we were all dead.

Our entire marching group commander was supposedly the oldest in rank in the U.S. Army. We were all mixed up now, and it seemed all the allied services were represented in our quest. We were warned not to try to escape, as the S.S. and other units were following on the flanks, and if we were caught trying to escape, they would shoot us, especially if we were caught in a prohibited area. There was also a rumour going around that we might be held as hostages for Hitler and his staff and taken to somewhere in the German Alps. No one knew where we would end up.

Also, on the march, I had a variety of fascinating experiences. Some included trading cigarettes with former members of the Afrika Corp for bread. When wandering off the road a short distance to a farmhouse, a woman gave me milk, bread, and potatoes. She said that her husband was a POW in the US and was treated well in a letter she had received from him. She wanted to return her gratitude by helping us. And at a spot where an old man was wheeling his son in a wheelchair, he turned towards Berlin and cursed at Hitler. He said that he had three other sons who had already been killed in the war, and how we crossed the Danube River with unexploded bombs on each side with S.S. soldiers resting on the east side. And now, I perhaps saved one POW from being shot who was sitting near me on a farm cart. He had hopped on the cart with a couple of us who were lame, and the farmer objected as the old horse couldn't pull the wagon. The guard told him to get off, and he retorted by calling the German a terrible name. Then, the man raised his rifle and aimed. I put my arms in front of the fellow and told the guard that he didn't mean it, which calmed him down a bit. The guard and several others had his entire family following behind him on the march; his wife, children, and grandparents. They had no place to go, and it was like some medieval procession from the middle ages, except with a few more updated weapons.

A few days before we reached Mooseburg, a German Captain told us that our chief, Roosevelt was dead.

Upon arriving at Moosburg, I lived in a tent, and it was a pretty miserable time. Compared to even Nurnburg, it was far worse. It was like camping out on an extended field trip. Glad we didn't have to stay there long. It was here I met a classmate from pilot school. He was now a major, and I was still a second Lt. I could hardly believe it! He had completed his bomber missions, transitioned into fighters and was shot down a few weeks before the war ended. Some guys had all the luck- and he wasn't even injured.

After liberation, General Patton came into the camp at Moosburg. He gave a speech and said, "Men, we are proud of you for enduring your experiences in Germany", or words to that effect. I did not get close enough to hear or see everything going on at the time. It was a glorious occasion and an excellent feeling to know that I was free again. I saw the German flag come down and the American go up. I cheered. So did hundreds of others. Later, I wandered outside the camp and into a small American military encampment. I believe they thought I was a Frenchman because of my clothes. They gave me food and cigarettes from their rations, but they had plenty.

We were taken to an airfield at Landshut not long afterwards to await transport to Rheims, France. Here at Landshut, I met POWs from all over, including a group from New Zealand who were captured at Crete. They had been shipped directly to the island and issued mostly wooden guns and wooden cannons. It was amazing to hear some of their stories. So it was a piece of cake when the Germans took them so unprepared for combat.

Several times at Landshut, we heard horrible screams. In one case, we were told that it was a German woman made to watch the live carving up of her husband. The woman, a farmer's wife, was bound up and made to watch while a Russian POW who had worked on their farm started cutting off the farmer's ears. He finally killed the farmer. And in another case, less horrible, I became involved again. Two American POWs were stealing the heirlooms highly prized by an elderly German couple in their eighties. The New Zealanders and I made these men give them back. I suppose there were thousands of stories like these.

On May 7, my group flew into Rheims on a C-47 transport plane. It was the first time I had ever flown in a military USAF transport after eight years in the Air Corps. We flew low the reasonably short distance, and I could see the extensive damage that had been done even to small villages in the battles and skirmishes that had occurred. At Rheims, we were deloused and given new clothes. And German POWs were already working to clean up the mess we had made. Most were young men who appeared utterly dismayed.

On May 8, the lame and wounded, including myself, were put on a hospital train bound for 'Camp Lucky Strike' near the French Coast. At about midnight, we passed through Paris and looking out of the window, and I could see the giant searchlights pointed towards the sky in the shape of a giant 'V'. It was quite a night.

At Lucky Strike, I was given a physical examination and classed as combat fit and ready- for possible action against the Japanese in the Pacific. There was some rumour that we might be shipped directly to the Pacific from there! But my government was watching over me? At Lucky Strike, I made a recreation trip by truck into the town of Fecamp. I was warned, however, not to wear my pilot's wings, as the Allies had heavily bombed the city, and the townspeople (those who were left) didn't look very favourably on these aircrews.

Here I met a Frenchman in a bar that had come to have German High Command papers in his possession. He was charming and not at all hostile. These were ones the Germans had not destroyed on their retreat from the area in their haste to depart. Amongst these papers were orders signed by Adolf Hitler himself, and although in German, of course, I recognized this. For some cigarettes and a few bucks, I was able to 'purchase' these from the genial fellow. I would love to have found out what the orders had been, but at another bar, this time in New York, on my return to the States, I went to the toilet and stupidly left my small case sitting on a barstool; when I returned, it was gone!

Finally, they put us on a military transport ship bound for the States. All the passengers were ex-POWs. It was the first time I heard the song "Don't Fence Me In", and it became pretty popular aboard ship.

We arrived in New York Harbour on May 29, 1945. It was the biggest welcome I had ever seen. The tug boats were blowing their whistles, the fireboats spouting water, and we could see the ticker tape flowing like water from the tall buildings downtown. Newsmen were allowed aboard the ship even before it docked, taking pictures and interviewing ex-

POWs. I decided to watch it all and remain quiet. Anyway, I was nearly speechless at the time. That night we were quartered at Fort Jay, given another physical exam and leave, and a train ticket (in my case) to my home via Atlanta, Georgia. I could have had 90 days of leave, but I chose 60 days. I tried to enjoy myself on leave but couldn't come to terms with all this freedom and some of the people I thoroughly disliked at home. Not my family, but some in my hometown and surroundings didn't understand the war and my experiences and were sometimes belligerent. I suppose if I had been killed, I would have been classed a hero!

In late July, I reported to the rehabilitation center in Miami Beach, Florida, and quarantined in a First Class hotel. A few weeks later, I chose an assignment to an airfield in Douglas, Arizona, where I had a wild and hectic time. I was promoted to First Lt. and flew B-25s for two months before the Base was closed. After that, there were two more assignments to other U.S. bases before returning to Boca Raton in Florida. Here I saw signs for Real Estate Agents plunged into the ground in wild speculation advertising $5 down and so much a month per acre of land to purchase. Even on my relatively low salary, I was tempted and should have bought all the land I could-ha! This land and swampland would become highly desirable property worth millions in years to come. But instead, it was spent on good times, crap games and radio parts.

I toured bases in Florida and The Mississippi Gulf Coast before being reassigned to duties overseas, returning to Germany for the Berlin Airlift.

Chapter 11

The Berlin Airlift and Beyond

The Russians became hostile to the Allies' intentions in Germany, specifically Berlin. Their 'territorial ambitions' became under threat, and Stalin and his cohorts ordered a blockade of the city of essential supplies and movement by rail and road in general. In addition, the Marshall Plan and the introduction of a new Deutschmark to stabilize Europe did not sit well with the Soviets. Therefore I was part of a group that flew C-47 missions into the city to aid the Berliners. Unfortunately, with many aircraft airborne and taxiing on the ground, there were casualties, and over 100 pilots and crew were lost. Fortunately, I came through, and the siege was lifted when the operation had concluded.

I returned to the United States. I went home to Tennessee and spent some time resting and recuperating. However, I was restless and wanted to return to Europe for duties in England again. The States did not quite have the rationing issue that Europe had, and meat and poultry, if not available in the stores, could be hunted in my part of the world if you were willing and had a mind for hunting. I wanted to do something other than this, however. The war was a long way away, it seemed to me now, although it was only a few years since I left Sargon and that particular part of my history behind. I went home for a brief stint of leave.

The Great Smoky Mountains National Park was and still is a great place to hike and watch nature, although, at the inception of the park, many of the old-timers were bought out and asked to leave by the federal government. One day, with a buddy, we drove and then hiked up to the highest point in Smokies-Clingmans Dome. A B-29 Superfortress had crashed there in 1946 on a routine mission from MacDill Air Force base in

Florida to Chicago. During an early morning flight, the area's poor visibility and bank of thunderstorms contributed to the accident. We could still see bits of the aircraft visible along the Andrews Bald trail, which was sad.

I heard the most significant part of the aircraft left intact was an engine. It must have broken up into thousands of pieces, and I believe there would have been no hope for the crew; all 12 died. Low-level flying in this area, together with the mist and fog the Smokies are noted for, have caused many accidents. Spatial disorientation is magnified in these conditions, plus the fact that you have nowhere to go if you have to make a quick and safe landing. As I have read, there have been many accidents, and in some cases, the planes are never found. The park is relatively small compared to other national parks, but it is still huge, and there is so much backcountry off the laid-out trails to deal with and the overhanging canopy of trees and shrubs. The trees and general shrubbery in the Smokies are dense. A beautiful location, however, and I always liked to return there.

Part 2

Chapter 12

England and a New Start
A Sons Continuation of The Story

Captain Fuller arrived in the UK in 1950 and toured several bases in England, coming to RAF South Ruislip in late 1951. He met my mother, who was working temporarily at the Base on the clerical side of operations of the base commissary.

Previously, she travelled by ship to New York in 1950 and spent time with a girlfriend she had met in London (Leanne), who was also returning by ship to the United States. The family was well off, and Mum stayed in the family apartment near Central Park. She was impressed by the sites and worked in the beauty department at Macy's for a time, which did not last too long. Listening to Ladies who were bored with their husbands and liked to talk did not suit her after a while. Mum moved on and, after training, worked as a psychiatric nurse in Canada after leaving New York. She didn't want to return to England at that time, which was rather drab after the war and had still not shaken off rationing and the aftermath of bomb damage in London and elsewhere. She became pretty disillusioned with the psychiatric hospital in Vancouver, however, as she once assisted an unmarried mother who had given birth to a child out of wedlock, who was sent to the facility because of her status and the fact that this had caused her distress and being considered a rebel. My Mother said she was a bright, pretty girl who didn't deserve this treatment. It had been enough reason for her to be incarcerated at the time! Also, electric shock treatment had been administered to some patients as part of a 'course of therapy', now known to be primarily pointless and have undesired side effects. Such actresses as Francis Farmer and Gene Tierney had been given this detrimental treatment in the USA for depression (and the loss of a child in Gene Tierney's case.) Gene Tierney was, in fact, one of Mum's favourite actresses.

After becoming involved in an accident crossing the border of the United States with a group of friends, she returned to the UK for family commitments.

Chapter 13

London History
and The English Side

My Grandfather Thomas, on our mother's side of the family in England, had fought in the First World War in the army and had some exasperating times in Europe. Once, taking shelter in a French barn with some other soldiers, he wrote a longing postcard to my English Grandmother about his and the men's plight-it is titled 'Somewhere in France', and we still have it.

Nan was a little suspicious in thinking he was having too much fun in France with the mesdemoiselles, which was why he was 'staying on and losing himself in the country'.He got a telling-off on his return to England! Their last name was 'Holder' on Grandad's side and Saunders on the matriarchal, and the genealogy is quite complex.

Dave Holder, my Nephew, is very interested and still trying to unravel the very long ago past, with a lot of near-European history being a factor in our history. After a DNA test of Mum, it is safe to say that we had much in common with Saxons, Jutes and Angles that came from the near continent in the areas known today as Germany and France.

The bulk of the Roman army left around 410 AD, leaving a maelstrom of uncertainty in their departure. This was taken advantage of by northern European tribes who colonised in a period known as the 'dark ages', meaning written records were scarce. It is a misnomer, because some of the jewellery and textile/tool-making was exquisite considering the nomadic existence of the invaders. After many battles with the indigenous, many of these people became farmers. However, the new settlers' image of 'camping out' in the magnificence of abandoned Roman villas was likely correct in the beginning. A possible climate catastrophe or outside agents like a comet or asteroid may have caused a cooling period, another factor in the gloom and scarcity of written records, and perhaps the sky and atmosphere were a little dark!

On Dad's side, apparently, there was a 'Fuller' or two on the Mayflower in which the pilgrims came to the New World in 1620. There is also talk of being related to Jesse James later. There was a paucity of people in the United States compared to Europe, so some of these families could be narrowed down a little more!

Our Grandmother and Grandfather had been publicans at The famous Enterprise Public House off Red Lion Square and High Holborn in London.

Grandad and his daughter Jean (Mum) had witnessed one of the first V1 flying bombs to hit London in the Woolwich area. They observed the red flame from the tailpipe and heard the eerie odd noise /drone it made, and at first, thought it was a bomber crashing into the city. Only later to learn of its true identity.

A year or so earlier, Mum frequented the Dominion Theatre on Tottenham Court Road to see the latest Hollywood 'flicks'. This she did by riding her bike from the pub and usually coming home via Red Lion Square. Mum said she had seen the film "The Tower Of London" starring Basil Rathbone and Boris Karloff. This time he was not Frankenstein, but the henchman Mord, serving Richard III of England as executioner. He scared Mum as he went about the Tower, removing those who might get in the way of Richard's becoming King and the ominous noise he made with his club foot on his approach to his victims. However, In the equally scary real world outside, she had taken another route home on her bike that evening. Unfortunately, a bomb landed that night in the Square. It decapitated a patrolling policeman while she would have been there- a fortunate escape.

Mum was evacuated with the many others during the war to a small village called 'Pidley' in Cambridgeshire (to the north of London).The name always gave merriment to the family, when it was mentioned. It may have lived up to its name, as mum wanted to come home to be with her Mum and Dad, which she did. Next they tried 'Whitemore' in Cornwall, apparently so named because of the 'white puffs of cotton' in the fields. It was was and is mainly smallholdings (small farmers or individuals). Mum liked the horses and nature, but again it did not work out. She was used to London, wrote letters to come home and did so after only a few months.

Later on in the war, she was out on her bike again, this time with friends, and they noticed something metallic near one of the bombed-out streets. Apparently, it was still warm to the touch and had some form of markings on it-not English. She quickly pocketed it, not wanting to raise the ire of an Air Raid Warden or Policeman. A V1 flying bomb had detonated on the spot, and it later was confirmed to be part of the chassis.

She kept it after the war, with her other belongings, but having returned from Canada, she had left it with someone and it was missing, along with some other goodies and storage, of which she was not too happy about.

Mum would have a small circle of friends in the later 1940s. There that surprisingly included a young German. They all went out together to the coffee bars and pubs together, and she was surprised about something; he knew London so well, like a local. It turns out he was a Heinkel pilot (The two-engine bomber used so effectively at first in the Battle of Britain). He had to know the topography and geography of much of England, including London. His name was Anton, and he was remorseful about the war, but he was just a pilot following orders. He wanted Mum and the others to go to Germany, but my Mother never did. Despite only a few years before being an enemy, he had a few friends in London, and the group had no animosity towards him. He left for home a few months later, and she never saw him again.

Red Lion Square has a history of odd happenings, and is a microcosm of the rich history of London.

Oliver Cromwell (the leader of the parliamentary forces during the English Civil War in the 1600s) and his military and parliamentary colleagues, Bradshaw and Ireton, were said to have been taken to the Red Lion Inn nearby before being taken onwards to Tyburn to be 'hanged whilst dead'! as a gesture and revenge against the English Civil War and the killing of The Monarch Charles The First. This period was during the restoration of his son Charles The Second.

Cromwell died in 1658 and had initially been buried in Westminster Abbey. However, following the Restoration of the Monarchy in 1660, the new Parliament ordered the bodies of Cromwell, Bradshaw and Ireton to be disinterred, posthumously tried and executed at Tyburn.

It is speculated that the bodies were buried in Red Lion Square or on the grounds of the Inn instead. Substitutes were taken on to Tyburn to be 'exhibited' and picked at by the crows' before rotting further, having been exhibited with their heads shown at Westminster Hall.

This may have been the start of the odd happenings that seemed to follow the Fuller and Holder family?

Mum and her brother (Uncle Frank)had always feared an attic room when living at the Enterprise Pub as children in the 1940s. Cold and foreboding, it had always felt like something was there, and they had never ventured into that place. A family pet alsatian did not like the site either, with the hackles on his back raised when it got near the room and growling simultaneously. Mum felt the bristles of his fur, which pointed straight up. Could it be the ghosts of Cromwell and his colleagues, their spirits not at rest, having been moved and disturbed so many years before? She said she did a bad thing to her slightly older brother Frank (Mum was 12) by scaring him in the basement with a rubber rat placed over the door and having it fall on him when he opened it when being asked to go down there and fetch something from the stores. He ran upstairs, terrified at this impromptu prank and thought it was a man laying a hand on his shoulder at first.

She said she was trying to get back at him for playing with her dolls and making them dirty when she asked him not to!

Later, I would read about a case in the 1970s of student nurses renting a flat and sharing the costs in Red Lion Square.

They were scared to death by banging and unusual noises late at night, especially when there was only one in the property whilst the other was out and working. The other flats around them apparently were not responsible for any disturbance of that nature. In 1971, a female guest at the small flat on the Square was woken by another girl who wanted to know why her bed was occupied. The guest apologised and explained that she was invited, after which the girl left the room, and the guest fell back asleep. The following morning, she mentioned the incident to her friend-he paled and explained his flatmate, who usually slept there, was in hospital after a suicide attempt. They later discovered the girl had died during the night. I don't know if this is the same flat or the same person or entity responsible. The book I read with the first account from the 1970s has disappeared, and I cannot locate the first story through research at this time.

On one occasion during the War, Uncle Johnny and Stanley, who always seemed to be in each other's company on merchant ships and spent a lot of time together in port, ventured into the pub with a female monkey, which one of the sailors had brought back with him from a trip to the South Seas. Johnny took ownership and even took her around on the buses if not driving. A strange site to see a Monkey strolling down High Holborn in the middle of a war. She would sit at the bar and eat peanuts with the rest of the customers and presented an unusual site. The cats in the pub would be terrified of her for some reason (the mating instinct?) and would usually take off to the cellar or parts unknown!

She was undoubtedly clever, as mum got some cups and a coin or pea and would hide one in a cup with the Monkey watching and move them around fast, as in the game of cups. According to Mum, she would invariably find the object and could understand the concept of play.

However, she could not be kept as she needed special attention, and the boys were leaving.

Also, she was becoming a bit jealous. There was friction even when John brought a girlfriend back to the pub. Jealousy was undoubtedly in her nature.
They decided the best policy was to take her to the zoo, and they rehoused the monkey there.
The cats were the most relieved.

Chapter 14

Family Life In The USA And A Visitor From Blighty

In 1952 Mum and Dad married and returned to the States, and Dad would tour various bases for the next ten years or so across the country.

As well as being a pilot, Dad worked in the communications sector and became a 'Ham Radio' operator and would later go on to teach my brothers Morse code.

They lived in Texas and Mississippi and places like Deluth and Minnesota.

Base living was quite good, and officers usually had agreeable habitations.

Mum became interested in performing arts and appeared in productions like the Student Prince and Cat on a Hot Tin Roof at the Keesler AFB Base in Mississippi.

According to her, although these were amateur productions, the rehearsals were quite demanding; you had to be as professional as the professionals, or it might devolve into unintentional slapstick.

She had other work to do too, looking after a young family.

Some years before, she had applied to Lucy Clayton Modeling Agency in London and been accepted.

Lucie Clayton College was founded by Sylvia Lucie Golledge in 1928 as a modelling agency and finishing school. It was bought by Leslie Kark, who owned a successful model directory. It became Britain's top modelling agency during the 1950s and 1960s.

Upon further investigation and later meeting our Father, she felt the lifestyle might not be suitable for her!

She had a place at the college, and she regretted not taking up the opportunity. Still, hey, she wanted to fly more than anything else.

In retrospect, she would have made a great professional actress as she had the looks too.

Life in the USA in the 1950s was very open and forward-thinking, with the rustic charm of frontier thinking and a dynamic attitude looking towards the future in a happy, fortunate mix. There was so much space too, unlike the environs of London, which however was still rich in history. Due to a lack of an earthly frontier, people have turned in on themselves and are far too worried now about what others think, from within and without. The USA did have its share of social and economic problems, and things were far from perfect, but things were beginning to change gradually after the watershed of the War Years. Dad and the family were mixing with test pilots and future spacemen, where the new frontier is, and one which could and should be explored more (There are, of course, vast oceans as well, but that is another story).

Time on base could be glamorous, attending parties at the Officer's Club and mingling with the 'Brass'! But there was also looking after the family and day-to-day life to organize.

At Keesler Air Force Base in Biloxi, Mississippi, the area backed onto what was known as the 'Back Bay', which was part of The Mississippi Sound, with barrier islands and waterways on The Gulf Of Mexico.

The family purchased a Sailing Boat and enjoyed days of Summer sun and trips on the Back Bay and Dauphin Island, a Barrier Island in Alabama. A little sailing training and getting used to the boom (which could knock you out of the boat!), and usually, the days were long and fun.

On one occasion, the family were all on one of the Islands, and relatives from Tennessee came down to visit. They said they saw dancing and smoke from a distance and thought some kind of a party or perhaps strange ritual was occurring. In fact, they were burning plastic bottles and the small amount of wood they could find to keep away the hoards of mosquitoes that were biting them to distraction!

These places were and still are subject to the destructive forces of Hurricanes and particularly Camille, in 1969, which devastated Biloxi and Dauphin Island.

In fact, It caused a storm surge of 24 feet and flattened everything on that part of the coast, and the Hurricane caused deaths even in The Appalachian Mountains of Virginia.

'The Hurricane Hunter' Squadron, which tracked and still does investigate and record weather measurements, which was based at Dad's base at Keelser, was involved in monitoring this storm and many others to this day. They use C-130 four-engine reconnaissance craft, which is rugged and durable. The wind Speeds of this storm reached a peak intensity of 175 mph.

Whilst in Texas, Bob and Roland got lost in a cave system, and Bob became trapped and had to be rescued by a passing man who found out that he had got caught when Roland pulled him up in his car. This was at a location near Universal City, near the house. In the San Antonio Times, he was described as the 'Young Spelunker', complete with a picture of him in a pensive pose.

The boys had got into trouble back in Mississippi when, as 5-year-olds, they found an axe in the garage at the house at Lamar Park on base and started hacking at the telephone pole outside; presumably, they thought it would give them some skills pre-scout camp! Mum, horrified at what they were doing, quickly ordered them inside, grabbed the little axe, and later met with a jeep of MPs who were doing the rounds. Their excuse, as young kids, was that they thought it was not used, as new poles were being put up and the old ones replaced in their defence. The Military Police said they would not report it this time and ordered a crew to assess the damage, which was light- a narrow escape. The brass and neighbours must have thought Russian paratroopers were in the area!

There was a tragic incident which did not end favourably when the kids all went out to play near the back bay and passed a relatively young child when they were returning home from the beach. They had been messing about on the shore, beachcombing and enjoying the weather after a spell of rain. Our parents didn't care for them to be put too long on their own, but they were independent-minded. As a caveat, however, Mum insisted that they all stay together. They had a feeling that the girl was much too young to be out on her own with her doll and skipping along and felt they should have said something to somebody, or tried to intercept her and ask her what she was doing out by herself. They found out later that either in a sand pit that had filled with water or a local quarry that was off-limits and posted, a young girl had drowned on her own. Though not showing a picture of the girl in the following newspaper write-up, the kids felt this was the same girl they passed, moving along in her own world and adverse to the dangers before her. From the newspaper article, it turned out that she had escaped the house and decided to wander off by herself, perhaps a little mad at something her parents might have said or just wanting to explore independently. It had not helped that previously, it was raining heavily, and any depression or place that could hold any amount of water was filled up and was not running off quickly or drying up. It was something they thought about for a long time and something that nagged at them, and they still recount the story to this day, though the little girl's face was a little unclear to some now, as much time has now passed.

On another occasion, one of many nuclear drills was about to take place, and Mum had become tired of these with 6 kids to get ready and move out in a semi-military fashion. There was a lot of nuclear panic at the time and paranoia about a possible Russian attack. As the MPs came around with megaphones raised from their jeeps, Mum told the kids to keep quiet and 'duck and cover' at home so they wouldn't see anything. Apparently, they got out and tried to peek in the windows, but the gang hid well, and the troops moved on. She didn't want to sit in a hot basement with the rest of the military wives today. Dad was on duty, so was not going to get in trouble directly if the brass found out.

The threat of Hurricanes was always a possibility living on or near the Gulf.

Whilst in the States in September of 1961, Hurricane Carla made Landfall at Port O'Connor, Texas, not far from Corpus Cristi and Randolph Air Force Base, near San Antonio, where our Father and family were also based for a time.

The family were away at the time visiting relatives in Tennessee, so they did not witness its destructive power first hand. The base was mainly left unscathed, fortunately.

Upon their return, they visited the outer banks and Corpus Cristi for some sun and a picnic about six months later, when things had primarily been cleared up.

They unpacked the car, and Mum and one of the children went down the beach for a quick reconnaissance and brisk walk.

Upon their return, an object caught my Mum's eye; she initially thought it was a stingray or crab that had washed up dead.

It looked odd. The picnic ended abruptly, however, when she had the suspicion it was actually a child's body part in the long grass of the upland dunes not far from the beach.

The Emergency Services were called, but the family only hung around briefly after that.

More than likely, whoever the person was was a victim of Hurricane Carla.

In 1964 the family lived in Hattiesburg, Mississippi, for a time off base. The kids attended the local Junior High School, Oak Grove, a bit like living in a Mark Twain existence in rural America as they described some of the kids from the poorer families wearing straw hats and didn't bother with shoes because it was so hot.

One day in October, the children were told to take cover under their desks. They thought it might be one of the 'old' nuclear drills of 'duck and cover', as the United States was still fearful over the Cuban Missile Crisis of the previous year and the possible prospect of annihilation by Russia. This time it would be different. This time my siblings said the floor rippled like a wave, even through the concrete, and the desk, chair, and inkwell undulated like being tossed on a stormy sea; this detonation was actual. This would be one of only two nuclear bombs to be set off east of the Rocky Mountains. This was near a little town called Baxterville, near Hattiesburg. There was obviously still paranoia about Russian and other powers testing their weapons and calling for test bans. But this one was therefore detonated underground in a salt mine. The idea was that any excess radiation would fuse into the salt and become less dangerous to man, beast and vegetation. Salt would also be more accessible to study than solid rock's effects, as it was easier to excavate. The bomb was put into position and plugged into 600 feet of concrete-.BOOM, BOOM, BOOM! This test was called 'Salmon', and the people of Baxterville, though aware of the tests, were treated to a party atmosphere with picnic tables, food and drink supplied by the local government. Later 400 persons would file for house damage to furniture and crockery! Two years later, the second was more minor, but the last test went ahead in the same cavity as the first was placed.

The perils and excitement of the Nuclear age.

Whilst in Mississippi and on base, Mum decided to get a lifeguard certification, as she thought this may be a good idea living close to the sea for her health, a willingness to help others and also something to put on her resume, should she want to return to full-time employment. On base, she attended the course for about 3 months in mid-summer to late autumn, and then came the day of her finals and attaining certification. The last trial involved rescuing three people who were pretending to drown in the pool and bringing them safely to the side and up the stairs. The first was a child; though mum said he fought a little bit, she managed to subdue and place him on his back, hold his head above water and make sure his air passage was clear. The second was quite a 'well built' man, who, though he struggled a little bit, was relatively easy to subdue (perhaps taking a liking to mum) and came along relatively easily to the pool's edge, although being a bulky prospect. The last proved to be the most tricky; this was a younger woman who mum said she had squirmed and resisted like a conger eel and was very hard to subdue (she was 'acting' very well and perhaps was using this space to demonstrate her talent; maybe having lost out to Mum in the part of 'A Street Car Named Desire' or 'The Student Prince' in a theatrical presentation at the base theatre.)In any case, Mum passed the qualification and could now call herself a 'lifeguard'.

Not long after this, my Grandmother from England came over to stay with the family. She travelled on the Queen Mary from Southampton to New York, and the family decided to go to Washington to pick her up. It was a voyage that could take up to a week, and the passengers had a dinner/dance on the last night to give you some idea of the relative luxury. I still have the pamphlets given to each passenger, which list the passengers, sumptuous food courses and entertainment for the duration of the journey; oh, so glamorous!

A very different experience from flying an economy flight nowadays to the East Coast. It would be a long trip to Texas for her otherwise and she said she would like to see some of the family in Tennessee and country too. Dad was considering his career in the military and decided to take a trip to The Pentagon, in Virginia to retrieve his records on the way up.

Mum and the kids were waiting in the car and got quite perturbed when Dad was too long. He came out and said they should drive to a diner as he was still waiting for a meeting with an official. After hamburgers and shakes, it was back to the Pentagon and a more relaxed security to pick up Dad.

They met Nan the next Day in Washington and drove back to Tennessee along some back routes and small towns as the interstate was only partially open. Quite an experience for the landlady of a London pub. They arrived in Tennessee and met the family.

Our Grandmother in particular got on unusually well with Dad's Father, who usually was sometimes quite distant to strangers, sometimes having the airs of a judge about to go into chambers for a murder trial; well he was a businessman. The rode the Ober, Gatlinburg together, a newly opened ski lift and resort in Gatlinburg, Tennessee and had fun, 'The Judge' was having fun too!

They drove back to Texas and had a good time, Nan helping to look after the children and meeting friends from Nogalles, Texas who she would later write to once back in England.

There was an incident on a trip to see the famous Alamo. They were driving in two cars at the time because of all the kids to carry and luggage during the school holidays. Dad was behind by a few hours after having to complete business at the base but was unfortunate to have broken down with the kids in the middle of the desert scrub somewhere behind with a cracked radiator hose. They had water and supplies and were not overtly worried. But, of course, no one had a cell phone. He was later picked up by a tow truck and taken to a local garage for repairs, as it could not be fixed roadside. Mum was obviously worried as they could not communicate. At the beginning of the trip, they said they would meet at a certain point to rendezvous and carry on, but this did not happen. In a diner restaurant, she spoke with a local sheriff who asked the local coffee-drinking community if they had seen a man and his kids in an old station wagon (Mum and Dad had one of those iconic American vehicles with the long wooden panels).They hadn't, so the Sheriff said he would follow this worried English lady and her 'mom' and help in the search, as Mum was fearful and she had Nan and some of the kids in her car. A little while later, along the highway, Dad recalls seeing a speeding Oldsmobile doing about 80 mph (the 'speed needle' rose quickly in a V8 if you weren't careful!) that he recognized and a cop car in hot pursuit. He knew that car and waved frantically with both hands, jumping up and down at the side of the mechanic's shop as Mum and Nan sailed by at speed, looking straight ahead as he recalls, and did not see him at all with the Sheriff in pursuit! A bit reminiscent of the comedy film it's a Mad, Mad, Mad, Mad World with all the American comedians of the day and the Brit-Terry Thomas, a British officer on a day out from Vandenberg Air Force Base with a liking for botany and cacti in particular. Our history sometimes reads like a comedy or Sci-Fi story. Twenty minutes later, the Sheriff pulled Mum over and said that he had a radio call from a deputy that he had found Dad at the shop. Eventually, they were reunited, and the Sheriff was thanked profusely for his help and for not giving the family a speeding ticket. The Alamo proved to be a welcome diversion.

At the end of her stay, Dad and Mum would fly her back to New York and a trip on a different ship, The SS United States back to Southampton with some stories to tell. Dinner dances and meetings with the Captain again were a veritable strain!

My Father received many awards during his career including in Radio Communication and received this report in a Duluth, Minnesota,
Paper.
Dated May 16 1957, Duluth Herald.

A Deluth air base officer has been awarded membership in the exclusive DX Century Club of amateur radio operators.

Capt. James A Fuller received the honour from the American Radio Relay League after making a two-way, short-wave contact with his 100th foreign country.

Fuller, communications and electronics officer of the 243rd fighter group made all the contacts from his station -call letters WWXJ -set up in his home.

Some of the countries Fuller has worked with his $300 homemade rig are Eritrea, Belgian Congo and Morroco in Africa, and Germany, Formosa, Liechtenstein and San Marino.

Fuller recalled an odd coincidence while working two ships in the South Pacific, and it turned out that the two ship operators were pals. Fuller spent about an hour relaying for the pair. He also had the occasion to let a Deluth couple talk to their son stationed with the army in Germany. The couple heard their grandson's voice for the first time in that contact. Operating on a power source of three hundred watts, Capt. Fuller can converse with other 'Ham' operators throughout the world. These amateur operators play an essential role in the Civil Defense network by relaying messages nationwide. As base communications officer, he is responsible for all telephones, fixed and mobile radio units, and the cryptography and teletype sections. He has approximately thirty men working under him in a job which he describes as 'very interesting and enjoyable'. Currently checked out to fly the C-47, Fuller holds a commercial pilot's license.

Also, from The Air Force Times, April 16 1958.

Capt. James A Fuller, WOWXJ Duluth Municipal Airport, lays claim to be the first DXCC radiotelephone certificate holder in the USAF while stationed in the U.S. He has contacted 120 separate countries from Duluth.

Chapter 15

The Great Blue Earth, Minnesota incident and More

In 1958 Dad was involved in an incident with a defective DC-3, which landed safely at a small regional airport in Blue Earth, Minnesota, and bought local notoriety.

This is a written account from The Faribault County Register of February 25, 1958.

"Comin' in on a wing and a prayer. Four relieved men stepped from a crippled air force twin-engine CS-47 (military search version of a DC-3) here Saturday morning after a close brush with disaster. "It was either find a spot to land or bail out," said Captain James A. Fuller, the pilot whose crew credited him with a 'superb' job of bringing the big plane in. The trouble started about two miles south of Fairmont as the aircraft returned to Duluth from Lincoln, Nebraska, where personnel were transported. A DC-3's average load is some 20 persons.

When the starboard engine suddenly quit, communication was set up with Waverly, Iowa radar station, which took a 'fix' on the plane. The decision was made to turn and head for Mason City, Iowa when, about five miles north of Fairmont.

However, an attempt to 'feather the propeller' of the dead engine (turn the blades with the wind instead of against it) failed, and the plane began losing altitude fast.

At 5,000 feet over Fairmont, the machine had now dropped to an altitude as low as 1,200 feet as it neared Blue Earth. Radar contact was lost at that altitude, and the Waverly Station alerted Sheriff Earl Fletcher in Blue Earth at about 9:30 am.

A few minutes later, the plane landed safely on a strip at the local airport. Crewman Lt. Ross B. Duckett, A2c Rober C. Murray and A2c Robert Woodward praised Captain Fuller for his skill at handling the machine. "We were ready to bail out just before we sighted the Blue Earth strip," Woodard said.

Checking the air map, Fuller noted that the next nearest Field would have been Fairmont, the place they had just passed over. "We could never have turned and made it back even that short distance by the time we approached Blue Earth," he said.

The C-47 landed on the 2,400-foot strip from northeast to southwest. "From the air, commented Lt. Duckett, the strip looked extremely rough because the sod showed through patches of snow, giving it a bumpy appearance. But it was a nice smooth landing".

Captain Fuller said the airport here "was in excellent shape", and the runway is adequate for the take-off. He said the DC-3 type requires only about 1,500 feet when no cargo is aboard. The CS-47 is a search plane equipped with considerable radio communication equipment.

It was the largest plane to touch down on the local airfield for many years, and hundreds visited the Field Saturday afternoon and Sunday to see it. Courteous air force men allowed many to go through the aircraft.

Airman Murray remained in Blue Earth after another craft from Deluth arrived Saturday afternoon to pick up the other crewmen.

He was joined Sunday by four maintenance men from Deluth Sunday afternoon who brought with them a new engine, a hoist and other major equipment. It is expected to take about three days to have the ship ready for take-off. A normal engine replacement at the Duluth Field, where equipment is handy, takes only about one day.

The crippled plane was towed from the landing strip to the west side of the hangar, where mechanics were making the engine change. The craft is too high and too wide to get inside.

The DC-3 (or C-47 in the air force) was the most popular craft used in World War II. It has been said that not a single one has ever worn out-some out-lasting as many as 60 engine changes. Moreover, they have been known to carry as many as 74 persons on a single take-off in emergencies.

Lt Duckett is as relieved as any to touch 'the good Blue Earth'! Unfortunately, he is a jet fighter pilot who only 'was along for the ride' to clock air time.

Dad was also involved in the rescue of a small plane in Minnesota, and this was the report from the local Deluth newspaper.

'In Fog A.F. Pilots 'Rescue' Lost Plane.

Air Force and Civil Aeronautics administration teamwork yesterday led to a lost private pilot to safety after a two-hour hide-and-seek search packed with tension and drama. The pair of Duluth air base C-47 pilots were credited today with preventing the crash of the small single-engine Cessna craft. Its pilot made a forced landing at the McGregor municipal airport.

Air Force personnel are trying to learn the flier's identity. They knew he was bound for Prairie Du Chien, Wisconsin, when he alerted the area's bases with 'The May Day' distress call about 10:25 am yesterday.

Control tower men at the Duluth air base heard the pilot's call. He was lost in fog and rain and had a limited fuel supply.

Airbase operations headquarters alerted Capt. Joseph Gambucci, pilot and Capt. James Fuller, co-pilot, who took off in a military C-47, a two-engined transport plane. The alert came so fast that Fuller stood guard against fire as Gambucci started his engines. Just as they were ready to roll, S-Sgt, Paul Jansen, flight engineer, boarded the search craft.

Runway fog was so low and thick that Gambucci had to make an instrument take-off. Once in the air, he switched over to radar control. The Ground Control Approach unit at the base gave directions, sending the C-47 32 miles west of the Duluth Airport.

Gambucci ascended toward the 6000-foot level and found an opening in the heavy cloud mass at about 5000 feet. He radioed the control tower, which served as a communications relay for both planes, telling Howard Dogherty and Russell Stafney, CAA controllers, that the C-47 would circle in an attempt to spot the Cessna. The circling continued for some time, during which the occupants of both planes saw one another only to lose sight as rain and clouds boiled around them. When contact was finally made, the Cessna pilot flew close to the giant plane." He headed in on us like a pigeon coming in to roost", Gambucci later said.

The troubles of both pilots were not yet over. With the light plane on his wing, Gambucci started to return to the Duluth air base. Then the weather became exceptionally rough, with visibility decreasing to the point that Gambucci and Fuller were unable to see their own wing tips. The tower ordered the Cessna to spiral down and find the emergency landing field. Meanwhile, most airport personnel in northeastern Minnesota had followed the three-way broadcast. Moose Lake tower men called immediately to tell that their Field was clear for a landing. At this point, the planes were out of Duluth base radar control. Finland air force base controllers took over and guided the Cessna to Mosse Lake, leaving the C-47 to fly alone.

The Cessna made it to McGregor at about 1:30 pm. Isedor Iverson, McGregor airport manager, said the pilot was almost hysterical from the strain. With this unidentified pilot was his son, about 10, and another man, Iverson said. The part took off again an hour later. Iverson said he thought they had continued toward Prairie du Chien.

Gambucci, Fuller and Jansen found themselves in weather trouble. They circled the Duluth air base for two hours, but the fog and clouds did not lift. Finally, they decided to make one pass for a ground control approach landing. They made it shortly after 2 pm.

Dad retired in 1964 with the rank of Lt. Colonel after many Tours of Duty in the United States and Overseas, including as a transport pilot and radio operator in The Korean War.

Chapter 16

Retirement and Back in the UK

The family moved back to England for the final time in 1963-64, having lived in the USA and Dad being based on and off in the fifties in the UK, and some of my siblings being born in England. After renting and living in Oxford again as they had in 1953, they settled at a house on Sweetcroft Lane in Hillingdon, Greater London. There would be visits back to the States, of course, but the family was based in England for now. The family returned to England on the SS United States, and Mum had a fright on the long voyage. Sister Josie was being chaperoned by one of the crews on deck, they were playing hopscotch, and Josie fell over; she slid and got perilously close to the edge of the rail, which had gaps below, and had it not been for some of the deck rigging she may have met the cold North Atlantic head on. Mum ensured she was always on deck when they were all 'topside' after that incident.

When they arrived at Southampton, Frank was mesmerised by the welders in their goggles and sparks from their arc torches as they toiled on ships, either fixing or making them in the great manufacturing nation of Great Britain! But Frank and the family were 'old hands' at this travelling game, having lived in London for a spell only a few years before with his siblings and parents.

We were welcomed at Sweetcroft Lane in Hillingdon, Greater London by a sweet old lady who used to live across the road from us along a quaint little path filled with flowers. Her name was Mrs Harrington, and she had lived there since the early 1930s, and perhaps before-a world away, and she had seen many changes. Her husband was a Captain in the army but had died some years before. It was sad for her, but she had her daughter visit occasionally. She was impressed by Dad's credentials and called Mum-'The Colonel's Lady', which Mum just laughed off; Mum and Dad weren't the pretentious type.

The house was built in the 1920s and had a concrete air raid shelter installed! It seemed unique for the area. It soon had a vast and impressive American fridge in the middle of it and a washer and dryer. These things were purchased at the South Ruislip commissary, which was given over to the 'Yanks' as a USAF Base sometime before. All these things, electronics/white goods and food, were usually brought over by US Transport planes or shipped on boats from the States.

Also, something that came over on a container ship was our Dad's huge Oldsmobile convertible which was quite a site at the time in London and England.

However, this car had been stored in the 50s for Dad when not in England, by my English Uncle Stanley. He was a merchant seaman, very smart, particularly with anything nautical or mechanical.

A separate book could be written on his world adventures, as with my other Uncles who served in World War II.

Years before, in the early 1950s, Dad, Stanley and some of my other Uncles had been frequent visitors to local pubs and parties held at respective houses.

We had a sunroom area where a piano was placed in the hopes of someone becoming the next Tchaikovsky, but it was mainly used for fun or school practice.

Everybody from different backgrounds and experiences seemed to mingle and get to know each other during the war and into the 1950s. Friends' and relatives' experiences appeared to perform on a more miniature scale of closely getting to know each other. Conversely, the countryside appeared to be an adventure in waiting as fewer people and fewer cars were on the road.

The world seemed to me a lot bigger to me from reports of those days, with the converse of close knit social groups.

When Dad had to spend time in England in the early 1960s, My Grandfather Thomas took the children around London, from Battersea Park to Hyde Park, and all the museums and attractions, which were a wonder to the young 'colonists'. Roland, Bob (twins), and Frank remember these long walks in particular and Grandad's attention to detail and kindness all those years ago. Also, a trip on the Serpentine boating lake at Hyde Park, which Nan expressly forbid, but he and the children did anyway being adventurous. It was created in 1730 when Queen Caroline (wife of George II) had the jolly idea of redeveloping Hyde Park and Kensington Gardens for beauty's sake and ordered the River Westbourne to be 'damned'! This early engineering feat formed the lake as it exists today.

The family explored England and drove out to Stonehenge with very few people around at that time. So you could touch and walk around the stones without them being cordoned off.

I recall a Ghost documentary from 1964 commissioned by the ABC network in the United States with famed British actress Margaret Rutherford, a stalwart and no-nonsense but hilarious lady of stage and screen from the 1940s and beyond, most famous as Mrs Marple, the slightly eccentric English detective. She and her husband drove by Stonehenge in an open-topped Roles Royce on a quiet two-lane road now, the busy A303. Its atmosphere was palpable as they drove past on their way to film eerie ghost lights at Longleat House. The road is still two-lane but quickly expands to a busy dual carriageway with an industrial estate and McDonalds just a short distance away.

On a trip to one Stately old home, she casually opens up a large shed. She discovers a perfectly intact British made Mosquito light bomber made famous in the film The 633 Squadron. A formidable little plane that was mainly made of wood. Anything seemed possible in the 1960s.

Mum and Dad once drove out to Bristol with my Grandmother. They stayed in the same hotel where Oliver Hardy and Stan Laurel had rooms- The Grand Hotel in Bristol. Stan and Ollie acted quite casually at Breakfast, though. On this occasion, Stan did not have to fill a hole in his shoe with a piece of tough meat from a wild west saloon sandwich to stop the rain from getting in. The food seemed quite appetizing! They met briefly and seemed friendly and happy to chat, though Mum and Dad did not want to bother them at breakfast.

On one occasion in 1952, my parents attended a party at a pub in Ruislip, not far from the American base, and Uncle Stanley (my British uncle) was in attendance. One of his English friends (a former pilot in the RAF) was a little worse for wear but asked if my parents would like to see the West Country. They thought perhaps, he would suggest a trip in the Summer for a jolly outing later that year. But their friend had a more immediate plan. Without taking no for an answer, they were whisked away in his Jaguar at about midnight, with an female admirer of the British officer in tow. So with five in this green Mark VII Jag, they were driven along the A30 out of London at 1am. With no one quite sure where they would end up, everybody was quite happy to just drive in this luxury car along single-lane roads engaged in light banter. Someone suggested Stonehenge, but it was dark and off the route a little bit -was there somewhere you could have a game of cards and a drink close? As it turns out, they eventually ended up at a small hotel on the Bodmin Moor in Cornwall!. The hotel manager kindly gave them rooms at such a late hour. The fellow was not mad at the intrusion as he was fascinated by the men's wartime stories and offered them a drink. Mum and the girlfriend had retired to the guest rooms, but the 'boys' chatted the night/morning away. By this time they were all pretty hungry, and so, as you do, retired to the kitchen and started cooking breakfast, guests as well. Dad liked his scrambled eggs a certain way, cooked longer and without milk, so was 'let at it' in the kitchen by the accommodating proprietor. Pots and pans started clanging and breakfast was later served in some confusion. The outcome was that half of The English guests coming down for breakfast were treated with 'scrambled egg-Yank Style' with their tea and toast in the heart of 1950s rural England! Later that day, a little worse for wear, they departed for the long trip back across the moors to London.

In those now misty, half-forgotten days, one of their acquaintances and that of relations had been a man named John

Godar. He was a cameraman/focus puller at the nearby Pinewood Studios in the late 1940s and beyond and had worked on such films as Great Expectations and Oliver Twist, directed by David Lean. He used to drink with my Uncles and was often in Uxbridge, as he worked at Pinewood.

At some point, Mum and Dad had given a lift to Godar to return him to the local town of Ruislip, after an evening when they were all together.

The morning after, they noticed slashes maniacally cut into the back seat of the Oldsmobile. For some reason, he got agitated and used his knife in a rage sitting in the back.

It is hard to know what makes people tick, and Brother Roland now says, 'You have to be on orange alert (like at the traffic light)' when out in public in any given situation, which I now think is valuable advice.

This would be portentous later and perhaps a lucky escape.

The following is a background of what happened next from a Police Report:

John Godar murdered his girlfriend Maureen Jones Cox 20 who he stabbed to death in a taxi-cab, Uxbridge, London on 6 June 1952.

He stabbed her in a cab and then asked the driver to take him to the police station. When he got to Uxbridge Police Station at 12.40am on 7 June 1952 he said "I want you to take me inside, I've killed a woman I think". There was blood on both his hands and clothes. As the policeman went out into the passageway to go outside John Godar said "I think you'll find she's dead".

The policeman then went in the cab with the body of Maureen Cox to Hillingdon Hospital.

Later at 2am on 7 June 1952 the police informed John Godar that they had just seen the dead body of Maureen Cox at Hillingdon Hospital and said that they understood that he thought he had killed her. John Godar said "That's right sir". They then asked him if he wanted to make a statement and John Godar said "I'd rather let it go, I want to get where she is quick". When he was charged he said "that's right, I just want to go where she is as quickly as possible and no messing about".

A sad case all around. His Mother had tried to get her son a stay of execution and have his court case retried based on diminished responsibility after the judge came down with a guilty verdict, and he was sentenced to hang on the 5th of September 1952.The plea was unsuccessful, and the famous Hangman, Albert Pierrepoint, carried out the sentence.

On a lighter note, concerning the Oldsmobile car. Dad had to get mechanical parts for it at the base because they were unavailable in the UK for obvious reasons. Years later, Dad sold the car to an Englishman who still had trouble getting things like tyres. So the tyres he put on it were 'English skinnys', often seen around the Town of Uxbridge with these thin wacky wheels. It resembled something out of an episode of Laurel and Hardy or The Wacky Races, with an oversized Yank car and funny wheels.

Also, the kid's bikes were shipped over to England. The American bikes often had thick tyres, like today's mountain bikes, which appeared odd in England then. You could call them the first English mountain bikes?

However, some kids teased my brother and sisters for these bikes and their 'funny wheels' and even punctured the tyres out of spite when parked at the bike sheds, along with calls of "Yanks go home", or some such.

Chapter 17

The Start of Strange Happenings

One late Autumn night in November 1971, a young woman showed up at the door of Sweetcroft Lane in a state of distress. She had walked from Hillingdon Tube Station, having met friends in London and spent the day and early evening there. All the way back, she had been aware of a man seemingly following her and hiding in the bushes as she nervously looked around. Finally, she saw our light and decided to walk the path to our door to seek shelter.

Dad went out with suitable protection (a baseball bat from the States) and walked the street for a little while. Whoever it was, they had disappeared.

He later escorted her home.

I will start with the disclaimer that the following 'probably' had nothing to do with the incident in Sweetcroft. In June of that year, a girl named Gloria Booth was discovered murdered on a recreation ground about half a mile away from South Ruislip Station, close to the US Air Base where dad was stationed and the family frequented for medical, banking and groceries. This was not the same underground line as the girl who visited Sweetcroft was on, but South Ruislip was only a few miles as the crow flies. Mrs Booth, a 29-year-old housewife from Ealing, had died from strangulation, and a scarf appeared to have been used. This led one journalist to refer to the area as 'Ruislip's Murder Mile' because of a similar incident nearly 20 years before.

This happened near the American base as mentioned, and to this day, as with the Booth Murder, they remain unsolved.

Jean Townsend was a theatrical costumier returning to Ruislip from London's West End. On the evening of 14th September 1954, she attended a local function in the West End, returning to South Ruislip on the last Central Line train later that night.

At around 11:45pm, she was seen leaving South Ruislip Station and walking along Victoria Road. Her body was discovered the following morning on the waste ground on the north side of Victoria Road, in the area now occupied by St Gregory the Great Catholic Church (Opened in April 1967).

The autopsy report stated that she had been strangled with her own scarf.

Some three weeks after Jean Townsend's murder, Mrs Doris Vennell reported being followed and attacked by a man outside North Harrow tube station(the same line that the girl who visited Sweetcroft had been on all those years later) while returning home just after midnight. Her attacker had boarded at Baker Street and sat watching her intently until following her off the train at North Harrow. Mrs Vennell challenged him and managed to get away, but only after a struggle during which she tore some buttons off her assailant's coat. The man was described as having a high forehead.

Three years later, in 1957, a young mother called Muriel Maitland was brutally murdered in Cranford Woods near Heathrow Airport (a few miles from Ruislip). Again, it was reported that police considered the possibility of a link with the Townsend case. Still, it seems nothing came out of this.

Unfortunately, suspicion fell on American Servicemen based at South Ruislip. These rumours intensified when a resident near the scene reported hearing a woman crying for help and two men arguing. According to the resident, one of these me sounded like an American. Dad had the alibi of not being there or in the country at the time of the murders, but as an officer and having some authority, he was asked to keep his eyes and ears open.

In the end, the murders were never solved, however.

Chapter 18

Posh Ghosts and More

My brothers in England attended a private school at first in Hillingdon (Near Uxbridge) called 'Rutland House'. They recall the history master, particularly a Mr Wells, as a well-liked teacher.

Unusually, for bored shifting pupils- this teacher made history enjoyable with tales of Henry VIII and his 'doings'. He talked about people like the Hero Black Knight (named so because of his armour) of the Hundred Years War in France and the creepy and malicious deeds done in the name of honour, religion and jealousy at castles, palaces and fortresses like the Tower of London. The boys said they could still remember the chronology of the Kings and Queens of England in detail because of his engaging style.

The Masters wore archetypal clothes: black mortarboard hat, matching gown, and wooden pointer.

Also, there appeared to be some odd goings in the realm of the supernatural at the school and that area in particular if you believe in that realm of existence.

It is not surprising as the history of England is saturated with interesting figures and events. Charles The 1st stayed at the Red Lion Coaching Inn opposite the School in his dash to the Royalist stronghold of Oxford. There was talk of secret tunnels to St John's Church, also across the road from the school in Hillingdon.

Mr Wells, the English teacher, lived at the school as many masters did then. Working one night and sorting through papers with a roaring fire, his door was open to the outer chamber, which led to a long corridor. This building is old, dating back to the Tudor period. As he scanned the pupil's work, he noticed something out of the corner of his eye. As he described it, an amorphous shape formed at one end of the corridor, which he first thought was smoke or condensation, and then consequently thought he was dealing with a fire. To his disbelief, it started to unravel itself and form into a human shape with the classic white billowing form of a woman with seemingly flowing long hair. It appeared to him as a woman, and I guess a man on his own, in the middle of the night, would know the difference. According to the Master, it kept forming and altering shape slightly as it moved and floated along (as he put it) towards him along the hall. Then, rushing to the door and banging it shut, Mr Wells didn't want to see her/it anymore or experience what would happen next! This encounter was a highly unnatural experience for one used to dealing with facts and logic. He relayed it to the boys, and they say he was usually a strict but caring person, who they thought would not be telling tales just for the sake of it.

At the same school, one of my brothers had an incident whilst getting changed for PE.

Frank was slow in leaving the changing rooms as it was group games (cricket), which he did not enjoy, and the weather was cold and dreary, and he was the last out of there and by himself. Even all the masters were out of the building. He said it was unnaturally cold in that place, and felt like he was being watched -that feeling when the hackles on your skin rise. That made him rethink his snail-like pace, and he joined his mates quickly.

The first year in England they attended a Junior School in Uxbridge called 'Whitehall' near the local River Frays. For the most part, they enjoyed the British-style lunches. However, they were a little taken aback by a dinner lady who served the much-liked pink custard and treacle tart; the only thing was, she was missing fingers on her right hand, and they all thought (in their young minds)she must have had a terrible accident in the kitchen and just carried on, and where were her digits?

When they left that school and went to the local comprehensive, they did not have an enjoyable time, though making friends and just getting on with it.

The Girls (my sisters) went to a grammar school in Ickenham. They did not enjoy it as much as their life back on the coast of Mississippi and Texas and the freedom it offered there.

Sweetcroft Lane went through some changes and had the touch of my parents put upon the place.

Good luck seemed to follow at first; whilst cleaning up, Dad found a Gold Ring in the attic and, unable to contact the sellers, gave it to Mum (having reached out to the police, they said they could not contact them either.)

Col. Fuller added something rather special and unique in the late 60s-a- a 100-foot beam/tower for his Ham Radio hobby with a figure H crosspiece resembling something out of a US intelligence facility! From 11 Sweetcroft Lane, he contacted countries all over the Globe. In addition, he had what is known as QSL Cards- (postcards from fellow 'Hams'-amateur radio operators) and companies from around the world plastered to the ceiling in the top attic room. He was highlighted in a local newspaper -' Just another ordinary day for Jim Fuller', in the attic room contacting people worldwide. Of course, there was no internet then, and telephone communication was expensive, so this was a big deal. The problem was that the early TV sets were tubes and valves and did not include suppressors for interference from big setups like Dads'. So invariably, his voice would come over the TV sets of households all over the borough-it was hit and miss. The next-door neighbour complained, and he went over there and tweaked something... Has this worked? Perhaps there was something wrong with their TV?!

Before this family, a family called the Bollingbrokes lived there; we now suspect they may have had links to aristocracy in the past, and through my schooling and later history degree, I found that the name had many Royal connections. Both teachers and Mrs Bollingbroke played the Harp, which you could hear on sunny days if their French Windows were open.

Elvis was a big name still in the 1970s, and I did a bad thing. Playing with my train set, I accidentally broke a couple of 45 records of Elvis singing 'Hound Dog' and another famous tune. Dad thinks they may have been first editions of his songs bought from the States. I certainly hope not and I was in the 'Hound Dog' House for a couple of weeks after that.

When I was at school in the late 70s and early 80s, we used to have morning assemblies and could often be found belting out sounds like Onward Christian Soldiers and other popular Hymns of the Faith.

This would be piped through the large assembly building, often with a backing track of monks or angels singing their hearts out and us singing in rapture over prominent large brown speakers and tannoys.

One morning Dad must have been on the Radio, and his voice belted out this id ""G5ACW, G5ACW (his radio ham identification call sign). I am calling from London. Is anyone on this frequency! Hey, what's going on."It was a deep voice, but it sounded muffled and tinny over the speakers, so you couldn't quite make it out, but I could.

Either they thought it was Jesus trying to get through, the Holy Father, or maybe even the Devil!

I tried to look as astonished as everybody else. 'THIS IS G5ACW, IS ANYBODY THERE'!

We had about finished with the service anyway. So everybody filed out-some of us walking like a groggy Douglas Bader trying out his tin legs for the first time because our legs had been crossed for some time; we had pins and needles, so we were walking quickly to the exits but hobbling! The teachers looked as astonished as everybody else. I don't know if they were expecting the rapture at some point. Did any of them know it was my Father!?

Ah, the 1960s-70s were a time for free thinking and expression.

A neighbour was living next to us (on the other side of The Bollingbrokes) called Mrs Ryder, whose son went to art college. She came over one day to show Mum and Dad a picture of a banana her son had painted at the college in oils and claimed it was a masterpiece; Mum and Dad just agreed. Sister Rhonda later went to Art College in Maidenhead, so she must have been inspired! He also liked to hang his transistor radio outside his bedroom window on a rope for the world to hear- free entertainment.

In Rhonda's first year at her College, she lived in student accommodation, an imposing old Victorian house, but there were reports of a 'peeping tom' in the area. Many girls sharing digs together may have attracted this type of individual, and they were all rightly a little unsettled. A dual occurrence happened when in the dark, having gone to bed in her room, she felt a presence and couldn't sleep; she felt 'something was watching her'. Later, in the semi-darkness, she thought she saw a very small undefined ugly little figure seemingly 'perched' at the end of her bed for a moment, almost like a gnome. What's worse, she thought it was 'smiling', not smiling, more of a grimace. She rushed to the shared bathroom and stayed there for a while. When she built up the courage to return, she felt pressure on the bedclothes later on, like a cat may be settling in for the night, but nothing was there, and it was uncomfortable. Rhonda brushed it off as perhaps the 'semi-dream state' between being asleep and being wide awake but wasn't happy with the set-up. A couple of days later, her roommate confessed something similar: pressure on her bed and a feeling of unease. They both didn't stay long at the place after that, and the threat of a more 'corporeal' peeper spooked all the girls. Was this all linked to an Ouija board session performed at the house at Sweetcroft, which I will mention later or just imagination?

It sparks a memory in that the serial killer Ted Bundy was active in this period in the United States, prowling around sorority houses and breaking in to do heinous acts on the sleeping girls. An odd coincidence.

After Mrs Ryder had left, in 1977, an Indian family moved in with a mass of children from Aden, where the father had moved as an immigrant worker, and I made friends with the eldest son Raginda Govind. On hot summer days, the smell of cooking was very pungent, and one could smell it half a mile away. Their spices were powerful, and their mother made ghee; a butter type. We invited Mr Govind over for a Christmas drink, and he fell in love with my electric train set. They also loved brother Bob, who helped them with the house's interior by acquiring reasonably priced carpets or charity items. 'where is Bob' they used to say!

Mum drove Raginda, I and Frank to the countryside and coast to show him England and bought us dinner or lunch out; it was a fun time, and Raginda thought of Mum as a second parent and 'an amazing woman' as she used to paint and decorate the house and do electrical jobs even better than Dad at times, or when he wasn't in the country or kitchen! Jim loved the Ham Radio and was on there as much as possible.

She took us to the local Coop store in Uxbridge and gave us pocket money to buy some sweets. I remember a guy in the shop was re-stringing tennis rackets on site. I wanted to get a racket to try to emulate McEnroe. What has happened to all those great stores, Amazon and Ebay I guess?

Something rather baffling was a big black object with red lights and protrusions seemingly floating overhead that had appeared in the shop. It reminded us of the ominous thing (mind probe) Darth Vader was about to use on the captured Princess Leia in Star Wars before a black door shut quickly. We were whisked elsewhere, only to imagine what was happening to the poor Princess. It turned out to be one of those new ' Close Circuit Television Cameras' (CCTV), which was now 'spying on you'. Even as a child, I thought it was pretty 'sinister' and bizarre, and, in most cases, I still do. A bit like being stalked by an unseen big cat in the forest, never knowing quite where it is and leaving one unsettled and on edge, especially in England, where there seems to be a camera on every corner. England was perhaps the world experiment for a control grid? What happened to all the store detective ladies in floppy wool hats and cloth caps for the men one avoided and occasionally gave us kids (and some adults) disapproving looks or watched over our shoulders. Police officers patrolling in long helmets and carrying notepads to take descriptions of possible wrongdoers. Things sure used to be a lot more innocent.

97

Chapter 19

The Ruislip Spyring
This Island Earth

The high radio beam in the back of the garden (which could be seen from the local public park, Hillingdon Court) may have garnered interest from the intelligence services-MI5, MI6 and probably others.

Well, it turns out there was some espionage going on in a sleepy town not three miles from us in the many streets, alleys, and back doubles in the streets of 1960s London suburbia.

Peter and Helen Kroger were a Canadian couple (real name Morris and Lona Cohen) who lived in Ruislip- a very conventional and what could be described as a dull middle-class area through the fifties into the sixties. They owned an attractive but average bungalow down a lane that turned into a pedestrian path backing playing fields.

Gordon Lonsdale (real name Konon Molody) visited them on weekends and transmitted information to Moscow via a hidden transmitter in the basement. He was a Russian spy who ran a ring and procured information from the Underwater Weapons Establishment in Portland, Dorset, via the civil servant spies there. The information included files on underwater weapon and detection systems, top secret, of course. Photos of documents were also reduced to microdots and placed in antiquarian books to be sent overseas-an audacious set-up.

The intelligence services finally caught on to them and set up a 'sting' operation in the house opposite that had a clear view of the front door. Men in grey overcoats and black hats were strangely visiting the neighbourhood regularly! This intelligence operation was done with the cooperation of the neighbours, and they were arrested in early 1961, tried and sent to prison.

Helen Kroeger used to carry some pretty expensive camera equipment and wear designer gear, unusual for the area.

I wonder what the locals may have thought about Dad's High antennae and Mum being a pretty snazzy dresser as a Colonel's wife.

Dad was based at the local South Ruislip Air Force Base (where I was born) and was acquainted with Larry Hagman, who served in the USAF for a period and did a tour in England in the 1960s. Hagman was only briefly there, but Dad said he loved the place and London/England when he had a pint with him and some of the other guys.

Larry Hagman was an actor, and his most famous role was that of JR Ewing, the oil baron, trouble maker and all-around villain in the series 'Dallas'. In the 1980s, when JR was shot in one episode, some people walked around with 'who shot JR' T shirts as the series was top-rated and a cultural phenomenon.

It was great, as Dad and Mum used to load up on American food and toys/gifts at the commissary and BX (Base Exchange). Giant Skippy peanut butter jars were always present at home, along with Tootsie Role candies, Moon Pies and other tasty things. Christmas was unique, as we used to get the extras from the base. I remember train sets and a big blue rocket one year, brought by Father Christmas of course.

As we had US appliances, we used transformers to step down the current from the 240 volts of the British standard to the 110 volts of the American system.

Not only could Mum use the US kitchenware, but we had giant Norman Rockwell-style bulbs. The only trouble was the lights were in series, and if one bulb blew, the rest would go out. So you had to hunt the rogue bulb, which was usually at the back of the tree, facing out the window, and the hardest to get at. We attained a massive transformer to 'step down' the voltage from Mum's eldest nephew (an Oxford Graduate, later to become a science professor and teach at Brunel Unversity) because he was moving from a house in Northwood that was oddly wired up for Americans, and Roy (my oldest cousin) needed it for the many American appliances in the home. This was 2 feet across and looked like something attempted to be built by Earth scientists in 'This Island Earth'-the 1950s Sci-Fi Film to show you were smart enough to work with the aliens seeking a way to use Earth scientists to defeat their enemies on Metaloona, and also escape from the Earth. Roy also looked like the Metaloona Scientist -Brac (The actor's name was 'Lance Fuller', my last two names) with a 'scientist type' large forehead.

The meat from the base was always top-notch (from Scotland, I believe), and for some reason, I liked the big blocks of processed cheese, which was sort of like astronaut food in big lumps.

November 5th (Guy Fawkes Day) was also a significant event in our house, and Dad enjoyed it the most, I think. Not sure why, as he was shot down on Guy Fawkes Day in 1944!

Before Guy Fawkes, around Halloween, I would make up a guy- an effigy of the man we were supposed to hate childishly and burn him every November 5th using Dad's old trousers, my brother's shirt and maybe a stocking from my sister or cousin to help make his head, an old pillowcase if you were in luck. Then fill his torso with more rags and old clothes, or if nothing else to hand, it would be paper. Paper wasn't so good, though, as our man would burn too quickly. He would be faceless with someone trying to draw some eyes, or we would get an ugly mask. Later, I would take him down to the local shops in Mum's old shopping basket, sit outside the shop, and yell "PENNY FOR THE GUY". Every lad expected more, though; we weren't living in Victorian England and inflation and all that! One guy stopped his car, got out, and gave me 50p before I had made it the half mile to the Coop to set up camp outside- a fortune.

At the house, we had an expansive garden at the back, so we could have a large bonfire. The food was plentiful, and Mum and family set up tables for the hot dogs (known as wieners), hamburgers and sweets.

The Fireworks were very powerful, and we had the devices known as 'airplanes' that were set on the ground and lit, made a whining noise and used to fly everywhere, with people running for cover with the more lively rounds! Like being at war, without actually being so.

Dad was upstairs in the radio room when a rocket exploded above the house on his side. I don't know if he was working the radio, but poor Dad must have thought he was at war again. Fortunately, being somewhat of a 'big kid' himself, he wasn't too annoyed by the festivities. In fact, at Halloween (which, at that time, wasn't really celebrated in the UK by most of the public), Dad put an effigy of a man in the tree with a noose around his neck, a hanged man for all to see. I think the neighbours thought that an offshoot of the American Munster family was living in the neighbourhood. My favourites were the rockets and the bangers. Bangers for the more wayward individuals or oiks (British slang for young ne'er-do-wells), a bit like cherry bombs for the American trouble maker. The rockets were more regal and powerful and went farther, the snob end of the firework fraternity. Catherine wheels were great, too...a bit like the show's clowns and could sometimes misfire or be duds and required more of a set-up-(usually a nail and a scaffold).We also like the aerial bombs, which travel to about 100 feet and explode in a big bang or with a high-pitched whine, a bit like impatient pissed-off rockets that never quite reach the upper atmosphere.

Of course, the police were called on one occasion because of the noise. We had a swing set in the garden, and one of my cousins was sitting with his back to the policeman. The policeman then blurted out, "excuse me, Madam, is this your fireworks party"? We've had a complaint". Gary had long hair, which was the style then, a bit like John Lennon or the average hippie. The policeman apologized as they didn't even think it was a big deal and met my parents, and we smoothed it over by giving them a hotdog and a drink. They might have been alerted by some of the antics of partygoers, who found that we needed more wood; heck, the fire required feeding. So they retreated to the wilderness area at the back and started dismantling an old decrepit shed to keep the big bonfire going! Not unlike the Marx Brothers' scene in 'Go West', when on inspection, they are running out of wood and coal for the boiler, Groucho starts to call out for 'more wood', and they proceed to tear the train apart. Someone putting a can of used-up hairspray or air freshener was always an interesting party trick, as it might explode and even pop out of the fire. But, if that was the case, people were still determining exactly which way it would go. Mum was not happy with this practice.

It would be fun to save pocket money and buy fireworks as a kid, hoard them till the big day, and keep some through the rest of the year. Dad would also go out and buy fireworks and store them, somewhat of a big kid himself.

Chapter 20

An Unfortunate Event

The following year after we moved in 1965, a lady who lived at the back of the garden in a large house was quite elderly (and some local kids unfairly called her a witch because she had a large wart on her face) and mysteriously died just after Guy Fawkes. We were worried that our and the neighbour's parties may have been a factor in this, but the medics confirmed it was something chronic and could not be cured. The kids thought they had heard a muffled scream in the dark, feint and far off one cold night. As a child, the story made my blood run cold.

The local nuns used to visit her and help out as best they could. The house became disused sadly, and my brother and sisters went in there to try and clean it up and play house, as they were at that age.

Later the residence was torn down, with only the massive 1930s garage remaining.

I remember playing on the site, where only bricks were left strewn about, and the remains of a black and white chequered kitchen floor were evident with the slight imprints and scratches of the long years printed on its surface. Also, I used the lady's garage as a den and used to explore it. It was huge; you could imagine an enormous swanky car from the 1920s or 1930s housed in it after a day travelling down to Brighton or maybe even a daring and eventful trip to Stonehenge, with a big Picnic basket strapped to the back.

It was to become part of the wilderness area at the back of our garden, a testament to the past and lived lives. It was sad to me even then, as the echos of laughter and sadness from what seemed to me aeons ago had long since departed this very spot.

Very often, near the entrance to Hillingdon Court Park, where the wilderness met the park, stolen motorbikes and other 'gear' would be left and abandoned. Also, one year, a stack of wet Playboys, which I swear I did not look at. The stolen bike and girlie magazines had somewhat of a sinister air-god knows what else there was, but the weeds and nettles tended to cover things up, and they may still be underground there. Someone's Royal Enfield, their pride and joy in 1968, buried, rotting and forgotten.

One year in the 1970s, a great oak tree fell over the back there. Every year in the weeks before Guy Fawkes, a friend of my brothers- Martin Weeden, would come with his petrol chain saw and cut the tree into logs for the Bonfire to stack. This went on for a few years until the tree remains had virtually disappeared!

After the lady's death in the 1960s, a strange and recurring situation happened with a local family. The neighbour a few doors down from us, Mr Lawrence, used to work in his garden practically all the time tending his roses. He always said he felt watched and would stand upright to look over his shoulder, and nobody was there. This was a person who I remember even when I was a child, would not be given flights of fancy. He had been involved in finance all his life and appeared to be very grounded. But this experience gave him the shudders. His wife and daughter had been wardrobe designers at Pinewood Studios and led an interesting life themselves, felt the presence to a lesser extent. I have spoken to the daughter, Jean Lawrence in recent times, who still lives on Sweetcroft Lane and we recall old times.

Chapter 21

Subtle Sophistication

Dad and Mum could fit in anywhere, modern-day 'persons for all seasons', though they held some solid convictions and ideas, most of which have held true. They did 'bang heads' invariably at specific points in some realms. Though a man of the world, Dad held on to some rustic charms from the mountains of Tennessee, often I think for affect.

In the 1950s, Mum and Dad were dining with a friend of theirs, Pat Renard, whose husband was a wealthy businessman and had contacts worldwide. The location was the Veraswamys Indian Restaurant on Regent Street in London, the oldest Indian restaurant in London, started by an Anglo Indian retired officer, which retained a very lavish and eastern decor. Winston Churchill and Charlie Chaplin dined in the place at some point, and other notables.

At the end of the meal, they had their coffees poured by a 'maharaja' type fellow in full dress. These small demitasse-type cups were tiny, held strong coffee, and often could be finished in one sip.

Dad, not thinking, held the cup with his small finger curled around the handle in the style of Hercule Poirot or some such (or maybe even Charlie Chaplin).This provoked howls of laughter from my Mother and Pat Renard, who could not, stop-especially Pat, who had a bellicose laugh. This went on, and eventually, it got so bad the management asked the party to leave, and they were forced out onto the cold, foggy London streets!

I also remember them saying they all went and saw the George Pal version of 'War of The Worlds' at the Dominion Theatre in Tottenham Court Road, as they were reshowing it there.

Mum had used to cycle to the same place as a child from Red Lion Square in Bloomsbury in the War Years and dodged a few bullets quite literally. After that, she cycled all over London; what a far-off and mystical place the London of that time and how it has changed. She often visited the old Natural History and Science Museum on her bike. Not the usual thing for a girl, then.

I am not sure what happened to Pat. Still, in the vagueness of time, I remember her showing up at Sweetcroft with her Chauffeur in the 1970s, fresh from Heathrow and some swanky place abroad, and I was most impressed but shy. This is the last I remember of her and her posh 'Lady Penolope' like visage.

Chapter 22

Famous People Just Wander About

The local Brunel University, quite a famous 'seat of learning' in London (where some of my siblings and cousins studied for a while as part of their coursework and modules,) had its fair share of bands 'just before' they were famous or just becoming so. In the 1960s and 70s' Fleetwood Mac, The Who, and The Kinks, to name but a few were performers there. Later UB40, and was the last infamous venue of the Sex Pistols! The family attended many of these, and ticket prices were usually low. Brunel ran a small bar, lager, and Rum and Coke on tap as these were generally 18 and up gatherings. I never attended, but it sounded fun and a genuine opportunity if you liked the music scene. Not the thousands of people trying to get a glimpse of their favourite bands with security everywhere and often remoteness from the singers.

The security was low-key, with half-drunk beers and cigarette ash abounding on hastily assembled tables. It seemed to be a venue where rock singers, as seeming anarchists or laid-back folk in general, would be at home? Presumably, some of the bands must have been going home in their old vans or even perhaps on the 207 red London double-decker bus!

Even the local Hillingdon Show, a sort of 'county fair with tractors and dog shows plus hamburger vans, had its fair share of celebrities in the 1960s. In June 1965, Marianne Faithful appeared at the show, and I think even the Kinks were in there at some stage- A, 'Waterloo Sunset' in Uxbridge in close proximity to the smell of English beefburgers and onions.
What a time to be alive.

We also had at least one famous person living near us on an adjoining road to Sweetcroft called Vine Lane. (where I went to school at the American Community School for some time). A

Dr Franklinburgh, who used to be a doctor to my Mother, was the father of Jane Seymour, who lived with them for a time. She first became famous in the James Bond Film- Live and Let Die as one of his many conquests, though she appeared innocent and reluctant to his charms. At first, the family would see her walk down the road with a friend towards the Hillingdon shops when she was relatively young. Later, she would drive along Sweetcroft Lane in her little sports car, and my siblings would see her often and wave. I don't know what she thought of the old boat and DAF car that used to sit on the property, but it would have been a memorable site. Later, she would appear in films and series such as Dr Quinn, Medicine Woman in Hollywood. The family moved to the West Country in the eighties, and she had a nice pad near Bath for a time.

One hot sticky summer night in 1980, while lounging and playing about in the garden at Sweetcroft, we could hear music and people talking, seemingly close, but still about three-quarters of a mile as the crow flies. Sound seemed to travel a lot in the 1970s and was intriguing, or perhaps it was the cooler temperatures.

We thought we would go investigate, so we walked through the big garden and the wilderness area to Hillingdon Park. To me, it seemed like going on a walk in deepest darkest Africa and an adventure. Mum and my brothers and sisters, and I trooped to the very back of another big garden and house and tried to spy on what was going on. People were having drinks on the veranda, and there was a music system blasting away at the back. All having a seemingly great time. We, however, did not try to gate crash but stood there like Ninjas for a while behind the bushes. Mosquitoes and midges were on the prowl, however.

We learned from the local paper that it was a party hosted by Jane Seymour (formerly Franklinburgh) and her father and mother. One of the guests was the actor Charlton Heston, who was filming the 'The Awakening' in town. In it, he plays an archaeologist who discovers that his daughter was possessed by an ancient egyptian queen, mummy. It was just another day in sleepy suburbia.

Chapter 23

' Is this Your Flying Kite Sir'

This park was also a great place for flying kites. I remember one time, my brother Roland and myself were flying a kite with the appropriate 'Apollo' Spaceman emblazoned on the front. Now, we had learned, or my family had learned through the family interest in aviation, that a long tail and the right balanced kite would get your Kite to great heights.

However, this was a relatively inexpensive one with just a really long tail. I think I remember ladies' tights and car rags being attached, but later long roles of thicker plastic proved better for lift. I think Dad supplied tail from the USAF stores.

Now this kite went up really high, and it was a little hard to hold on to due to the winds aloft. It must have been thousands of feet up at one stage.

On the periphery of our vision, a little bit later, we saw a blue light atop a little white police van driving in the park towards us, (This was an unusual site, what could we be doing wrong.)

It turns out that the kite had gone so high it had appeared on the local Northolt RAF Airfield Radar as it was nearing the flight path! We should have known, as planes flew across the park, landing and taking off quite regularly. This was a military base where often 'big-wigs' and politicians would fly in, as well as private jets for the right price. Then they sent out the policeman in his little van to tell us to reel it in.

In reality, the string would have done nothing to the aircraft as they would just cut right through it.

We also used to attach messages to the kites we sent up. On reflection, I don't know why we did that. Perhaps we thought it would be nearer space and perhaps more interesting on its return, or maybe politicians would read it as they zipped by and perhaps be persuaded to give us more 'tuck' at school (tuck shops were snack vendors at British schools, whereby you could buy things like crisps and chocolate, which were the tuck-as in ' tuck-in'?-I'm not sure.)

Even after that, many hot summer days would be spent flying kites, perhaps at a slightly different location or not too far up into the blue.

Later in 1978, we lost another 'spaceman' kite in one of the 100-150 foot tall Oak Trees that dotted the park. It was so high up that it could not be retrieved and we could still see it up there years later. I don't know if it ever did came down of its own volition, but the world changed again while it was up there and it didn't take any notice.

Chapter 24

Unwanted Hauntings?

One day the 'meddling kids' (to quote Scooby Doo) did something they probably shouldn't have.

Sometime in 1967, the Children decided to construct a homemade Ouji Board. They tried to use it in an attempt to contact the Spirits or whoever was listening. Not a bought one from the shop(which was on sale to children in the 1960s), but a cut-out paper version with letters and numbers written in felt tip pen and a drinking glass replacing the planchette.

I know the subject is contentious, with some people thinking it is harmless or absurd and others thinking it is a direct line to The Spirit World. And perhaps a middling group who think it's a good idea not to meddle with it just in case. I tend to fall into this middle group.

They attempted this at the big bay window in the middle bedroom with its ornate curled clasps and fresh white paint on a generous window seal. It seemed nothing happened at first, and they didn't try it again in any case. Some odd things had happened before the 'seance', but certainly afterwards.

One day, Mum was moving between the kitchen, and former air-raid shelter come pantry, which was partitioned by a concrete hallway which joined the front and back garden/yard. Taking some washing out between the two areas, she stood momentarily, somewhat aghast. The big American fridge was also in the air raid section.

From the floor upwards in this hallway area, something stirred from the floor, and a definite shape formed, which she described as smoke, at first quite small, and it appeared to get larger, as you might imagine a genie arising from a bottle in the Arabian Nights stories. By this point, it had reached about four foot tall and was a bilious mass. It grew more extensive, and she stood back as it eerily moved down the hall and seemed to disappear into the garden. This was more shapeless than the boy's teacher's sighting of a misty woman's form. She went through after a minute or so (she was somewhat shocked) to see where it had gone, but it had vanished.

According to Mum, it was not like condensation or smoke you might get from a burnt-out motor or car exhaust or temperature layers; it was somehow different and glided along with a seeming unknown purpose through the partition. Perhaps something that had exhibited intelligence.

Other things were seen at the back of the garden, odd shapes near twilight and sometimes caught in one's peripheral vision.

Maybe a taste of the future or warning?

Once, Mum and I were blackberry picking in the early Autumn and at the point where the back garden meets the wilderness area. There were a lot of stinging nettles, thick bushes and dark spaces. A roughly dressed guy with a shopping bag on his own suddenly appeared and kept edging towards us, which she did not like. Mum said he was now on the property and asked if he could leave. He ignored her and said he was just "collecting blackberries for a pie as well".Not until the family dog (Cookie) came bounding up barking ferociously he left; she felt something was off and had a good 'nose' for people's character, as dogs often do.

On another occasion, Roland, one of the twins, was alone in the house one evening approaching Christmas and had gone to relieve the call of nature in the middle toilet on the house's second floor. Now there was the attic room on the third floor, which Dad used as his Ham Radio cabin, and both Roland and Robert had bunk beds in there. Also, this small room had ample loft space on both sides. Leading to this attic room was a tight winding staircase which led from the second floor to the attic past a window. The toilet was right next to this staircase.

Next, Roland said he heard definite footsteps run up these stairs and then seemingly pause and frantically come back down, as if intending to find someone or something, but whatever it was returned, and, perhaps in thought and with intent to the landing. He also heard a 'sort of rustling' noise. Mum had put up those crate paper decorative chains overhead in the hallway. Some of the curves in the chain were low, and tall heads would brush against them. Could that be the noise? There must have been someone in the house.

He finished up, came out expecting to see Dad or one of his siblings, and even called out. He searched the attic and the house, but nobody was there. He even looked to the front and back gardens to see if anyone was resident-nothing. Perhaps someone was playing a trick? However, when everybody filtered back later, they said they hadn't been at the house at the time. Also, the front and back doors were locked, so nobody could have gotten in via that method. The incident certainly creeped us out.

Chapter 25

Local History-The Key?

One day, when I was at school, my primary teacher gave us a history class about the local area.

Included in this 'lecture' was a story about Sweetcroft Lane and its surroundings. Apparently, there had been a river below the foundations of some of the houses along our street. As a result, there was much red clay in evidence, which the Thames Valley is noted for. However, this river had long dried up.

Apparently, during early Saxon times, there had been a 'Folkmoot', where the local elders and people met to discuss the moment's business. Even tribes from outside the area would come along to have a good old chinwag as was the custom. I know about a mile away, there have been Roman and later period pottery shards found on Hillingdon Hill, next to the Church of St Johns (and coincidentally opposite the Rutland House, in which other odd happenings had occurred.)Perhaps they had been present, too, trying to create a dialogue. A skirmish and fighting may have broken out?

Another strange and poignant occurrence was about to unfold. Oddly, my sister Jane had awoken in the middle bedroom one night to see what she said appeared to be a man 'with silver on', as she described, next to the bed and staring forward. She was pretty young at the time. Could this be chain mail on a man's torso, like the armour Knights used to wear? I was recently fascinated by a 'mudlark' (someone who scours river banks in search of treasure.) On the Thames River, She found five tiny silver ring-shaped objects linked together, which turned out to be chain mail from as far back as a thousand years.

It was sort of dismissed at the time as perhaps a dream or her imagination. She swears she was not dreaming or making it up.

Perhaps the ancients were disturbed, but this would not account for the presence of the old lady, who lived at the house at the back, and whose presence may have been trying to make itself known.

One day in 1976, near dusk, a traumatic event occurred. Some of the family was at home when they heard a 'blood-curdling scream outside'. A woman directly opposite the house had fallen on the sidewalk grasping her chest. Mum and Dad rushed out to see if they could help. They called the emergency services while someone stayed with her, but it was already too late when they arrived. They tried to revive her in the ambulance on the site. It was too late; they said she had virtually died on the spot anyway, with a massive heart attack.

A gypsy/fortune teller had also called at the door one dreary afternoon and was trying to sell some kind of a dried flower with its stem wrapped in tin foil and told my mother to buy it for good luck. Mum did not have the change and was not inclined to accept the bundle anyway, and the woman went away, mumbling something under her breath. The woman looked like the typical crystal ball reader you might meet in a tent at the local fayre or circus. Mum occasionally brought up this incident and felt she might have tried to curse her. The late 1960s and early 1970s were unusual, with many strange events happening to the Fullers and the wider world in general?

Now these occurrences happened in a span of a 20-year period, so though mentioned together, they were not happening every day. At least if they did happen on a more frequent basis, we might not tell each other? Although an opened minded family, on the other hand, we were all relatively grounded and would not be in the habit of making things up.

After these occurrences and the death of the old lady at the back of us, the family suffered some bad luck and usual teenage years troubles for the family.

Chapter 26

Hot Remembered Days, But Cracks Appear

In the Summer of 1976, there occurred in England an exceptionally hot period from May all the way through to September. The foundations of Sweetcroft Lane started to become unstable and the house began to 'crack up' inside too. This over the next year required supports to be set up on top of the garage, which were heavy and bolted to the side of the house. Cracks occurred in one of the front bedrooms. To confirm the story about the stream/river bed the surveyor confirmed this was the case and the red clay below was becoming unstable, partially due to the extreme heat and the clay cracking underneath, but was a little puzzled why other houses were not affected. We were not aware of this happening to any other house in the area, or even next door to us on either side of the street. It brings to mind the scene in the 1982 film Poltergeist, where the spirits of the dead come to haunt the living because they developers built the new housing project on top of a graveyard, and only moved the gravestones, leaving the bodies underneath the development.

The house was built in the 1920s. Perhaps any bodies had been obliterated over time or the builders of the house might have discarded any remains or not noticed the signs of death.

As far as I can ascertain in old local records, a strict archaeological survey of the site of the house and environs was never done. We always surmised that after the meeting of the warriors of Saxon tribes with perhaps the Roman invaders, there might have been a minor skirmish, and the bodies might have been left or hastily buried. It plays into the theory of sister Jane seeing the figure with the 'appearance of armour'.

The house really deteriorated after that and the fissures in the walls became bigger, but it was still habitable and we stayed on, with much of the family later moving out to pursue their own lives and careers.

On one occasion, in 1977, we had high winds, and the big Ham Radio tower in the back garden blew on to the side of the house in a diagonal fashion and stayed that way for a few days!

Uncle Stanley and Dad devised a block and tackle method of restoring the tower to the upright situation again-quite a feat! The winching action took a while, but the tower was eventually returned to the vertical. Dad would afterward still clamber up the huge tower of 100 feet to turn the beam to get an optimal signal to the continent that he wanted to most speak to. At that time, he didn't have a remote automatic electronic method of doing so, and was quite a site at the top with this huge monkey wrench, almost like a miniature version of King Kong atop the Empire State Building.

Another 'supernatural encounter' occurred one Autumn when brother Frank and sister Rhonda were walking on the far side of Hillingdon Court Park whilst they sat and chatted. They say it was at dusk, and upon redirecting their gaze to the point where the park meets the wilderness area, which used to back up to our garden; (the park bench was about a quarter of a mile away) they noticed figures, about four or so with one carrying what looked like a baby. The odd thing about these figures, was that they were all absolutely white in appearance, and not only white, but they appeared to give off a 'glow', as if ethereal in nature. Two of the figures moved through to the back where the old lady who passed away lived, and the one with the infant passed the child to them and proceeded on through also. It was all very strange.

There were cricketers who used to play in the park at times, but Rhonda and Frank swear, they were not the wandering white entities. Cricketers usually (especially in those times)dressed in white for matches. Also, why would they be headed to the over grown area behind our house? There was an overgrown driveway through to Sweetcroft Lane, but this was rarely used, as it was difficult to traverse. Because of all the greenery, you would have to usually fight your way through nettles in order to get through on foot. Going through by car would have been much more difficult as well. The figures seemed to just disappear, as they moved through the hedge. After some initial trepidation, they made there way back after the white figures had gone. They scanned the area and even went through to the main street, but whoever, or whatever it was had vanished into thin air!

In March 1968, Mum was 'carrying' me and up late at night; early one frosty March morning, she came down to the kitchen in search of the vegetable radishes, which she used to crave, maybe a lack of iron. She returned upstairs to the bedroom with the big bay window with a bottle of milk and a punnet of radishes. She stood at the window, stared at the blackness, and spotted something. About a quarter of a mile from the house runs the main road called Long Lane, and Sweetcroft was a road off this thoroughfare and bisected it at a 90-degree angle. Moving slowly along the road, three abreast were three eerie lights emitting a green/whitish glow around them as they moved. Mum thought at first that it might be helicopters from nearby Northolt. She opened a window, but they were moving very slowly and didn't emit any noise, as expected from aircraft. The orange sodium street lights did not emit this light, and she was perplexed. Telling the family, but perhaps thinking she might have dreamt it or it may be a reflection from the moon, but still retained an open mind. Later that week, it was reported that a local man in Ruislip (a town about three miles away) had seen a similar thing on the same trajectory following the course of Long Lane in a southerly direction. Significantly few people were around at this time of the morning, and it was not widely reported. Especially then when UFOs were considered more a fringe topic, and some were reticent to report odd occurrences. She still recounted the sighting years later, which has always intrigued us. Are some UFO sightings linked with reports of ghosts? That is a whole other can of worms.

Chapter 27

Adventurous Travelling
and The Holder Family

A certain degree of eccentricity has been part of the Fuller and Holder (matriarchal side) makeup for centuries!
The Uncles and Aunts in England had led some interesting and exciting lives. Although, of course, I know more about some than others or was physically closer to some of them.

Henry (Uncle) was the eldest son to survive and can be seen astride a horse and an officer in the army whenever we look at his pictures. He and the family loved animals and particularly horses. The family lived in one of the oldest thatched cottages in London (Cowley, near Uxbridge) dated from the 1400s, and you had to watch your head because of the low ceilings of the property whenever visiting. People were shorter in the middle ages! The family had a donkey in the garden, fowl, chickens, etc, but the area had been encroached on by flats and offices, so the English hamlet nature and feel of the place was no more starting from the mid-1970s. Uncle Henry had the countenance and manner of a squire from a Jane Austen novel and always appeared as a gentleman, perhaps with a touch of roguishness, like an English Clark Gable. Because the area was becoming too crowded with new development, he and the family decided to move to Somerset and find a house with more land available for country pursuits and horses. Uncle Frank was too young for service and the beginning of the war but would serve later. Later in life, he became a successful businessman and was manager of a local petrol station and mechanics shop for a long time, where we usually bought gas, and some of us worked for him pumping gas for a while too.

He and Uncle Albert would also run a driving school for many years and taught nearly all of us Yanks how to drive, except for me. One of Albert's pet peeves was learner drivers treating the gear stick like 'stirring a pudding basin', which made us laugh. In the end, we all passed, even some of us on the first time, unless we got an examiner that resembled Basil Fawlty -John Cleese. The local Ruislip testing center had one of the most demanding bunch of driving testers in the whole country apparently.

Not to say we hadn't visited nearly all of the family at some point or they would have come to us. But they were all great and generous people. As mentioned, Uncle Stanley had a varied career as a merchant seaman. Here is one of the incidents that occurred during his life at sea as recalled by him years later.

But before, let's mention the boat he had intended to 'fix up', but because of space constraints, he had asked to put it on the Sweetcroft front lawn in 1976! It was a former fishing boat, by the looks of her, but it had a massive hole in the side. It looked like an extra from Jaws that had been attacked by a real 25-foot shark at some point. The boat was called 'The Compass Rose' and had provenance because it was told to us as being owned by Nicholas Monsarrat, who wrote The Cruel Sea in its more seaworthy days. The novel details life aboard Navy and Convoy ships and the sailors fighting in the Battle of The Atlantic, each chapter describing 1 year of conflict in World War II. The fictional Compass Rose is a Corvette that is eventually sunk by a U-Boat. It describes their battle for survival in the cold waters.

Uncle Stanley was actually in those convoys and often sailed with another Uncle of mine-John. The submarines formed the so-called 'Wolf Packs' and hunted together often as one unit. Seeking out and destroying allied ships that, before 1942, had usually sailed separately and being easy targets for the German Reich to destroy. The answer was, in part, to sail together and be escorted by the Royal Navy, thus making it more difficult for them to be picked off. This was only sometimes the case, however.

Stanley and John were in one of the boats that, due to persistent mechanical problems, had fallen behind the other ships; apparently, it did this a lot, and they were lucky not to be a casualty of war, i.e. sunk. Though Stanley often joked that Uncle John had probably fallen asleep shovelling coal in the boiler, and thus, this is the reason why they had slowed down!

The fishing-type vessel, The Compass Rose, was very much in reality on our lawn and was never restored. It was in a far too much a state of decay, and rot-it was a shame. It remained on the grass for ages with its big hole in the side, attracting some quizzical and often snooty looks from the passers-by. Mum was irritated by it, as she had the back garden looking lovely with hundreds of flowers and vegetables. It became a place to play for myself and my friends, pretending it was a sinking boat and we were trying to save it and ourselves from sharks.

At the back portion of the garden, there were all kinds of fruit trees. This house was built in the late 1920s, and it must have been an orchard at some point, with homes built around the trees. Today, they would tear them down.

In fact, they were taken away for profit when the house was torn down in 1982, and a set of mock Tudor and tiny up-close dwellings were built on the site. Also, some handsome trees and a wilderness area bordering the 60-acre park built over it were removed. It still makes me wince when I return there.

I remember sitting with Mum and our grandmother and having tea outside with all the animals running around on hot days between an apple tree and a peach that would never fully ripen because of the English climate. (I think some horticulturalists were hopefully experimenting there in the 1910s).

Sometimes my Aunts would visit for tea and bring over goodies (if they were in the area.)We would all go to the back of the garden and the wilderness area to gather blackberries when it approached the autumn, and my Grandmother would use her apron to gather the blackberries up in her lap and if a bag or colander wasn't available, would take them back to the house.

As I was a young entrepreneur, I had a bright idea one day at 10 years old. We had loads of plum trees in the back garden, and so many, all the windfall could not possibly be picked up and became food for wasps and other insects. In fact, one of the puppies of my Dog 'Cookie' was eating plums and got annoyed with a wasp, and one stung him in the mouth- he had to be consoled after receiving a blown-up jaw, and after a vets check, he was just fine and didn't complain much. I decided to bag the plums, wash them and weigh them on the family scales for distribution. Mum would supply the bags, which was cost-effective for me. There were golden and red plums, the red being more popular and tastier-I had a thriving business for a while. I even sold them at my sister's apartment complex; she was expecting a discount or sometimes didn't answer-ha! The old folks liked me, and business boomed for a while, replacing the odd plum gone bad to keep customers.

Inside, we had one of those old gas fires with a grill that appeared like plastic waffles with an accompanying orange glow and a black and orange plastic facade where shapes would seem to move and glow underneath. Like some sort of pagan or wicker ritual with witches involved was in progress. This was not unlike the kaleidoscope bedside lamps with cut-out silhouettes that children often have. I remember getting my one-quarter-inch plastic army men too close to the grill, and a platoon melted; the other side did have a soldier with flame thrower tanks, so this was apt. On one occasion, when we had an old fireplace and were burning wood upstairs in the room with the big bay window, the flu and chimney caught alight, and the fire brigade had to be called. My older sister Jane, who must have been about 8 years old, was excited to see firemen in the house and thought it was quite a lark.

At Sweetcroft, Dad had put a substantial swing at the back, nearing the bonfire site. It was attached to a sturdy oak tree branch and high off the ground and somewhat difficult to raise yourself up on for very young folk. I can remember even now the smell of the twines of rope (hemp) on a hot summer day as if it was rigging on a pirate ship. Then, a plate of Skippy peanut butter sandwiches with grape jelly and a glass of milk, perhaps set to the side when you had finished swinging. You could almost grab the ripening pears from a tree on a particularly high curve.

Giant jars of peanut butter were not available to the mass in England then. However, the alternative British 'Sun Pat' did taste a bit weird once you had tasted Jif or Skippy! The peanut content was low? Some of us got up to high altitudes on that swing, that had you been thrown off, one could have been ejected on the fire had it been alight and you miscalculated.

Great fun, though!

Everybody made Airfix and Revell model plane kits, including me. Frank made a C-130 four-engine transport in such detail, and the back would open up and allow vehicles or small soldiers to be placed inside and gave it to Bob and Roland. I remember making a Lancaster bomber that took me ages, and I was proud of it; it was so well done even if I say so myself, and I, a kid, had done it and remember staring at it before going to school with pride. It all seems like a dream now. I used to go horse riding in some posh stables in a local town called Northwood every Sunday without fail. I was really into horses for a long time and houseplants for some reason. Someone had even bought me a Black Beauty Revell model horse kit based on the novel by Anna Sewell for Christmas. I dutifully made it but managed to get glue in the tail and on the body, and the horse came out a little the worst for wear. One of the long-haired boyfriends had a good laugh at this, but hell, Action Man needed a horse if he had run out of petrol for his jeep with Rommel's Panzer Corp following him! Or perhaps an early version of Indiana Jones.

We always had a lot of animals, including a 'bitch' brought over from the States in the mid-sixties. She was called 'Beauty' and a constant companion to Mum. She had a large brood of puppies, some distributed to the 'greater family' and a boy given to Aunt Gladys. His name was Sancho, and he was also very loyal to Aunt Gladys.

The Rabbit population grew at the house, and we were in the newspaper again:

The Middlesex Advertiser, Thursday, May 30th 1968 WHO COULD guess that four pretty white Himalayan rabbits could mean big trouble. But unfortunately, the phrase "Breed like rabbits" is no empty boast. Once, James Fuller, a retired Colonel of the U.S. Air Force, had two white rabbits. Now he has six. And, if something isn't done quickly, he's afraid white rabbits will be arriving in his house faster than from a magician's hat. And there just isn't room for hundreds of rabbits in the Fuller household at 11 Sweetcroft Lane, Hillingdon. For the Fullers have seven children, a guinea pig, a cat, a dog and a goldfish. So the four two-month-old rabbits will just have to go. "They will be getting round to breeding in another couple of weeks or so, and then we will have more rabbits than we know what to do with", said James Fuller, who's getting rather anxious about finding homes for the four bunnies before his back garden becomes a maternity home for rabbits. So if you have always wanted a white Himalayan rabbit, James Fuller is your man. Absolutely no charge!

We gave away some rabbits that week.

The kids had also found a young kitten outside a flower shop in Ruislip, and the owners said he was a young stray and would we take him. A good-looking tortoiseshell cat that somebody names 'Titmus' after the famed British cricketer! At first, he was at odds with our Labrador named Brindle. One day, Brindle came bounding up to him, barking in an attempt to show the cat who was boss. A yelp was heard, and Titmus swiped the dog with his paw, creating a light scratch on Brindle's nose, and Brin' ran away. After that, they became pals, with Titmus as boss, and would often be in each other's company as slightly antagonistic but good mates.

Mum and Nanny would go shopping together and return with excellent British food, including cakes and cake ingredients. They also marked off their items on huge till roll receipts. They looked like what a pharaoh's priest might use to calculate the items and jewellery for the afterlife and mark them off in a similar manner-the Papyrus scroll of the Fuller family. The flower, eggs, and milk would fly, and Nan would come up with Spotted Dick and custard for Tea-very tasty. The only thing that was a bit unpleasant was the smell of the fish when I went to the fresh fish stall in Uxbridge with Mum. The Uxbridge market sold a kaleidoscope of things and was situated at the old corn exchange with massive Romanesque columns. The place dates from 1793, the height of the French Revolution. The mail and passenger coaches with a team of 4-6 horses would stop and pass the place in their droves, sometimes procuring fresh horses and travelling either east into London from the cities of Oxford or Bath, and vice versa.

I remember Mum buying me a brown leather wallet with rhinos imprinted on it from the bag stall. I had been a pain about it, and the last 50p was paid to buy it. We did not have a car at that point for some reason and she had left her chequebook at home, so paying for a cab or bus was tricky-somehow we made it all home with the shopping and walking across the park.

Uncle Stan would visit if, at any time, a car required attention. 'Make a d'Fix' as he used to say. He was the sort of person who could fashion a fan belt from 3 rubber bands tied together with a pair of tights or hammer something and somehow make it work, with usual success. On one occasion, brother Frank was trying to locate a water pump in a hurry for his British Austin 1300 (The very type Basil Fawlty would thrash with a stick in the British Comedy series 'Fawlty Towers'). This car was not too reliable. Having seen a burnt-out mini in a local field and thought it would prove useful, he went with Frank to find a water pump-"from that burnt-out thing, Uncle"- "sure, it will work", came the reply! The water pump was extracted from the burnt-out car and placed in the Austin, and yes, it worked well. He was having more trouble with the boat, however.

I don't know what happened to the Compass Rose, as the house started to subside in 1976 and was towed away a couple of years later. However, Dad kept the nameplate and the giant compass we have today. Unfortunately, it was too far gone and rotted to be restored.

Chapter 28

Urban Legends and Long Haired Boyfriends

I enjoy Urban Legends. Some may be based loosely on fact or changed over time. Like Chinese Whispers, whereby the original story is distorted, intentionally or unintentionally changed when it is passed on from person to person. One of my sisters went out with her boyfriend, that was very good at recounting Urban Legends. He was a bit of an Urban Legend in the flesh himself in the fact that he drove around in a white dune buggy with butcher's style plastic that replaced glass windows. The heating in these vehicles was poor or non-existent. If winter was cold, one would have an oil heater in the back to keep oneself warm on those cold British evenings. He also bought a blue and red old-time-style police siren that he used to place on top. This upset the local constabulary, and he was pulled over by the police several times.

We would go to the many cinemas in the area, watching films like Peter Pan. Bedknobs and Broomsticks, or 'One of Our Dinosaurs is Missing' (brilliant film).

One evening, over hot milk and cookies and listening through the bannisters, I overheard a 1970s' story about a couple that had gone to a Kentucky Fried Chicken Restaurant in London and, because they were late, decided to take the meal into the cinema and eat it in the stalls! The smell must have been legendary in itself. The girl noted that the 'chicken' tasted rather odd; (she could not tell what she was eating in the darkened auditorium) but carried on eating the chips and coleslaw. Upon the film's ending, they came out bleary-eyed yet enthralled by the movie they had just watched but decided to look at the remnants of the meal to see what was up. After gazing into the greasy box, a moment later, the girl let a cry out and unexpectedly fainted, and a medic had to be called. It turns out that a rat had gotten into the batter somewhere in the process and became 'Kentucky Fried' itself. This is what she had been chowing down on in the cinema. A little grisly story for a young lad, I gulped on my milk, but this wasn't the end of it. This was like the trilogy or separate stories the iconic British film Studios Hammer' used to make. They were well-known then (and still are) for making mainly horror and suspense films. I loved them.

The second story recounts how a group of motorcyclists had gone out on a jaunt and stopped at a motorway service area for some grub after weather conditions had become poor to wait out the storm. Motorway service areas in those days differed from the 'expensive chain affairs' you have now. They were of varying quality and were hit-and-miss. Sometimes called 'greasy spoons' or 'mungy tossers' (as my uncle used to call them), they were great and individual, unlike today. They used to be called Blue Boar or Blake's Seven, names like that. I remember travelling up the M1 Motorway in the strange in-between Christmas period in England in 1980 for the New Year's celebrations with my other sister Josie and husband Dave, who had moved up to Coventry. He was one of the new 'software computer engineers' and, with the help of Dad's sponsorship, would travel and live in the United States the following year. It turned out the services were closed because of a power failure. Nevertheless, hot and cold food was sold in a portacabin (the door kept banging open because of the howling wind and ice outside). Cakes, scones and hot mince pies were served by a group that appeared to be headed by a vicar (and perhaps his flock!), and prices were low. I assume the Blue Boar corporation had enlisted their services for Christmas Period. Back to the story. The group of motorcyclists had decided to brave the weather. However, it was still icy and cold, but they took off into the country towards the coast anyway. It was treacherous because of the dearth of traffic and the fact that the roads needed to be treated with salt. One of their number had lost control, skidded and had a nasty encounter with an oak tree at the side of the road! Because there were no mobile phones available at the time, someone had to ride to a call box or go to a house and ask to use the telephone. In the meantime, miraculously, the rider had regained consciousness, and his mate had wanted to take his helmet off because the injured man was mumbling something. Stopping for a moment as the man gesticulated frantically- he wanted to leave his helmet on, his friend asked another rider to carefully listen to what the guy was saying as he could not understand a word. The fellow came over and put his ear to the motorcyclist's mouth and, this time, understood. He was telling the assembled for gods sake not to take his helmet off for any reason and had apparent fear in his eyes. The ambulance had still not arrived, and they were in a quandary about what to do. They decided they must remove the helmet to make the incapacitated man more comfortable. They ignored his plea, thinking he had trauma and was rambling. They eased the helmet off, and the unexpected happened to the horror of the onlookers; the man's head split open like a watermelon; the moment the helmet was free, his brain virtually spilt out onto the dark, icy and dreary road. How in the heck did he know what was going to happen? I stealthily crawled back up the stairs, grabbing my last cookie and had nightmares the rest of the night. The first story was maybe true, but the second- no!?

Chapter 29

1969- A Strange Year?

A year before 1968, Dad had enquired about going on the great North Pole expedition of 1968-9 organized by Wally Herbert and the British Trans Arctic Expedition (BTAE). With his radio and navigation knowledge, he thought he might be in the running. He believed in the end; however, Herbert wanted an all-British team to make an attempt, and it was not to be. Wally Herbert made it from Point Barrow in Alaska to Spitsbergen, being the first team to mostly 'walk' the terrain to reach the North Pole and make some history over 18 months of travel.

Later, back in the USA, Dad was visiting Aunt Gladys and the family in Tennessee. He had been taking his Masters' Degree in Political Science at USM (University of Southern Mississippi) and decided to take a break. He stayed with Glad' at her house next to the strange cabin on the hill that he was to rent and eventually buy 10 years later on Rocky Branch Road in Walland. They went hiking to the Smokies and the Cades Cove area and beyond in June. They enjoyed a bright day in the hills, wandering around the old cabins and 'primitive' churches (no ornamentation here) that dotted the valley. A few days later, they heard about a missing boy Dennis Martin as it was Statewide news, eventually becoming quite a famous missing person case. Aunt Gladys incidentally married a man with the last name Martin, and the boy may have been a relation. Dennis and his family had gone for their annual hike in the mountains, and they climbed to Spence Field this time. Spence Field is a small grassy meadow that sits at an altitude above the river valley.

The famous Appalachian trail runs right through the location. Dad went on a short trip with a small group of the many searchers but couldn't stay long as he had to return to Hattiesburg and the University. He wasn't trained in search and rescue but had enough military experience to know a little of what went on in the process and could navigate himself reasonably well.

Even The Air National Guard became involved in the search, and the numbers reached about 1400 overall. This was later thought of as odd years later, as apparently, the military usually didn't become involved in these types of operations, and it was very rare if they did. Dennis Martin was never found, and the case has become quite famous to those who investigate and read about missing persons and mysteries. Theories range from the boy falling down a cave shaft, being taken by feral pigs, abduction, etc. It was so quick as Dennis and his friends were very close by playing a hide-and-seek game. Any noise or screams would usually be heard, but there was nothing, and nobody was seen (It was hectic, being a holiday weekend). Later, in Cades Cove, a family called the Keys was visiting the park, and the kids wanted to see bears. They got out of their vehicle on a trail just off the Cove. Moments later, the family heard a 'horrible scream' on a bluff or forested ridge a short distance away. They saw something. It appeared that a shadowy 'hairy' person was running through the trees. It was odd, as it seemed that there was something 'he' was carrying on his back. It was over very quickly, and they brushed it off until being interviewed later by the FBI- but perhaps just a bear or park visitor with his family. Cades Cove was several miles away, and this setting was close in time to the disappearance. I remember Dad briefly mentioning the case, but I read more about it in a book entitled 'Unsolved Mysteries in the Great Smoky Mountains', by Juanita Baldwin and Ester Grubb, which I bought locally in Tennessee. It touched on other missing cases, local folklore, and the Martin case.

In 2005, I hiked up to Spence Field by myself from the Bote Mountain trail from the Valley floor, which was a relatively easy climb up until the last mile, where it became steep; I was glad to have carried a supply of water, coffee and saltine crackers with peanut butter and cheese! I learned later the path was used to cross the mountains by the local Cherokee tribe for hundreds, if not thousands, of years. It was strange to be at the actual spot, and I moved on quickly back to the car, not really wanting to hang around. Nobody else was around either, and I remember it became hushed with a lack of animal noise. This I thought was a little strange. One odd occurrence related to the story happened in a nightclub on the Kingston Pike in Knoxville. Kingston Pike is a long 'strip' of bars, hotels and clubs (a bit like a mini Las Vegas) in Town. One night, the lead FBI investigator on the case at the time took himself out on the dancefloor of a club and committed suicide. An odd case all around.

Later that year, Dad was traversing through Mildenhall USAF/RAF in 1969 on one of his long haul trips back to England. He was usually able to wander around the outlying Hangers of the base but noticed the security was 'ramped up' somewhat from previously. He spoke to a master-sergeant who told him about the night of the theft of a C-130 Aircraft. A Sergeant Paul Meyer, a Chief Mechanic on the C-130, had ordered it to be fueled and ready to go. The ground crew, below him in rank, prepped the plane, and on a cold morning on May 23rd, he took the aircraft out, taxied to the runway and took off. Flying low to try to avoid UK Radar, he got as far as the English Channel, where near Alderney Island, he unfortunately crashed, and the body was never found or the wreckage until 2018. A Vietnam veteran but disillusioned with life at the base and the fact that his wife wanted him home in the States to be with his new family, he decided to leave. He had been in contact with his wife on the plane and told her he 'was on his way'. Dad had misgivings and felt the possibility was there for him to have been shot down. A French interceptor and one RAF Hawker Hunter were scrambled, but he may have proved elusive to locate? Years later, it was reported by the ground crew that the atmosphere felt 'off' when working in the hangar the plane was housed in and the ramp (tarmac) outside. An eerie gloom and the feeling of a malign presence, but there again, it could have been imagination. The initial incident was the talk of the base for a while afterwards. Mum had kept the papers and gave them to Dad on his return to London.

Life went on at the house as 'normal' approaching the new decade. Uncle John used to come over to Sweetcroft and do some woodwork at the house and bring furniture, as he was a driver for a large cabinet firm; as well as being 'good with wood', he gave us some discounted pieces, including a lovely Chippendale dining set, which one of the dogs chewed the leg of one of the chairs of course. They were all sitting down one day, and John bought up the subject of the recent book 'Chariots Of The Gods' by Erich Von Daniken, and a discussion was held. Von Daniken postulated the theory that ancient astronauts had visited Earth in the past and influenced ancient cultures and even created old structures, such as the pyramids. Also, the Nazca Lines and petroglyphs in the deserts of Peru were ancient landing strips for extraterrestrials. I think the consensus was from Dad and brother Frank, at least(the astronomer of the family), that it was not credible.

Frank sent off for a map of the Solar System given to you by the cereal Weetabix as he had saved all the tokens in concert with the celebrations of the up-and-coming moon landing. On July 20th, 1969, everybody was enthralled and sitting around the Black and White TV set and watching The Moon Landings. The next day Dad bought the Daily Telegraph with the big spread-'Man Lands On The Moon' emblazoned on this and all the other newspapers of the era, even in England.

A few weeks later, he bought the same newspaper with different headlines. That the beautiful, fledgling actress Sharon Tate and her friends had been murdered in Hollywood, California. Sharon had been watching the same Moon landings weeks before with probably similar awe. She was also from a military family, and her father had been stationed in Italy. She got her start as an extra in the film 'Barrabas' starring Anthony Quinn, filmed in Italy in 1961. She can be seen briefly in the amphitheatre scene. Possibly, Sharon had a premonition of her death, which can be researched if desired. It was later found out that the 'Manson Family' was culpable for the killings. Having read about the event myself, I believe it contributed to a significant change in attitudes and the zeitgeist of the free-thinking hippie era, and in its place, paranoia, security, and guard dogs replaced it, and it was all so unnecessary. On the same day, the murders took place, eerily, the Beatles pop group had their photograph taken on the Crosswalk in Abbey Road, London, for the Abbey Road Album Cover, and a willing policeman even held up traffic for a moment. Manson was obsessed with the Beatles, and it was an odd coincidence.

The ad hoc music festival Woodstock would still go ahead a week later, but it was, in some ways, the end of an era as mentioned.

The A40 Road Junction at Hillingdon Circus on Long Lane, half a mile from Sweetcroft, was dangerous. Fast traffic driving into London used to traverse it every day. For some reason, it gave me slight creeps when walking to the shops to get sweets. A young girl on her bike was crossing the road and was literally flattened by a lorry in 1969 as she was halfway across at the junction, and the driver was traumatized. I recently read this in Dad's correspondence home and remembered that story along with another about a girl of about 20 who crashed in her car in 1980 into the bridge erected because of the other girl's death and other accidents. She was planning a new life in the States and had much to look forward to. I used to go over the cement bridge they erected and then removed years later on my British Raleigh Grifter bike and moved across quickly.

At the local common or 'square' in Uxbridge that was part of a housing quarter called the 'Lynch, ' Protestant Martyrs were burnt at the stake in an act of retribution by the Catholic queen and daughter of Henry VIII, Mary, in the mid-1500s. The description of their horrible deaths can be found in Fox's Book of Martyrs. Not far from this spot, a number of girls would die in a fireball, trapped in a mini before the emergency services could reach them. Again, at an early age, coincidences like this I found weird and a sad event of course.

James and Jean Fuller.

Albert Holder Marine Commando 1940.

Alice Springs, Australia 1973.

NTY REGISTER

Two Sections, Twelve Pages

e Show Dated

ttending will register at
and will not need be pres-
win,

nection with the show, the
amber of Commerce will
"Farm and Home Week"
and also will provide cou-
customers to allow them
a show at reduced prices.

ainal fee will be charged
loor out of respect to the
es who are thus assured
se visiting the show are
y interested in seeing the
ems for farm and home.

ednesday evening perform-
Livingston, incidentally,
timed so that those at-
Lenten church services will
me to get to the auditor-

dition to the main stage
local talent will be per-
at various times in the
n and evening.

e Faribo nners In row Show

Faribault county hog rais-
ced among the top five
me classes with their ani-
the Minnesota State Spring
show at Austin last week.

were headed by Ted Goltz
n, Elmore, whose hogs
in four classes: third in
hree and fourth in class
the open division for in-
s; third in class two and
class three in open di-
ons.

countyans placing were
Garlick, Winnebago, fifth
one, open division indi-
and Donald Scheid, Dela-
rd in class two, open di-
dividuals and second with
three in class two.

AIR FORCE CREW ponders next step after surveying crippled engine at left shortly after the emergency landing. Left to right they are Airman Murray, Lt. Duckett, Airman Woodard and Captain Fuller. "We had only one chance at the field," said Fuller, who was relieved enough at just finding it. — Post-Register photo.

'Ready To Jump'

Blue Earth Is 'Good Earth' To Four In Crippled Plane

"Comin' in on a wing and a prayer."

Four relieved men stepped from crippled air force twin engine CS-47 (military search version of a DC-3) here Saturday morning after a close brush with disaster.

"It was either find a spot to land or bail out," said Captain James A. Fuller, the pilot whose crew credited him with a "superb" job of bringing the big plane in.

A few minutes later the plane landed safely on a strip at the local airport.

Crewmen Lt. Ross B. Duckett, A2c Robert C. Murray and A2c Robert Woodard praised Captain Fuller for his skill at handling the machine. "We were ready to bail out just before we sighted the Blue Earth strip," Woodard said.

Checking the air map, Fuller for many years, and hundreds visited the field Saturday afternoon and Sunday to see it. Courteous air force men allowed many to go through the airplane.

Airman Murray remained in Blue Earth after another craft from Duluth arrived Saturday afternoon to pick up the other crewmen. He was joined Sunday by four maintenance men from Duluth Sunday afternoon who brought with them a new engine.

Blue Earth, Minnesota Crippled Plane 1958.

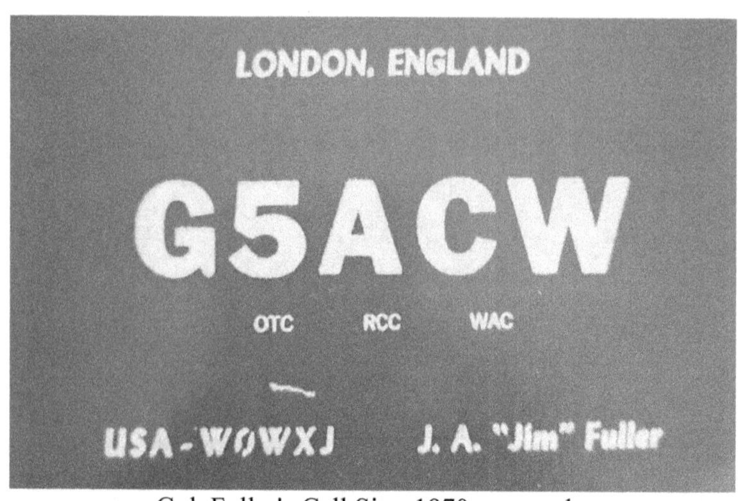

Col. Fuller's Call Sign 1970s onwards.

Dad and Bob at Sweetcroft 1977.

B24 Aircraft-Dad and Crew 1940s.

Dad 'Radio Room' Sweetcroft 1977.

In Fog

AF Pilots 'Rescue' Lost Plane

Air force and Civil Aeronautics administration teamwork yesterday led a lost private plane pilot to safety after a two-hour hide-and-seek search packed with tension and drama.

The pair of Duluth air base C-47 pilots were credited today with preventing the crash of the small, single-engined Cessna craft. Its pilot made a forced landing at the McGregor municipal airport.

Air force personnel are trying to learn the flier's identity. They know he was bound for Prairie du Chien, Wis., when he alerted the area's bases with the "May Day" distress call about 10:25 a. m. yesterday.

Control tower men at the Duluth air base heard the pilot call. He was lost in fog and rain and had a limited fuel supply.

Air base operations headquarters alerted Capt. Joseph Gambucci, pilot, and Capt. James Fuller, co-pilot, who took off in a military C-47, a two-engined transport plane. The alert came so fast that Fuller stood guard against fire as Gambucci started his engines. Just as they were ready to roll, S-Sgt. Paul Jansen, flight engineer, boarded the search craft.

Lost Plane: Part 1 Deluth, 1955.

Deluth Herald Lost Plane: Part 2, 1955.

At his Post! A happy phone call.

Florida 1999.

Ham Radio Beam the 1970s, at Sweetcroft Lane.

Harriet Sexton Fuller the wife of John Rufus Fuller was sister to
the well beloved Thomas Sexton... The blacksmith preacher.

Jane 1979.

Josie, Frank, Rhonda and Jane 1959.

Korea 1959.

Mum with Beauty's Puppies 1970.

Jean (Mum) Working at Cabin in Tennessee 2001.

POW Badge awarded by Air Force.

Precarious Air Travel; Christmas 1954.

QSL Ham Radio Postcard USSR.

Roland, Matthew and Bob in Bath March 1993.

Rutland House School, Hillingdon 1966.

Outside Sweetcroft, England 1969.

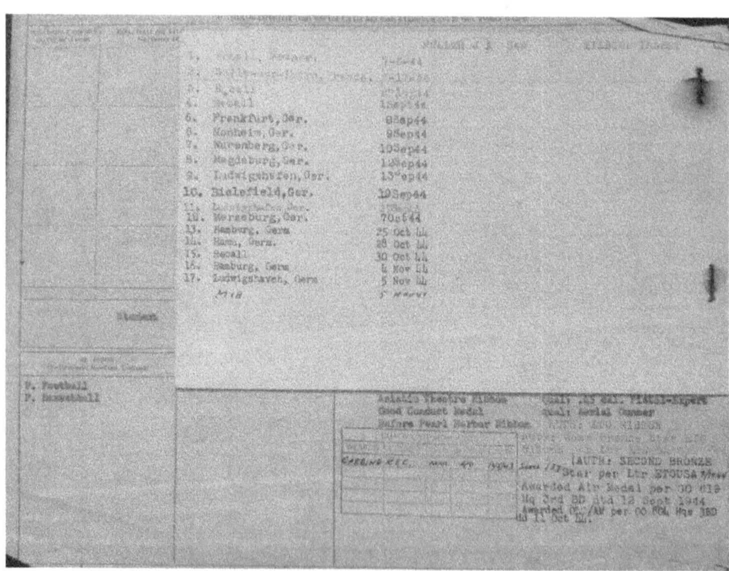

WWII Mission List, Europe.

The Holder Family 1918.

Thomas Holder, Grandfather; The Great War.

Uncle Edwin, London, Early 20th Century.

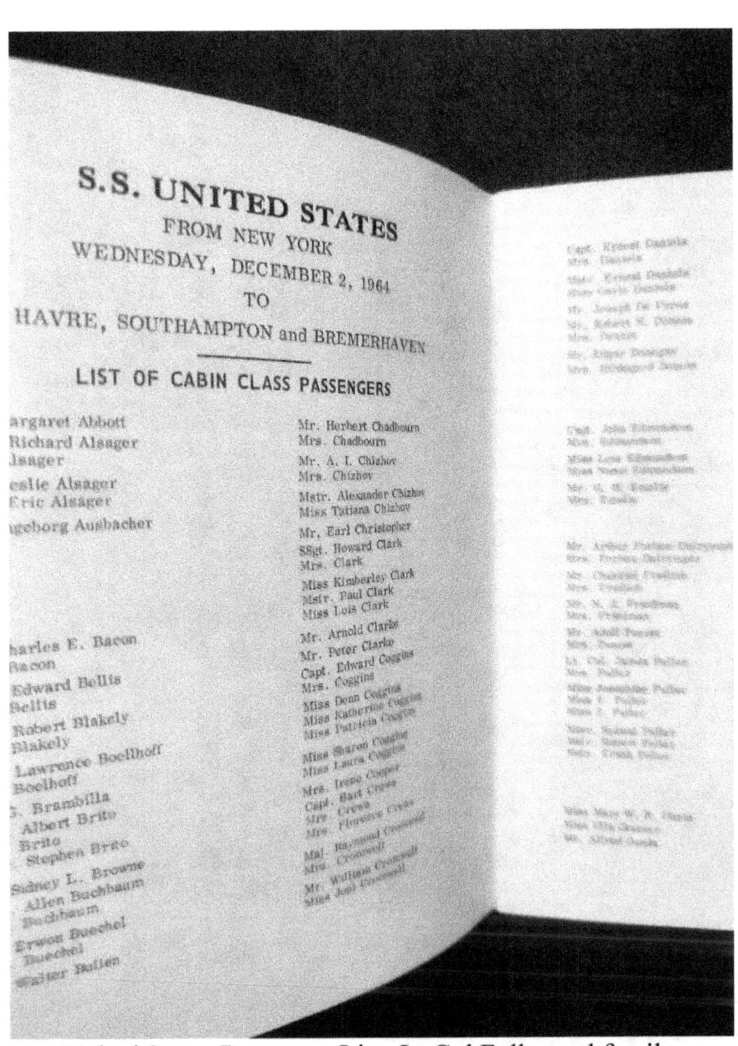

United States Passenger List -Lt Col Fuller and family.

Winter 1977 Sweetcroft Lane, England.

Stanley and Frank 1950 London.

Lt Col Fuller.

Chapter 30

India Trip

During the Summer of 1976, my brothers and their girlfriends embarked on a spectacular road trip to India. Eventually, they met up with a former tutor in London, a Dr Durrani, who became a family friend and gave homeschool lessons to a couple of us back in England. He was a good tennis player, and we often went to the local court for a few sets, but he could have gone professional. The problem was, his favourite foods were the cakes and sweets my mum and sister Jane would make for us all. He would otherwise wander down to the local 'Coombes' (British Bakers) and buy fondant fancies and the coconut pastries, which consisted of icing and strings of coconut baked in. A real character from a famous lineage, from an offshoot of a line of rulers founded in 1747 by Ahmad Shah Durrani in Kandahar, Afghanistan, though he made little reference to this and wasn't the type to brag. One of his ancestors, Ahmad Shah invaded the remnants of the Mughal Empire in Northern India in the Punjab and Kashmir regions and defeated their armies. He even went as far as Delhi but allowed the Mughals nominal control of the city after their defeat. China was considered for attack because of the Qing Dynasty's expansionist policies towards the sub-continent. Attempting to unite the other Muslim tribes, he eventually ran out of money. He could only send delegates for talks to Beijing, not exacting a physical assault on the country, a relief for China, I imagine. The Dynasty of Durrani was still a force well into the 19th Century.

The boy's trip to India I will leave for them to explain for themselves in another book perhaps, but here is a short 'projected' itinerary of their outbound trip in a Volkswagen bus-HGJ213N.

21st July: Hoverlloyd Hovercraft Ferry from Ramsgate, England, 2000 Hrs.
22nd July: Austria!
23rd July: Belgrade (Capital of Serbia, then a part of Yugoslavia).
24th July: Depart Belgrade-Stay for a while in Sophia, expecting arrival in Istanbul tonight.
25th July: Expect to reach Yozgat, Turkey or the vicinity.
26th July: Stop at Erzurum, Turkey.
27th July: Leave Erzurum for the border and arrive at Tabriz, Iran, the same night.

28th July: Tehran?
29th July: Leave for Mashad.
30ˢᵗJuly: Mashad to Herat, Afghanistan.
31ˢᵗ July: Kandahar to Kabul1st August: Kabul?
2nd August:: Leave for Rawalpindi.
3rd August: Rawalpindi to Amritsar, India.
4th August: Amritsar to Srinagar in Kashmir, India!

Though they kept a few of these dates, it was a complicated and wild route-best laid plans of mice and men. It was a fortuitous journey in terms of timing. Only three years later, in 1979, the Shah of Iran was overthrown by Islamic revolutionaries and the imperial State of Iran was ousted by The Islamic State headed by Ayatollah Khomeini in a coup and takeover.

Dad had flown into Tehran on a diplomatic plane at one point and described most of the town as being relatively modern, with female university students at a campus he visited for coffee having the mannerisms and the dress style of their Western counterparts. He was going there for a job interview, something to do with the diplomatic service and possibly hush-hush. Being very young, I never really knew much about it, and I don't think anybody else did.

They would never have been able to make the journey after this, and people still ask about it until this day. Even as it was, border crossing and meetings with officials came with risk and they certainly had some hair-raising times. They eventually met up with Dr Durrani, and they gave him my kite! Some months before, I had bought a kite that had emblazoned on it a spaceman in full gear. They took it with them to fly in at the journey's end. However, Dr D. liked it so much that he took it and, in exchange, gave me two wooden and carved catapults, which we still have to this day, one of which is slightly damaged from a chewing incident by my collie 'Cookie' in 1978. We don't know what became of Durrani. Still, I will never forget him playing a classical piece on a violin at my birthday party when I was eight years old whilst opening presents and eating wobbly jelly and cake and chatting with my friends. We were more into disco or pass the parcel for the expected gifts, but he was an excellent musician and we as kids never appreciated his talent.

We just carried on and blew paint bubbles onto a white canvas to make some psychedelic drawings; it was all very strange.

Meanwhile, a 'friend' wandered upstairs and stole some 'precious stone eggs' that had been polished and made into gifts from India. They may have contained precious stones; I can't remember now.

One day, I was at the back of the park getting ready to go through the wilderness area with this 'friend' and another to play games or watch television at my house. He knew about the old lady's story and whispered to the other guy to leave me. There was another pathway to the main road, which you could walk along to reach the house. They ran off this way, and I was left to run through the wilderness at top speed in fear of being taken by a witch and looking back to see if anything was chasing me. I didn't stop running until I reached the back garden and the house at the back. I can't remember why I just didn't go along the path back to Sweetcroft the way they went. Ah, I was drawn in! A strange and lost time now. Well, not all lost; I am currently in contact with one of my old friends from the past.

Chapter 31

Life at Sweetcroft Lane

Dad was a collector and kept much memorabilia from the war, with personal /Air Force items and, afterwards, perusing antique shop wears as he wandered continents. He would even buy stuff from my school jumble sale.

One early morning at the house in 1977, Dad came down in the morning in one of the old heater suits from the old B-17s he used to fly. The cabins were not pressurized or heated at altitudes of 30,000 feet, and it was freezing, so the men had to wear heavy-duty weather gear as well as oxygen. It was a frosty morning, and Dad put the light on and peered out the kitchen window just in time to see three men proceeding up the garden path, eyeing up the shed and the house to burgle it. Dad came to the kitchen door's entrance alongside the air raid shelter. They caught one site of Dad in his quilted, puffed-up one-piece 'boiler suit' and took off running down the back garden! He had also put on some heavy military boots; a frightening sight for the uninitiated. He called the police, and I believe they caught them as they reached the road on the other side of the park. The police called in and spoke to Dad for a report. One officer mentioned they looked confused and bewildered; I guess so!

Dad could lose his temper when it came to his radio gear or, let's say, furniture, for instance. On one occasion, he had been given a desk by Uncle Frank for use in the upstairs attic room. It was a big desk and a small space, for starters. Also, the attic room had creaky, freaky smallish stairs you had to negotiate in almost a hairpin. One person was at the top, and two others at the bottom trying to push, prod and generally cajole this desk to get upstairs and come quietly. Finally after an hour had passed, it wedged itself and didn't move; it was an immovable object.

Dad got so frustrated he just started kicking it (he was also late for an appointment), and someone else started kicking it after trying to rock it free. It finally ended up in a heap of matchsticks at the bottom of the stairs, a lousy day for wood. Even at a young age, I felt sorry for them, and Mum cooked some extra pork chops to keep their spirits up. He was also not a fan of the then-modern pop music and trying to speak on the Ham Radio to a distant nation, he could hear noise from somewhere, and down below, my brothers, sisters and cousins were playing David Bowie and then British group Slade in the kitchen rather loud on a portable radio. He came down and, in a fit of temper, picked up the radio and shook it with both hands caveman style, and 'The man who fell to Earth' was about to do so a second time.

Dad was interviewed at home for the local newspaper because of his Radio Ham notoriety.

In January 1977, there appeared a story in the local newspaper in Hillingdon, The Post.

Quote:

Header: HELLO…HELLO….IS THAT YOU TREVOR IN ANTARCTICA? SAYING HIGH TO CHUMS ALL OVER THE WORLD.

Wednesday was a normal kind of day for Jim Fuller. He spoke to a man in Siberia and a couple of friends in America, before he contacted Trevor in Antarctica.
Jim is a 'Radio Ham'. He has £300 worth of ultra sensitive radio equipment at the top of his house in Sweetcroft Lane, Hillingdon.

Jim, an American and ex-military pilot, has been in England for over 12 years, but has been in the 'radio ham' business for

30 years. He admits to be addicted to his hobby, and has instilled his enthusiasm into two of his sons, twins Roland and Bob.

I was lucky to be with Jim last Wednesday, as he managed to make a new 'contact' in Antarctica.

He was trying to contact one of his regular operators off the Southern coast of Africa, but instead picked up a strong signal from a man with an Australian accent.

As Jim shouted his call sign, an unintelligible muddle of Qs and Ts, the Australian accent came through and informed Jim that his name was Trevor, and he was Trevor and he was in Antarctica with 22 other compatriots. And it was 1:30 in the morning!

Jim and Roland couldn't believe their ears. Although they were in regular touch with Siberia, Japan and Australia, they had never before contacted anyone in this particular part of Antarctica.

Again, Jim sounded off in Radio code, before telling Trevor he was calling from London and he had a young lady from the press with him, who was excited as he was picking up that part of the world. With that, Jim plunged the microphone in to my hand and told me to go ahead and speak.

Well, what would you do when suddenly asked to say something spectacular to an Australian in Antarctica.

I summoned up all my journalistic wit and said "Hello Trevor, really great to hear you..."and faded off into silence. Bang went my radio career!

Trevor said that, contrary to belief, the previous afternoon had been hot and he had been swimming. With promise of a future contact, Jim signed off.

Roland explained to me that the radio operators world was divided into 40 zones, each numbered. The most difficult to contact were zones 19 (parts of Russia) and 23(Mongolia), but Jim had managed both. A certificate hung on his wall confirming he had contacted all 40 zones. The only country which cannot be contacted at all is China, who forbid such activity.

As I reluctantly departed on Wednesday evening, I left Jim in touch with a slightly more familiar contact, a British Airways employee talking from Ashford!

By Alison Cameron.

The expectation of talking to somebody in Antarctica back in the 1970s was quite a revelation, not that easy to do now, but with the introduction of the internet and satellite phones, it is much more accessible. However, Ham Radio is still as popular today with hobbyists and used in front line military communications, as is the use of Morse code. Speaking to China and Russia was more difficult, and Dad used to complain about the Russians using a jamming signal. I heard it a number of times, and it was quite loud, reverberating through the room.

Dad would even contact the wife (a female Ham Radio Operator, which was rare) of the director of The Musee De L'Homme (Museum of Mankind/Anthropology) in Paris, who she assisted, having qualifications in the evolution/pre-history side of things. Her name was Andre, and Dad even visited the museum and both the director and his wife at the museum and their stylish Romanesque apartment in the city, which Dad said was quite sumptuous. We all thought she contacted people amongst the bones and relics jars of the museum basement- an exciting picture.

When my Father acquired the cabin in 1980 in the Smoky Mountains of Tennessee, he mentioned he was out 'berry picking' previously in the hills whilst speaking to Andre on the radio later. I think she thought that was his main diet in the mountains and advised him to take care 'foraging for food' in the foothills. I imagined she thought of the pre-historic hunter-gatherers with clubs and stone tools. However, there was a Southern' Piggly Wiggly' grocery store to shop at in town, so he had other means of sustenance!

At Sweetcroft, he also had the opportunity to speak with King Hussein of Jordan from the top room. The King's call sign was JY-1, which was pretty short and unique. This he did for a while, and Dad was invited over (he never took up the offer). Later, brother Roland was to meet his son and wife in a strange synchronicity of events.

Chapter 32

English Family Life and Adventure

Uncle Stanley was always at the house, fixing cars that were broken.

He and his family had decided to emigrate to Australia in the 1960s to seek a fresh start and a different perspective on life. He was a mechanic and driver most of the time and made the best of it. Along the dusty trails, a little ways from Coober Pedy, he picked up a hitchhiker who had broken down on the Stuart Highway. There were many broken-down vehicles all over Australia in the outback. Stan didn't want any money, but the guy offered him a bag of something, insisted he took them, was let out at a service station, and went on his way. Stan peered inside and found a bag of opals!. Coober Pedy was the place for opals as many deposits and prospectors had claims to different parcels of land. The hitchhiker must have been one of those early men. Stan visited 'Coober' and was met with some odd looks from grizzled men in a cafe. He thought about prospecting and even bought a book. The guys in town probably thought this 'newby Pom' might want a piece of the action'. Stan left and thought he would leave it to them or try somewhere else to buy in, but he decided against it. He gave my sisters an opal each on his return to England and one took it to school to show the teacher and her classmates at school, and nearly lost it. Stan and his family had to return home for family reasons.

He was born in London in 1919, one of a large family; my grandparents on my English side had brought up through some difficult times in London and England in general.

Two of my uncles from the period did not make it to adulthood, through poor health and one acquiring the horrible disease tuberculosis or consumption as it was called.

These were Edwin and Sydney, Sydney died as an infant.
This was just about the end of The Edwardian period in England.

I remember another uncle of mine, Uncle Albert recounting when he was a boy how Edwin was so weak that he had to carry him back home from school on one occasion. It reminded me of Tiny Tim in the fictional 'A Christmas Carol' whereby Bob Cratchet, having just locked up for an ungrateful Scrooge on Christmas Eve, takes Tim on his shoulders to play in the snow in the town square with the other boys. It was regrettable. We still have a picture of Edwin, who lived until he was 13. He was a handsome fellow with long brown hair and delicate features.

Stanley had a wandering spirit and decided to join the Merchant marine in 1939. He wanted to be a fighter pilot in the RAF and passed the first selection process, at first as a mechanic, and then pilot training. At this point in the early stages of the war, the recruiters for the armed services were looking for navy personnel or general seaman for the Merchant navy. He was slightly early, and the need for pilots just before the Battle of Britain and other duties abroad, say in France, were considered less urgent at this time.

Uncle John was training at the base during the same period before he was also selected for the Merchant marine and paired with some Stanley, for better or worse! They both made friends with a young cadet from Canada named Luther, who had come to Uxbridge for training in 1940. During their stay at the base in Uxbridge, billets were sparse, and they had to train in tents. Because of the damp climate and lack of hygiene, he developed pneumonia and died in a foreign land far away from home. My grandmother Elsie kept in contact with Luther's mother. For some reason, because of the war and confusion/lack of facilities for the storage of the deceased, he could not be returned home to Canada. The family organized and buried him at the local Hillingdon cemetery near Uxbridge. He had been a frequent visitor to Nan's house and the Holder family and was considered a friend. Since my Uncle and Mother, Jean, have passed, I don't know the location in the cemetery where he is buried. Mum wished to go there and place a more permanent marker/refurbish the stone and inscription. I hope at some point to go to the location and perhaps locate the priest/warden to show me the site. Stanley returned to Uxbridge Camp in 1944 and was involved in a large parade, where dignitaries, including the then King George VI, were in attendance. He gave a speech with Admiral Cunningham on hand (Commander in Chief of the Mediterranean Fleet). On the same day, Cunningham was reviewing the men on parade and singled out a number of men, including Stan. Admiral Cunningham reviewed him and asked, "Where are your medals, man" to which my Uncle replied "I don't have any because you have them all" in the form of a joke (or words to that effect)! Apparently, there was quite a bit of 'tin wear' on the fellow's chest. Stanley had seen some unpleasant things in the war up to that point and was a little blase about it all and authority. Especially as his friend had died at this very camp and he was assigned to ships when he wanted to fly. He was reprimanded and sent to the Guard House to cool off for the night. No extra charges were brought, and he apparently didn't appear to lose any medals.

Uncle John and Stanley were in convoy to the South Seas during the 1939 as a part of a group delivering perishable goods like meat and also textiles like wool to and from Australia to all points of the compass. Soap was a valuable commodity too. Even electrical generators for some of the Island nations like Tonga as well as foodstuffs.

Tonga is a series of Islands in Polynesia, the central Island being Tongatapu, which has a rainforest-style climate. News of foreigners and their whereabouts was to become widely known quite quickly whilst in port. There were rumblings from the Empire of Japan at this point, and the crew had to be careful, but this was difficult. At Port in Tonga, the boys generally enjoyed the bars and Island life. Uncle John somehow caught the eye of the royal family, and especially Queen Salote and her kin folk. Because of the Islander's fascination with the British and John's good looks and easy wit, the family wanted him to stay on the Islands and perhaps even become part of the family and a trusted confidant. Although Uncle John enjoyed the life and the comforts it offered, I don't think he wanted a permanent stay. The Queen was insistent she liked Uncle John, and so the boys thought it prudent to leave, preferably at night, on a small boat back to the ship and stay there. The family guard might try to persuade them to stay. After all, there was work to be done aboard; they set sail a couple of days later and said farewells to Tonga for the time being!

Stanley mentioned that he was considering staying in the States when he docked in New York on one occasion and joining the then Army Air Corps to become a pilot. This never happened, however. It would have been interesting and a feat of synchronicity had this occurred, and he would have met Jim (Dad) at this point instead of later on in the 1950s!

His exploits would require a book of their own. There was a lot of stuff he just didn't want to talk about, as with my uncles, who you had to often 'tease out' the stories, as they often gave you snippets on a visit or during a tea break in remodeling a kitchen in 1981, or at a party when I was a kid. Some of it could be quite dark, as war mostly is.

Albert came in one day to our condominium on the other side of Hillingdon Court Park. He had just started to remodel the kitchen area. What had once been a dingy cupboard that cut off the lounge/dining room was knocked down, and an arch that you could walk through and a smaller arch you could sit with bar stools was constructed. You could now have breakfast in the kitchen or sit on the other side on bar stools.

It was now virtually a Spanish villa.

One day in April 1981, my Mum, Frank and I went on a day trip to the Tower of London and returned later, and it was finished! It was like a part of the house was now a space that even Salvador Dali would be impressed with. On a clear day, it was a feature of the condo' that you could see the Post Office Tower in London from the large windows that adorned the living room. Now you can see it from the kitchen. It was about 10 miles away as the crow flies. It was certainly not a massive place, but my Mother extended the feeling of it being more extensive by putting a relief setting (massive painting) in the background of a large conservatory, which was very effective.

Uncle Albert was also a veteran of World War II, having trained as a Marine Commando in Scotland for the push into occupied France in 1944 and the D-Day Landings.

The formation of the Marine Commando units at this time was unique, and Albert, being quite agile and thin, was an ideal candidate.

Whilst training in The Highlands and resting for a break, he swore he and his company saw a bobcat, or perhaps a wildcat; the bobcat is thought to have gone extinct in the middle-ages. He said it was too large to be a regular house cat and had whispy, sharp ears, which narrowed and reached a point..It must have been wondering what was happening with the shooting and such and quite disturbed. The manoeuvres may have brought it out of its hiding place.

At this point, they were using live ammunition, and things were quite tense, even in training.
On a break, he recalls one guy messing around with a hand grenade. He kept flipping the pin, mimicking the action of removing it and about to throw it to the receiving unlucky set of individuals in a future combat scenario.
Apparently, he had fallen out with the commanding officers and had become somewhat sullen and perhaps felt he was being singled out for reprimand.
Albert and the other guys in training decided to remove themselves from his company for a spell. They were becoming a little jumpy and had previously cajoled him to stop, which did not work. He was still laughing, apparently, when they walked away.

And then it happened, what they figure is that he released the pin by mistake, and the grenade just dropped where he sat, likely in his lap.
BANG; it went off, and you can imagine the rest. Safe to say, Albert and his mates did not want to be involved in the cleanup operation and the guy had blown both his hands off, and this was something that Albert did not want to see. The fellow was

stretchered off, and Albert lost contact and didn't know if he had survived.

Albert also relates an amusing tale whilst on the coast getting ready for D-Day and his glider hop to France.

He was part of a convoy that headed to the south coast and a seaside location for billets.

Somewhere along the line, it was assumed that Albert was at the head of the convoy and unbeknown to him, the leader with the map, who was confidently navigating his way to barracks, thus providing the soldiers with enough daylight to set up, have some food and hopefully get an early night. They had been on the road from the North of England for a long time.

Albert, however, did not know where he was going and came upon the back side of a troop transport lorry like his.

He thought this guy was the leader and started following him, but in fact, he was not, and the guy in front with equipment and troops was following another driver; he as it turns out was the last in line.

Albert, by chance, stared in his mirror and viewed a long Convoy following him. It turned out they were following my uncle, thinking he was the scout and knew where he was going.

In reality, it turns out that they were going in a ginormous circle with Albert as the leader, but really just following the truck in front of him!

Eventually, I think they made it to the barracks after this Laurel and Hardy-type escapade. Still, late for dinner and Albert was blamed.

Later, he was to become involved in the famous battle of Arnhem in the Netherlands.

He was brought to France via towed glider, a very hit-and-miss affair. Although most made it, the vagaries of the weather and the somewhat fragile nature of the gliders made for some accidents.

The Allies had pushed through Belgium and France with relative ease after overcoming the toil and horrors of the French coast and finally establishing a bridgehead, cleaning up pockets of German resistance as they moved forward.

Field Marshal Montgomery had proposed the operation Market Garden to push north towards the lower Rhine and attack the very industry of Germany, enabling a quicker passage into the heart of Germany and bypassing the Siegfried line to the East. The proposition was to secure bridges over the lower Rhine River.

The problem was the 1 British Airborne Division was dropped by a glider some distance from their objective and had to make up ground to the river and Arnhem and Nijmegen.

The paratroopers moved north of the river, moving through Arnhem town and the waterfront house by house and trying to force an element of surprise at the bridge, but their cover was blown.

Support was slow in coming and bogged down by the German counterattacks.

There was heavy resistance by the 9th and 10th SS Panzer Divisions that moved in from the North East and on the other side of the bridge.

Albert was in support, but the small detachment that made it to the bridge could not move further and was trapped after 4 days of fighting. Finally, the majority of the British at the bridge surrendered to the Germans.

He and his small company were besieged in a foxhole as the Germans counterattacked and made ground.

The big fear for most of them, according to Albert, was the German mortar attacks, which could be trained around a small area, but were often indiscriminate and unnerved the soldiers, even in a foxhole position. For example, during the height of one of these mortar attacks, he was called to another dugout to assist in the moving of a wounded man, as there were not enough stretcher-bearers and medical personnel to go around.

Upon returning to his fox-hole, the officer with them could not be found, he had disappeared in a blast and was never heard from again.

Albert fell back with his platoon, having not made it to the bridge, luckily, as he would have been captured.

Fierce fighting occurred, but Market Garden was only partially successful, and the Allies had to retire for the time being.
But Albert would later be part of the unit that made it all the way to Berlin.

Stanley relates this story of travelling in South American waters in 1941 and sailing up the Orinoco River basin to escape the possibility of attack by the Kriegsmarine and German U Boats.

He was an acquaintance of an Egyptian who signed on the boats in Algiers and was employed as a deckhand. He had ideas of making it big in the United States after the war and going out west to explore and make some money oil drilling. Stanley used to read many old Zayne Grey books like 'West of the Pecos' that Mum had given him funny enough, as she enjoyed the stories about the old west. Tariq (the deckhand) had been intrigued by this, as Stan often recounted the stories in it to the crew.
They would all be jovial, play cards, and drink when work finished.
Stan remembers Tariq asking about England and life back there. All in all, this crew appeared jovial and, except perhaps for the odd rivalry and usual issues aboard ship, got on well.

One twilight, whilst travelling back up the Orinoco (The Delta Amacuro), a squall blew up, and the boat; although a large craft with some serious tonnage, it started to rock back and forth.
Tariq was on deck but had had a few drinks, and Stan was down in the engine room.
Suddenly, there was a commotion up top and my uncle and another crewman rushed up to the rear deck to see what was happening.
It appeared that Tariq had been blown or perhaps tripped in some cabling on the ship, as he was in the water now at the back of the boat and floundering around.
There was no one close enough to grab him and save him.
It would take ages for a ship of that size, requiring a large turning radius, to turn around.

The boat was steaming on, and the crew yelled to get to the bank, throwing out a life ring, but he could not get to it. They decided they might jump in and save him or launch the life boat.

Then something, perhaps not wholly unexpected, happened. Two guys saw turbulence in the water in the gloom, noise and fading light, but this differed from the choppy water. Suddenly Tariq cried out and was presumably attacked from beneath by something and struggling with whatever it was. Orinoco Crocodiles and Black Piranha are known to inhabit those waters, but it could have been that or something similarly insidious. Stan and other crewmen considered still trying to save him, even jumping in, but were overruled by the Captain, and it was a long drop. The commotion continued for a moment, with his mates unable to do anything before it was too late.

The last thing they saw was the man's outstretched hand, clenched in a fist, perhaps resigned to his fate, struggling and trying to stay afloat but shortly disappearing below the water and finally gone. Nothing could be done; it was also wartime, and the local officials were only sometimes friendly. The ship returned to the North Atlantic.

I always have in my mind, when Uncle Stan recounted that story, a vision of the man's outstretched arm, perhaps trying to cling on to life, and the fear that must have engulfed him in those last few moments.

Chapter 33

Back To The Future

The 1960s progressed onwards, and my brothers and sisters were still at school but enjoying the music and fashions of London, with just a little American influence.

One Christmas, they had a showing of 'The Great Escape' movie at the comprehensive school my brothers were now attending, Abbotsfield in Hillingdon.

This was a Christmas treat, but it had been on at the cinema and now on television. It always seemed a staple, usually on Christmas Day in England. Most people were watching only 3 Channels, but as it was a great movie, it was always prevalent. Contemporary schoolmates of my brothers, Roland, Bob and Frank, were amazed at seeing Retired Col. Fuller, as they actually thought he was the actor James Garner, as he sported a resemblance to him!. They knew Dad was a POW, but probably not one from Stalag Luft III- I am not sure how they didn't separate the two from fact and fiction, but would not take no for an answer when the boys insisted they were two separate people!...”yes, your Dad is James Garner”, they said, and would not differentiate between the two!

It added a mystique to schooldays, but they couldn't wait for the short English summer to get out of the place. The juxtaposition of a relatively carefree life in the States (granted, they were younger) and the sometimes hostile reception at a British comprehensive school was miles apart. Though they made some good friends at Abbotsfield to counteract this nicely with some excellent and not so excellent teachers as well.

There were interesting new words to learn, like 'watcha', 'bagsy'(meaning it's your turn, I think?) and 'He's a Spaz'(if they didn't like a person), short for Spazmo if they couldn't be bothered to add the MO. I often hark back to a Pink Floyd

Song-'Another Brick In the Wall' and the lyrics 'Dark Sarcasms in The Classroom'- which was often true.

However, Bob, Roland and Frank had some unique teachers along the way.

There was the ex-RAF squadron leader who used to teach a geography class and took a dislike to the boys and mentioned one day that all Americans ever ate was corn cobs and peanut butter, and it seemed to irritate him that they didn't always take the corn off the cob to be eaten separately in quiet contemplation.

Then there was Mr Street, on the other hand, who loved the taste of Root Beer, which you could only get in this country at the time for love and money, perhaps from a US Airbase.

He would pay Mum when she went to the South Ruislip commissary to buy him cases of the stuff.

There was Mr Pendrey, the art teacher, who was so impressed when one of the boys made a plasticine mobile of the solar system, which he then displayed in the classroom.

Things got really interesting when a substitute teacher at Abbotsfield was brought in as a replacement to teach English, substituted that for tales of his conquests with girls and the acquisition of his latest sports car. On the door, as you went out, was a picture of a naked woman and man embracing, perhaps a reminder of the coming story the next time you filed in for class.

I believe he was fresh out of Art College.

This was a little too spicy, even for the 1960s. There were complaints from parents, and the Headmaster soon cottoned on to this. The substitute teacher was quickly substituted.

Finally, there was a Mr. Maddon (who lived up to his name) who was there in the 1960s, even when I was there nearly twenty years later. He was a metal shop teacher who once didn't like a pupil so much that he threw a vice at him and almost brained him, and the projectile just missed, according to my brother. Having him as a teacher would likely put you off metal work for life. This guy looked like a homicidal bulldog stung in the mouth by an Asian Hornet, with glasses that magnified his eyes to extremes. He wore a dirty white coat that usually had stains, probably blood. I couldn't imagine him going home to a wife and kids but perhaps retiring to a small closet at night with a meat cleaver in his hand and a pork pie drip feed.

Also, on one occasion, at Christmas time to amuse the kids near the break, one teacher showed another 1960s film 'The Manchurian Candidate' for a 'treat'. This was a film about brainwashing and assassination done to American troops by a Chinese and Russian unit during the Korean War. It was a strange choice to show kids at Christmas. It gave me Alex vibes from 'A Clockwork Orange'. Perhaps the teacher just pulled it off the shelf and it was a mistake bound for a university, or possibly it was to brainwash the kids-Ha!

Roland and Frank had trouble with some unpleasant bullies but fought back, and on one occasion, Roland was pushed and punched. He pushed back, and the guy hurtled backwards into one of the industrial glass windows forming part of the corridor. The window cracked under pressure; throughout their school careers at Abbotsfield, it remained a cracked window. When I went to this school in 1981, they described the 'bundle' location,' and a window was still broken! Reminders of the morbid moments of schoolhood and battle damage the school didn't bother to replace. There were bullies at my Junior School (Elementary School), of course, but there was one sort of ' high priest' bully who was remote to the lower order of bullies, and even they were scared of him. He was also quite mad in the head. He had bushy lanky blond hair and National Health glasses with white surgical tape where they broke around the middle often, and that magnified his eyes about 20X (A relative of Mr Maddon)? That alone was scary enough. Also, a pungent odour followed him about the place as he marched about, looking generally frightening. I didn't really come into direct contact with him on a 'one-to-one' as I was quite a 'large lad' then, and perhaps he was a little intimidated at that. I amused Mum at a school jumble sale by saying not to mess with him, and she still laughed at this years later. My personal battle with bullies occurred on one or two occasions, but I can't even remember most of their names now; I think one or two were supposed to be friends. Ah, 'the joys of a London school life'.

I preferred my time at Junior School on the whole and then later at the American International School, virtually sitting in the park opposite Sweetcroft Lane, where we lived. It was the grand old mansion constructed for Lord Hillingdon in the Victorian Era.

I was lucky enough to receive a scholarship to go there. In fact, I got closer to it, as after Mum left Sweetcroft, we lived virtually next to it, just off a street called Vine Lane near Uxbridge.

Jane, Rhonda and Josie were going through the same thing at Swakeleys School in Ickenham, and girls could often be worse than boys at that age.

Frank was an amateur astronomer from an early age and used to observe the planets very late at night or in the early mornings at home. He got bored once at school while the teacher was away and started to give a few lectures on the planets; I don't think the master was too pleased. Anyway, back in 1971, at about 2am in the morning on a cold and frosty night in October, he said the world went 'green', and it was like a 'green daylight'. A meteorite had crashed through the atmosphere and left a trail for a short time. It may have contained copper/magnesium burn off and turned green when it collided with oxygen in the atmosphere. It must have been relatively solid, of nickel-iron consistency too. There were reports of it crashing into the North Sea, but only a few people had seen it, perhaps because of the lateness of the hour.

Frank had the dogs on leashes tied up to a post that night. They sometimes tended to wander out through the back to the wilderness area and even onto the park if they were together. He was so engrossed in what he had seen and realigning the telescope that he hadn't noticed that our little whippet cross had chewed, not only through his nylon lead but also his labrador mates (Brindles)! They both had gone off together towards the park on a jaunt, and Frank had to retrieve them in the lonely and cold darkness. A few nights later, he was about to make more observations with the telescope around midnight when he heard a knock at the door. Nobody else was up, and he answered the portal with a bit of trepidation to find one of our cousins at the door. He had got off the tube from the local Hillingdon Tube Station, arriving from a club in London and had walked to the house. Frank said he seemed a little spacey and saw colours, not the meteorite this time, but even some coloured animals in the mix. He had a little bag of something, and it was probably LSD. Frank said he didn't partake, and the cousin helped him set up the telescope with the hope of having another 'groovy' experience!

Reported in the Uxbridge Gazette in 1978 was the story of a 'flash' over the sky of Hillingdon, a totally different incident to the green fireball. Apparently, residents near our local park heard a thunderous noise and saw a flash; even windows rattled, and it was reported that a local resident, Mr Rick Locker, had found a black object that 'felt warm to the touch' in the park in a wood copse. Frank, being interested in such things, and I (a small boy) went to his house and asked if we could see the space visitor (Just across Hillingdon Court Park). Frank explained he was an amateur astronomer, and Mr Locker was very obliging. He viewed it and was a little dubious about its origins. Roland and Robert studied geology and bought various 'rocks' at home as part of their university work, and the boys, were somewhat familiar with their appearance. It looked a little like the slag remains we had seen in the park occasionally. Slag is a byproduct of coal when heated to temperatures over 2500 degrees. We thanked a bemused Mr Locker and left. Were parts of the actual meteorite still out there?

Dad and I enjoyed treasure hunting, so much so that we dug a hole in the back garden of the house next door, which became unoccupied, and there was a rough patch at the very back, part of the wilderness area bordering the park. We kept going. He mentioned something about crystals and minerals being found in clay, and we both thought we might find diamonds or some

Anglo-Saxon or Roman treasure. It go so deep that we had to place a board across it to save people or animals from falling in! I think Dad enjoyed it because of memories of looking for diamonds in Arkansaw when he was younger, or perhaps he was reenacting the escape from Stalag Luft III. At about 6 feet, we stopped, as the clay was becoming harder and harder to dig through. We did find a rectangle shape object, about "1X2." in size, that felt like bone or ivory at about five feet, but it did not have any markings but a few indentations. I had found something similar 3 months before in the crater of a 300-year-old tree that had fallen over in the park. We put these items in a box together and were going to take them to the British Museum for them to have them looked at. However, they got misplaced in the move from Sweetcroft, and I still haven't found them. They may be an ancient game piece, perhaps Roman or later. In the 1980s, I bought a metal detector and found a rusted pistol in the park. We figured it was from WWII, which a local historian confirmed. The army had set up tents for manoeuvres here as there was a lot less housing, and because of its proximity to RAF Uxbridge, it was a good spot for training. Probably an officer's weapon. Also, lots of old half pennies and Victorian pennies and farthings. Later, we filled in the hole, and that was that. I wanted to 'open up' another one, but Dad had other ideas. In the wilderness area bordering the park, near the surface, were massive disused (he hoped) black cables, probably from the 1940s. He thought he could use them as a power source for the Ham Radio antennae and worked on getting this cable out for two weeks! In the end, he did, but as negotiations were going ahead to sell the property, he just stored this mighty role of cable that was probably connected to Battersea Power Station at one point. With the help of Stan, I think these two would have got it to work, given enough time. Dad should have been a miner; he loved prospecting!.

Dad, Mum and I would also go on fishing trips, usually to the River Pinn, and we usually caught sticklebacks, which I insisted we take home for the pond. Later, I would catch frogs and bring them back to the pond! They formed a little frog community and would sometimes eat the fish and insects- I was upsetting the local biosphere.

On a hot Summer afternoon in 1976, we were all playing badminton in the back garden and something prehistoric looking descended and made the dog bark. A huge flying insect went into the garage and made such a noise, and my sisters were petrified. We concluded that because of the scorching summer and prevailing winds (Sahara dust lay on the cars), this must have come from Africa and arrived on the southerly winds, and we thought it may like to bite. It was much bigger than the average British Scarab Beetles we had known (which can get big too). It eventually moved on to scare the neighbours after someone tried to capture it in a jar. A grand specimen it would have made.

Something that sticks in my mind encapsulates our time at Sweetcroft and the 1970s. My sister playing-'There's A Ghost in My House by R. Dean Taylor, an old 45' speed vinyl disc, and either her or my mother baking homemade doughnuts in the kitchen with an old arga-type cooker and copper pipes protruding from it. And the sweet smell and icing sugar flying around. I remember watching old home movies on our old 16mm projector of the family without sound, the family, boyfriends and girlfriends in and out, partaking in said doughnuts and everybody with long hair(including the men). It was like a snapshot in time, and you're unsure if it's real from a child's perspective or if you've squashed it all together in a strange floating thought capsule. Stan thought the men at the time were all trying to look and behave like 'Jason King', the investigator, a stroke dilettante detective who had an eye for the ladies in the eponymous series of 1971-72. Some even sporting the Mexican style mustache as well as long hair!

Cousins would float in and out of Sweetcroft and spend some time with us and thought it was cool to be with the Fuller gang. Everybody would watch Star Trek, Lost in Space and marvel at the new ideas and hippy lifestyle. And later in the 1970s, you were either a 'Mod' or a 'Rocker', whatever that meant.

In the late 1970s, one female cousin, for whatever reason, became very religious and came up to the bedroom one day to listen to records with the girls and chat. Just beforehand, I had recently been to Uxbridge and visited the stationer, toy and record shop called John Menzies. In the complex that it was located in, they had designed the passage/shopping center to the shop without consideration of the wind tunnel effect caused by the outside pressure. Consequently, it was like being at the BA jet aircraft testing facility and quite the experience, especially in winter.

Posters were a big thing then, especially for teenagers, and you would peruse the racks and find the number of your favourite singer or movie's picture and find the corresponding one at the bottom rolled up in a frame. I bought one with all the monsters from the Greek Myths. You had old Cyclops, Medusa, various dragons and others. The cousin thought this quite evil when she saw it up on the wall and tore it down; a bizarre thing to do, especially at someone else's house. It is still around in storage somewhere.

One day, cousin Roy (Professor Stainton) and my brothers were chatting at Sweetcroft about astronomy in general and the progression of NASA and its Moon missions in the kitchen on one of those occasions when everybody happened to be there at once ad hoc. The 1960s and early 1970s' were very communal, or perhaps everybody was just young and friendly. This identical cousin of the poster stripping saga came in and stripped down to her bikini when the boys were chatting. The focus shifted from one heavenly body to another, which caused the tea things to rattle and indigestion on Mum's serving of tea cakes and her being scuttled out for some reason. Mini skirts were all the rage then too.

I remember a three-dimensional board game called 'Lost In Space' that was put away in the attic that they all played, but it was old even then, even when I was young and put to rest in the attic, with some of the pieces possibly missing or scuffed. Some of the old dolls not secured in lockers or secure containers had their faces chewed by squirrels, and this was quite a macabre sight when poking around for radio tubes or old records to the uninitiated. These may have been worth money now as they were antiques from the States, and a couple of Barbie dolls were involved in the massacre by squirrel. Of course, there were now the new games too, Risk, Buccaneer and Tank Wars! Two I remember vividly were Roundhouse and 'Feely Creatures'. Roundhouse was an arena, and you activated 'spinning tops' cast by string, tightly bound and launched from an anchor point. It was based on the Roman Colosseum, and each top was like gladiators sparring it out to the death with names like 'Spiteful Spartacus and Agony Augustus'! The object was to knock your opponent down and outlast the rest by spinning at a hectic speed for the longest. The excitement of the Roman Arena and fight for survival Rollerball style. The feely creatures were rubber monsters that glowed in the dark, and you placed them in a bag. You turned the light out and grabbed some out-some apparently were worth more points than others, the bigger and uglier ones-bizarre but fun. I was also fascinated with lawnmowers and Daleks (from the British science fiction BBC TV series Dr Who.) I made a couple of Daleks out of Ski yogurt pots and later wanted to make a full-size one. Someone wrote away for the plans/schematics of a full-size replica, but unfortunately, it was never completed; and I didn't take over London! I had to make do with a shop 6-inch one. I am unsure where the plans are now, and I remember the bump protrusions and eyepiece prominent in the plans vividly.

Eventually, family and extended family would drift away, and the bubble of cooperation and wanderlust would disappear and drift away into memory. Of course, sometimes we would all meet at weddings and special events on occasion, but everything was different, as it is the way life goes. Dad would give my cousin Frankie a sixpence when he came over to Sweetcroft one day to buy sweets in the 1960s, and he later moved with his wife not far away from us and eventually settled in Spain after becoming quite successful in business in the UK. He recently passed away, one of a few to do so in the last ten years. Time is short.

Chapter 34

Going to the Cinema

Going to the movies was a great pastime in England. My brothers and sisters remember being taken to the likes of Mary Poppins, The Great Escape, Battle of the Bulge, The Disney version of Robin Hood and even The Bridge at Ramagen, an eclectic mix for sure.

The local Odeon Cinema in Uxbridge was quite palatial, even for a medium-sized town, and there was also the Regal. You had a balcony and stalls, which seemed vast to me as a young boy and quite exotic. A bit like the theatres that put on stage shows in central London with ladies in feathery hats and an imported can-can troop. The strange orange drink Kiora would appear with choc-ice, popcorn, and even Smarties (the cousin of M & Ms). Usually brought in the dark auditorium, buy a pretty usherette in a short skirt with a flashlight. Charles Bronson seemed to smile and wink at these girls from onscreen. Even Harrison Ford seemed impressed when I saw 'Indiana Jones-Raiders of the Lost Ark years later with a friend. Next to the art deco building with a short sweeping parking lot were curious bespoke little shops on either side, selling stamps, toys and sweets, and you really didn't know what-some fantastic toy in the back or just a gloop of green goo in a plastic trashcan could keep me amused for hours, I don't know why! It was like living in the street in Hogwarts most of the time when I went shopping with Mum and later on by myself or with friends. We had the space virtually to ourselves, and it seemed magical.

The family would see some of the more giant box office movies in Leicester Square in London, a big movie hub with three cinemas on each face of the square. Before or afterwards, we would visit the local steak house and later be mesmerised by what was on the screen and be taken away from the streets of

London for a few hours. I remember a particular restaurant called the Golden Spoon, where we would grab a late-night steak and later return to the multi-level car park (near China Town), give the valet your ticket, and then drive back—going through London and onto the A40 and home. As a former Central London resident, Mum knew the streets very well. The parking at the time was relatively reasonable, with no 'zone charging,' fewer cars and missing the proliferation of CCTV cameras. Now it is expensive for the car driver and generally unpleasant. The Uxbridge Odeon cinema became box-style and corporate later on. Eventually, it closed and moved to a shopping center, a gym in its place for the people who lived in glass houses; the new apartments going up nearby and virtually on top of it.

Chapter 35

Flyboys

The Northolt Aerodrome was close to us at Sweetcroft, and on one occasion, Dad got a 'hop' out of there on a USAF C141 transport plane. The base was usually exclusively for RAF aircraft or dignitaries, however. Roland and Bob were on Long Lane one day, and the limousines approached them whilst walking on the pavement. They were shocked to see then-President Nixon and Prime Minister Ted Heath in the cavalcade. They said Nixon smiled and waved. President Nixon was on a state visit at the time in 1970.This is down a suburban, leafy street in Jolly Old England and not something one would see every day.

Bizarrely enough, my Mother and sister Jane were walking through a passageway in Uxbridge one day in the early 1970s to catch a bus at the local depot. They were 'brushed' by a Rolls Royce moving through the lane driven by a chauffeur with an old man sitting in the back (not unlike the Mr Burns character in the animated American TV show 'The Simpsons',- slightly wizened and hunched over.) As it pulled over, the man got out and hurriedly went down the stairs to catch an underground train into London. Mum thought about berating the driver for the close call in the passage, but the guy seemed pleasant enough and asked where he could get a coffee and snack, before returning to the old man's house to pick up one of his relatives. It turned out the man was J. Paul Getty, the oil tycoon and founder of Getty Oil. He wanted to 'ride the train' up to London and spend some time in charity shops/vintage clothes for items, as according to the driver, he was quite frugal, and did not want the hassle and expense of driving to London on that occasion. One of the wealthiest men in the world, taking the tube and frequenting charity shops.

Upon leaving Northolt, the Helicopters of these VIPs virtually flew over the garden, and you could see people in the windows. The flight path of Northolt often tracked over the back garden if the wind was in the right direction and the aircraft approached from the West. On one occasion, A T-29 two-propeller driven engine transport plane almost landed with gear up as we saw him approach. A few minutes later, he was back with the landing gear down; he must have reflected on this and then rectified the problem!

In the 1970s (I was too young, but would go later), Dad took Roland, Bob, and Frank on around-the-world whistlestop tours courtesy of the US Air Force. If you paid up the princely sum of $10 each, they could go to the United States, Spain or Japan, for instance. This was a retiree perk, and dependents up to 21 (23 in certain circumstances if at University) could travel with him. He also took my sister Jane to Greece, and she stayed there with a family as a nanny and to see the sites for a few months.

The only problem was they were category 4 (the scale goes up to 1), in which 1 is pregnant or very sick service personnel, and 2 is active duty serving soldiers and so on. So in 1973 they flew from Mildenhall RAF base in Suffolk to McGuire Air Force Base in New Jersey and on to Arizona to stay for a little while in in Scottdale AZ, and later on to Phoenix. to embrace US culture again.

Whilst in Scottsdale, Dad and the boys stayed at a realtor friend's house, which was in a pleasant area. The pad had a swimming pool and a high diving board for the more adventurous. During one swimming session, one of the boys started making the archetypal 'Tarzan yell' when jumping off the board. A few doors down the road lived Buster Crabbe, famous for playing 'Flash Gordon' and Tarzan in the early years of Hollywood. The saw 'Buster' a day or so later, and he had a smile on his face; I don't know if he had heard them or not.

They also stayed in Phoenix. The chaps had not been back since they were kids. The boys all got jobs at the Goldwaters Department Store in town (Barry Goldwater was the US

Republican nominee in the 1964 election, losing to the incumbent Lyndon B Johnson).

On one occasion, whilst trying to leave the Yokota Airbase in Japan at Christmas, they got stuck as no planes were going for the States and hopefully back to England for a traditional Christmas spent with the family. A large plastic Santa seemed to be spouting Christmas Hits 24/7, and they got tired of staying in the terminal listening to the same Christmas music on repeat, but not going anywhere!

Dad was retired by then and happy to spend much time on the Ham Radio, speaking to people from the other side of the pond or hiking in the area. He later got a Realtor License to get back into work. A 'stop gap', as he wanted to return to university at some point to get his Master's Degree in political science and perhaps get a government job. He taught at the University Of Southern Mississippi after attaining his degree there and often made trips back to England.

They had some adventures in the desert.
Once, the boys went on a night camping trip to the mountain called Camelback, so named because it resembles a resting camel, not that far from downtown.
Even though in the desert, it gets cold at night due to radiational cooling and the sand reflecting the heat back into the atmosphere, especially in the winter months (The terrain around Phoenix is not all sand. It incorporates hardy plants and cacti, more of a 'scrub' desert.)
Also, the wind was picking up.
So, to get warm, they lit a small fire to stave off the cold and put rocks around it to stop it spreading. Though there was little underbrush to cause a potential spread of the fire.

A little bit later, something was going on in downtown Phoenix. No, something unusual must have happened in the outskirts, as they witnessed multi-coloured light weaving through town. They thought little of it until those lights started progressing up the mountain towards them!

Someone in town had seen the fire and reported it to the authorities, who were now approaching their position on Camelback Mountain.
Not wanting to be caught, they quickly hid away from the site behind some boulders.

Tough and grizzled firemen were now nearly upon them, saw the fire but realizing it was not a significant threat; they then put a little water on the embers. Frank, Roland and Bob had bought water with them and only built the fire up a little and doused it before the trucks could arrive. The winds picked up and probably exaggerated the size in the fading twilight. However, the fire team put searchlights on the surrounding rocks! Frank remembers one beefy guy scanning the surrounding area but not searching for them by foot en masse. They probably figured someone was nearby, but as now it was fully dark, but they did not explore the terrain. A lucky escape.
They hiked further into the wilderness but realized they had left their sandwiches and Little Debbie cream pies on a rock a mile or so back.
They went back to retrieve them, but they were gone.
It was concluded that before the commotion, a mountain lion had probably spirited them away while they were busy, or a hungry fireman had nabbed them!

In the morning, they decided to bury some English coins in the ground as a particular time capsule for bewildered Americans or aliens in the future or themselves to find. These were the big hefty 50 'pees' and 2 pee and 10 pence.
Not the old tanners, guineas, and farthings of old England pre-1971. Since they did not return for them, presumably, they are still there.
Also, on the way back (following a slightly different route so as to avoid meeting irritated firemen), they spotted a curled snake with a large red and emerald green stripe the length of it and a silver underbelly that they could never identify.
They searched the University of Arizona library through textbooks for this 'rare' snake but could never find it. A little odd.

Later in the year, they left Arizona and hired a big Plymouth to drive to California and Norton Air Base.

The boys had to give up their job at Barry Goldwaters Department Store but had made enough spending money for the trip, but still, money was tight.

Dad apparently had bought bags of oranges at a fruit market in Arizona as they made their way to make the trip to the Pacific and onwards, hopefully to Japan and even Australia.

There were and still are strict regulations about importing fruit and vegetables to California (or even plants) that may harm the local flora and fauna.

Dad got a bit irritated with the official at the checkpoint at Needles (a small town on the Arizona/California border) because the oranges were from California anyway.

Everybody (initiated by Dad) stood there and ate oranges for a while, so they weren't handed over to the official to be 'disposed' of.

Orange peel flew that day, and everybody got their quota of Vitamin C for the month.

Once at Norton Air Force Base in California, they were lucky enough to get billets at the Officer's Club because of his retired rank.

Flying on the C-141 or C-5 transports of the US Military often involved sitting on the canvas netting often used for regular military transportation of soldiers and personnel from one theatre to another or for paratroopers in live or simulated operations. If you were lucky, they could be configured like regular commercial passenger aircraft for medical or dependents (families), usually, the seats facing backwards.

Dad knew some of the runways were relatively short relative to the size of the aircraft, but this always depended on the plane, the cargo weight and placement. If not appropriately secured or distributed correctly, this could prove catastrophic for the aircraft if items shift and cause the aircraft to unbalance, particularly at takeoff. Crashes are rare but do still happen. Dad got a little nervous one time when a C-141 was taking over a minute to reach V1 (takeoff point of no return) at Mildenhall, which does have a reasonably long runway. When brother Bob flew military missions to places like Afghanistan in the 747 years later, he would always be present when the 'load master' and team were securing heavy army equipment, armoured vehicles etc.

Box lunches were given out (no flight attendants), which consisted of big white oblong boxes, usually filled with ham and cheese sandwiches and pots of chocolate and vanilla pudding for dessert (my favourite when I later flew with Dad).
It was basic fare but often more appetizing than the cooked meals on those little plastic trays on regular airlines.
However basic it was perceived, it was great for $10 bucks a shot!

'Space Available' (or Space A as it was abbreviated) often involved waiting around for long periods if you were unlucky not to have any available flights to your chosen destination or close enough bases out of state. This was because the category status of retired persons and their dependents is lower than active duty personnel, as previously mentioned.

They ran into a stroke of luck on the trip out from Norton Air Force Base in California to Hickham Field in Hawaii.
They managed to get passage on VC-118, a military version of the DC-6 (Civilian aircraft), often used for diplomats and Air Force personnel of rank.
This plane was the personal transport of A Rear Admiral of the Fleet, which was a lucky break and sirloin steaks and sauteed potatoes replaced the white lunch boxes and usual fare.

The first VC-118 was used and designed for President Harry S. Truman (who christened it Independence after his home state of Missouri), and others were built after this. It was a propeller/piston-driven aircraft, and over 150 were made for the US Navy.

As the flight was silver service, Dad, Frank, Roland, and Bob sat at white-clothed tables and enjoyed a champagne breakfast with steak and eggs, plus orange juice, served by a steward/waiter dressed accordingly.

The boys said it was similar to the pictures of the airships with open space and waiters in white serving wealthy, smiling patrons as they flew from Europe to the United States, except planes were a little safer than the early airship design. The plane also had a well-stocked library and even couches and this aircraft had fewer seats, obviously configured for comfort.

They got to Hawaii but found no space at the base facilities or NCO billets.

The terminal was pleasant at Hickham Field, with wild birds flitting about in the terminal building. Usually seeking food or welcoming tired passengers from points unknown.

They didn't mention if they got the flower garlands placed around their necks by beautiful Hawaiian ladies on touchdown. I didn't with Dad, probably because we were all business military types!

However, there was space on the big couches in the old terminal building, but someone had to sleep on the floor too. The sofas were near an open veranda, and Frank took the short straw and slept on the floor. He remembered giant bugs and centipedes moving past, not far from his head, but he couldn't care because he and the family were so tired.

Much time was spent on the beach at Waikiki, where the rest of the tourists were. Two of the boys swam out to a floating platform but thought about sharks; there were many species in those waters, including the Great White, and there were no shark nets. Apparently, there are a few attacks each year. Still, considering the number of tourists that visited, even back in the 1970s, your chance of getting attacked was low, or let's hope it was. As I have found, it's just that feeling of your head just above the water, a vast horizon of sea and you perhaps out of your depth and treading water that makes the human land animal feel vulnerable. Their land in the bay, was just a tiny floating wooden platform.

They took a hiking trip up to the spectacular Diamond Head, an extinct volcano.

The volcano is seen a lot in popular culture, and you've probably had a glimpse of it in an Elvis movie.

From there, they flew on to the U-Tapao Thai Navy base in Thailand, where the Americans had their own facilities as they had wanted a base in the mid-sixties as a mission stop and fuelling facility for the B-52 bomber fleet. And to serve these colossal aircraft there was also a fleet of KC-135 air refuelling tankers which backed up the B-52s and other military transports that flew in. So this was a convenient base for missions during the Vietnam War and USAF logistics backup.

On arrival at the base, they found the billets full. So they moved on to Bangkok to see the sites driven by a very hyper Thai taxi driver who was playing the latest American music on an 8-track player, which included the Don McLean Song American Pie about the deaths of Buddy Holly, The Big Bopper and Ritchie Valence.

This fellow was doing 80 mph through busy streets with vendors and market stalls. The trouble was that the tape spool kept coming out of the plastic spindle, and Dad kept feeding it back so that the driver could concentrate on the road and not on it. The more he tried to feed it back in, the more it started coming out, and Don McLean was getting more frantic, and his voice was becoming more high-pitched at the situation.

At the time, they thought they all might perish, not in a plane crash like the singers being remembered, including Buddy Holly, were involved in, but a regular car crash-Goodbye American Pie!

They finally arrived at a place which looked like a regular bar and restaurant on the outside, recommended by the driver.

As they moved through the bar area to the rooms upstairs, it became evident that ladies were running around with very little on with black stockings and suspender belts. This was indeed a strip club.

They were all so exhausted by now they couldn't really care by this stage and wondered upstairs looking for a 'flop'.

All night there was music and loud talking, but they had a reasonable sleep considering!

Later on, on the second day and returning to the base from a general site-seeing tour and time away from the Base, Frank forgot his Military ID and was not allowed back on site.
The proximity of Vietnam and the heightened fear of repercussions in Thailand kept the Thai and US militaries alert. Though a Peace agreement was signed in January 1973 between North Vietnam and The United States, disgruntled elements and the possibility of lone-wolf attacks could not be discounted.
Machine gun nests were trained around the proximity and stared out of the base and down at Frank too.
Beyond the base were jungle and dark bushes to hide in, which was frightening.
Eventually, Dad retrieved his ID from their rooms on base and was only let back on the US side of the perimeter and guard box after verification of his identity. Stern looks were replaced with smiles of "Oh well, these things happen"!

Having seen the 'sites' of Bangkok, bathing on Pattaya Beach, and viewing the 'strip' (so to speak), they moved on to Australia and New Zealand. Going further inland in Thailand at that time was probably not a wise idea, as there were still active bands of soldiers and cross-border groups who could be in the area between Vietnam, Cambodia, and Laos. Other groups that may be sympathetic could also be on the lookout for foreigners. The boys, however, liked Thailand and thought the inhabitants were friendly.

They flew on to Sydney, Australia and after spending a short time there, proceeded on to the Pine Gap /Alice Springs US installation. The great wonder of the world, Ayers Rock (Uhuru), was pretty close, but they could not make their way there due to time and delays. Pine Gap is primarily a surveillance base responsible for monitoring satellite and intelligence signals, anti-missile and anti-aircraft radar, among other things. At that time (I don't know if it would be possible now), but because of Dad's rank possibly, they could get a tour of the facilities, which was quite enlightening. Now at least, an alphabet of US security agencies is stationed there.

Alice Springs was a small settlement first seen by the first European in 1862, John MacDouall Stewart, who assessed inland Australia for potential settlement for farming and general agriculture. The 'Overland Telegraph' followed him out there, allowing communications between Australia and Europe and surveyors to be brought in. This was considered a major engineering achievement in 19th-century Australia. Alice was originally named Stuart, but the name 'Alice Springs' came from one of these surveyors who found a waterhole in the area. He named the town after the wife of Sir Charles Todd, Superintendent of Telegraphs, who was overseeing the whole project. In 1887 the town became popular when alluvial gold was found in a town called Artlunga, and Alice became the supply for water carried to Artlunga on Camel trains 110 Km east!

Dad and the boys enjoyed the town with its dusty sidewalks and interesting bars. Also doing a little hiking on the MacDonnell Ranges a few miles away.

From there, they flew back to Sydney on a C-141 transport and, after waiting some time in Sydney, caught a flight to Christchurch in New Zealand.

Upon arrival, there was a vast group of people waving at us from barriers. "Either they were very curious about us arrivals from the USA, or they thought we were famous-The Beatles perhaps?" remarked Frank.

New Zealand was very colourful, and Christchurch was in a scenic spot on the coast. The boys remembered pictures of the Giant Moa Bird being prolific on their arrival and figured there might be some about. Flightless, these birds were very large, however. Hunted to extinction in the 1400s by Polynesian hunters, unfortunately, so there were none to be seen in the flesh! They were again so tired that they figured they would probably conjure some up in the form of hallucinations anyway. Money was becoming a little difficult to access at the bank. Communications between New Zealand and the USA, and the UK were a little sporadic. Add to this; there was no room on the base. So everybody wandered off base and were so weary, but kept walking, maybe hoping to find inexpensive digs. However, they just kept wandering and virtually sleeping whilst walking, and eventually, sheep started to follow them, perhaps thinking they were the leaders and looking for new pastures.

Eventually, They got so exhausted, they all just went to sleep in a field and woke up with sheep all around. The flock must have wondered what these new additions to the group were up to. Afterwards, they headed back to the base in search of some coffee and maybe a bowl of chile.

Having attained digs and some cash on hand, they walked downtown, which was quite picturesque.

There were many Gothic-style churches in Christchurch, and they appeared to them as very English or European in styling and were easy to access and wander around. The inhabitants' attitudes seemed quite familiar, and it appeared to the boys that this could be an English town in many ways.

When flying 'Space A' with the military, nothing is set in stone to be absolutely sure of getting to your next destination at a fixed time, and this suited many of the retirees who were able to wander the Pacific and beyond and had plenty of time. So, there was a wait of a few days to get to your next destination, or if the departures board was on your side, you might be able to get out quickly, or if not, often visits to the snack bar or commissary and BX (base exchange) was the order of the day. The trouble was they could not access a car and would often have to walk everywhere.

Because of Dad's rank, he could go to the officers club, which was sometimes a pleasant distraction from having to wait around at the terminal building. But sometimes it was a good idea to hand around, as flights would come up fast, maybe within a span of 1-2 hours, and you had to be there to catch it.

From there, they flew from Christchurch on to The Phillippines and Clark AFB, but at Clark, they could not get off the base because of the ramifications of the ongoing situation and aftermath of Vietnam. Some disgruntled groups might at any time attack, and Americans were not always welcome. The next stop was the Island of Guam.

Guam has a tropical rainforest climate and is very picturesque, with some lush beaches and hiking trails. Although all born on the Island are American citizens, they do not have the right to vote in the mainland's elections.

The first European to travel to Guam was Portuguese navigator Ferdinand Magellan, sailing in the service of the King of Spain. However, the Island was not claimed for Spain until 1565 by adventurer Miguel Lopez de Legazpi. It was a stop-off point for the Manila Galleons, a fleet that covered the trade route between Acapulco and Manila. Until the late 19th Century, Guam was a stop-off point and happy haunt (in some cases) for adventurers and pirates, including Thomas Cavendish and William Dampier. I wonder what treasures are buried there, but the boy's luggage didn't carry any 'gardening equipment' or metal detectors.

The Island suffered a bad earthquake in 1849 and the resultant loss of life from the accompanying Tsunami in the Caroline Islands. The United States occupied the Islands after Spain's defeat in the 1898 Spanish American War, and then became US territory. In World War II, the Japanese took the Island in the Battle Of Guam on December 8th, while the attack occurred at Pearl Harbour.

The United States returned and recaptured the Island in the Summer of 1944 in the Battle of Guam.

Part of the long and arduous battles US troops would have to endure in their trek north towards the Japanese mainland. The Japanese turned out to be resilient and tenacious all the way up through the various Island chains. However, the recapture of Guam assisted in destroying Japan's naval air power. It allowed the US to establish bases to bomb the Homeland of Japan using the modern strategic bomber, the Boeing B-29 Superfortress.

It was in Guam that they met (yet again) the 'Guam Flyer,' as he was nicknamed. This was a fellow that, being retired and fancy-free, would travel everywhere on Space A for the $10 'a pop' charge and cover the Pacific and Atlantic in quite a short span. More of a latter-day Phileas Fogg on his jaunts worldwide, but without the 80-day clock. He was a good drinking companion and raconteur, but for the life of me, I never knew his name, and my brothers can't remember either.

They had seen him in the States and Thailand and could often be found in the various terminal snack bars ordering a bowl of chile from Los Angeles to RAF Mildenhall in England.

They said their goodbyes from Guam as he headed back to the States, and Dad and the boys headed to Japan.

On a DC9 from Guam to Tokyo and Yakota AFB, they experienced clear air turbulence, and the plane seemed to halt in mid-flight. The pilot maintained altitude,' went with the flow of things', and did not make too many radical moves to lose too much speed or gain too much. The wings were shaking violently, and the engine pods too, but they are built akin to giant springs so as not to make them too rigid in air pressure when they might snap off. The worst thing that happened on this occasion was that the stewardess had spilt hot coffee, and someone got a soiled suit; not her fault, though!

Later, the gang spent some time in Tokyo, and Roland met a soon-to-be girlfriend who was to be coming to London to study at SOAS (University of London) in Asian and Middle-Eastern studies; Miss Masako Mochida and visited the family home. They were fascinated by the houses made of 'wood and paper', using paper partitions for different areas and rooms. Not the same paper used for writing or printing. It is made from the mulberry tree and is more robust and durable. It is easy to move this paper and change the shape of your room without the need for a Feng Shui consultant! Traditional Japanese homes also are more minimalist in nature, which is a good way of reducing clutter. This type of design allows for more light and quick construction if changes are needed. Also, they hold up quite well during an earthquake and are cheaper to replace if there is damage or total destruction than a house made of bricks and mortar. Stone and bamboo are also popular building materials; obviously, stone will last longer and is more durable.

The drawback is that many of these structures (now with stricter building codes too for earthquakes and tsunamis) have a short life span, often only lasting 30 years on average. From Yakota AFB, they flew on back to Alaska and eventually the States.

On the C141 transport from Alaska, Dad met a rear admiral and his wife, and they chatted about Vietnam and WWII. The admiral was not afforded anything of first-class travel on this trip, and the famous white boxes of a packed lunch with my favourite 'chocolate pudding' were the only option available. Dad had bought a big jar of Skippy peanut butter at the commissary in Alaska and some saltine crackers for extra nourishment. The only problem was Dad only had a broken white plastic knife to 'dish out' the peanut butter goodness. I don't think Dad cared or figured the RA would mind, things being what they were, and offered crackers and PB to the admiral and his wife with said broken knife whilst standing with the open peanut butter jar for the VIP to dig into, the other hand hanging on to a cargo strap because of mild turbulence with a little swinging from side to side like a slightly flustered primate at the zoo. However, the dignitary accepted this kind offer; I'm not sure about the good lady wife!

They arrived in the States and got a hop from Norton AFB in California to McGuire AFB in New Jersey on a C-5 transporter. McGuire was a well-known C-141 base, with a good proportion of the fleet based there. Dover AFB in Delaware was the home port of the bigger C-5 aircraft. McGuire is also a main refuelling stop with tanker operations. The 438 MAW (Medium Attack Wing), which operated from the base, transported personnel and equipment all over the United States, Europe, and the Mediterranean.

I remember McGuire for the rows of plastic seats and the big clock in the central departure hall, where you could wait for a week or perhaps get lucky and depart in 30 minutes to the deepest, darkest Suffolk in England. They did have a friendly little gift shop, and the cafe served tasty chile and saltine crackers-Dad's favourite. The double cheeseburgers, fries and root beer were my favourite to chow down on! Dad would always keep an ear out for muffled announcements and kept an eye on the departures board. Shortly before Dad and the boys were there, McGuire had served as an embarkation point for those eventually flying on to fight in the Vietnam War, with many receiving training at the nearby Fort Dix Army Base. It was tough at this time for the retired military to get flights out because of the volume of personnel passing through.

Through the 1970s onwards, when Dad was traversing through Mildenhall and the nearby Lakenheath (fighter squadrons were based there, and the facilities included the Large American hospital), he sometimes went to RAF Bentwaters and Woodbridge, which had a MARS(Military Auxilary Radio System) radio station and sometimes billets if Mildenhall was full. Also, commercial and military transport to London occasionally went through. He used the radio and chatted with friends and acquaintances in England and overseas. When I was younger, I thought somehow the Americans had superseded the moon and now had facilities on the planet Mars.

The twin bases were later to become famous for a possible UFO encounter that occurred over three nights at the twin bases, one of the witnesses being the deputy base commander. This happened over the Christmas period of 1980, and the case remains controversial, even today. The UFO's being spotted in the nearby Rendlesham Forest, hence the incident's name. Shapes are described as red-winking eyes emitting molten metal and laser beams being shot onto the ground. Also, bunkers at the nearby Bentwaters base, having been scanned by lights that may have contained nuclear ordinance, thought this was never admitted. This was the time of the Cold War, and tensions with the Warsaw Pact were high, with the ongoing freedom movement in Poland causing upset for the Iron Curtain countries apparatchik. Details of the incident only came to light much later by one of the airman supposedly present at the incident; otherwise, it would have remained Top Secret. Dad knew nothing of it and assumed it was either a test of the base's personnel and readiness or a natural phenomenon when he learned of it later. Even though we only talked about it once, he still held an open mind and did not commit himself. It was such a bizarre case with 'higher-ups' being involved and many witnesses who seemed credible.

Chapter 36

1980s USA, Flying and The New York/New Jersey Scene

I went to school in New Jersey, staying for a year with sister Josie, travelling to New York, and visiting with brother Bob on the weekend. Bob successfully ran a computer maintenance business after coming over to the States in 1977 on the Camp America Program, a Summer Camp for kids and teenagers, whereby the counsellors would teach swimming and other outdoor pursuits. The family helped in the computer business for a time. Bob decided one day to take flying lessons at the nearby Ramapo Valley Airfield and was living in Bardonia, New York, after sitting there watching aircraft and daydreaming and was hooked. He eventually became an instructor pilot, as did his brother Roland and they have since made aviation their career. I had fun, and Bob, his girlfriend, myself, and others flew over New York and the top of The Statue of Liberty and New York Harbour at 10,000 feet! I don't know whether this is possible nowadays after the attacks on The Twin Towers in 2001, but it may have been relaxed now.

In fact, Dad mentions that pre-1973, before all the terrorist attacks worldwide in the form of aircraft hijacking, one could virtually zip through security with little hassle or delay. It has always been somewhat more lax with the military, but the civilian carriers were worse. Now everything was tinged with paranoia when flying, and images of movie stars with big hats and lovely clothes enjoying sumptuous service on airplanes are scarce. The optimal thing would be to have your own jet, where the paranoia is on a smaller scale, or park your plane up to your house like pilot and actor John Travolta!

Dad drove up to New York on a few occasions and sometimes brought Aunt Gladys, are colourful Tennessee Aunt who lived next door to Dad at the cabin. Dad usually kept to the speed limit now he was older, but on one occasion, a lane closed abruptly at night on 81 near Hershey, PA, and he was forced to cross three lanes of traffic. This time, we were in a Grand Torino, made famous by the TV series Starsky and Hutch. The 'Big Coke Can' as Mum called it. Dad put his foot down to about 90mph to clear the three lanes of traffic with a margin of safety. He said the 'Pennsylvanians' all had their mouths open after he had pulled this manoeuvre off and must have dropped their chocolates (Hershey is famous for the chocolate factory). Smoky and the Bandit with their Tennessee plates were in town. On occasion, Dad would take the controls on the Cessna aircraft, and we flew to places all around the New York metropolitan area and even out to Nantucket, about 30 miles from Cape Cod.

In 1982 The Worlds Fair was held in Knoxville, Tennessee and Bob and his then-girlfriend Jay flew from New York to meet Dad at Knoxville (McGhee Tyson Airport) in a Cessna 172, about 800 miles. The Fair was unique, and the glass 'Sunsphere' was built especially for the occasion. They had a good time, and occasionally at the cabin, I find ashtrays and stickers with the World's Fair flaming Logo emblazoned on them, even a six-pack of beer that's probably not fit to drink.

It was a bit like 'Showcase of the World' at Epcot, though more fun as it seemed more spontaneous, like a County Fair setting up for the week, but more sophisticated. Everything was on offer, from British bangers (sausages) to Chicken Teriyaki and the new 'slimline' computers of tomorrow; seemingly a strange place for a Worlds Fair in sleepy old Knoxville, with its gentile style and old theatres and country music scene; a lot less than Nashville of course. The Sunsphere stole the show; however, it was a golden ball on a gantry and looked like it may take travellers into space at any moment!

They flew over the mountains for a little scenic tour in the Cessna and Dad took over the controls for a 'spin'. The weather can change quickly over the hills, and the haze from the foliage(which is why they are called the Smokies) can decrease visibility in daylight and the fog, which is deadly in certain circumstances. You have to watch for sudden weather events like downdrafts from the topographical set-up of the mountains, which can cause a sudden loss of altitude. This is increased by thunderstorm activity and micro-bursts; a highly localized extreme downdraft can cause you many problems. There have been many crashes in the mountains, and many of these sites can be visited, but many are remote and in the 'back country'. Dad hiked to the area of one of these crashes not long after the war, and it is mentioned earlier in this book. A few of these aircraft in years past were never found, and the pilots weren't heard from again.

Bob and his girlfriend Jay hiked up in the hills with Dad, seeing more evidence of a tornado or high wind event twisting trees to a pulp. They walked the Walland section of the Foothills Parkway- a roadway that travels towards Gatlinburg and beyond that was never finished, well, that part of it anyway. The other direction travels around the edge of the park to the south. It was great for running or taking the dog out for long walks, and I was doing this 20 years later because it still wasn't open to car traffic! It is one of a few great USA highway projects never finished. Seeing that The USA could be better for assisting those who like to walk (a car country), this was a great boon for hikers, and you didn't need to venture into the park.

In 1993 a tragedy occurred in which a guy wanted to live off-grid, away from people like Grizzly Adams' the fictional character from the 1970s film. Unfortunately, he did not make it and was found not too far from the trail deceased. Some people can survive in the mountains, and several fugitives did this for years without detection or walked out and were never found. Again it is a place where sometimes you feel you are being watched, and other times it is okay. One should trust one's senses and do what one feels is right, even if that means running a little faster or leaving earlier! The guys flew back to New

York after a pleasant few days and had good weather flying all the way.

Roland and Bob would later become flying instructors, transition into jets, and have further adventures. Bob flew the Boeing 747 for some time and enjoyed living in France, doing passenger and cargo work. Roland returned to India for a time and taught aviation at Ahmedabad in Gujarat, India. Later he flew Julio Iglesias (who has, probably, a couple of private jets) before teaching in New Jersey for a while and then moving to Jordan in the 2000s to be one of the pilots for King Abdullah of Jordan and Queen Noor, which I suppose is something good to put on your resume. It was a strange coincidence, as Dad had spoken with his father, King Hussein of Jordan, at Sweetcroft in England many years before.

Chapter 37

Back In England

The 1980s rolled on, and Dad and Mum had separated. Mum stayed in England, looked after me, and became a Health Control Officer at Heathrow Airport.

She had worked before in local government but did not care for the rigidity of the post. She had also worked in a company that designed military equipment, helping design kit-bags for troops. This involved using black pitch to seal the bags for harsh terrains, such as extreme cold or warm climates.

Mum suggested a design change to the bags and how they were sealed, and management and the engineers incorporated this into the equipment design.

Dad would sometimes come over, and we would fly back to the States from RAF Mildenhall to McGuire AFB in New Jersey. Then, from there, drive down to Tennessee to the cabin in the Smoky Mountains. On several occasions, Mum came along, and it was good-spirited and usually an enjoyable trip.

On one occasion, the family drove up to Mildenhall, and I believe we even had a cousin aboard. Before visiting the terminal to see what the score was regarding flights departing to the States, we all 'pilled in' to the Officer's club and sat in the sumptuous Georgian lounge. It was a 'help yourself to chile day', and they opened the kitchen area. The chile was served from large vats with saltine crackers at the side. Dad got a little nervous trying to accommodate everybody, and trying to put some piping hot goodness into a small, not fit for purpose bowl, dropped some onto his suit trousers. My brother Frank could not hold in his mirth as Dad walked off down the kitchen isle with meat steaming from said trousers like a miniature steam train which did not abate. He continued into the sophisticated lounge with officers and their families relaxing, clutching his coffee and bowl. Frank was running behind trying to tell him, but he was slowed down by his own plate and couldn't do much anyway. I think Dad had twigged by now but stoically tried to carry on, like someone who had put the last $10 of their rent money into a slot machine. Fortunately for Dad, we at the table pretended not to notice, and some missed it. He went to the bathroom still steaming to wipe some of it off with paper towelling, with only partial success. We all left later quite discreetly and went to the terminal. When we found no flights, we went to the bar for some beers and popcorn. To our delight, we also played the slot machines and won a couple of jackpots with rows of triple black bars. This was a stroke of luck and made up somewhat for the earlier chile incident!

I remember flying to Goose Bay in Labrador and on to McGuire on an Arrow Air DC-8 from England in the Summer of 1983. This was a civilian airline, often contracted to the military to move troops about from far-flung places.

It was one of those moments in time when I remember having fun talking with the three stewardesses about something long forgotten and laughing and joking as an 'interested teenager'- they were all very attractive. But unfortunately, I can't remember the conversation, although I can visually see the discussion. Military guys in fatigues were also on the flight and getting passage back to the States from duty overseas.

The pilots were accommodating, too, giving updates and information as the flight went on.

The flight attendants seemed less rigid and weren't portraying false sentiment, like the some on regular commercial flights.

They seemed genuinely interested and chatty, and it was a great flight.

It was to my dismay that a couple of years later, a military contract Arrow Air DC-8 (flight 1285R) flying from Cairo and stopping in Cologne, West Germany, bound for Fort Campbell, Kentucky, crashed on take-off from Gander, Newfoundland, on a refuelling stop and all 256 passengers and crew were killed.

It was later concluded that a mix of a thin layer of ice on the wing and an overweight aircraft (all men with heavy army kits) caused the crash. The plane was just too heavy, and it hit me how even a thin layer of ice and perhaps the dynamic configuration of that particular aircraft could cause such a catastrophe.

There was a counterargument that there was evidence of an implosion, with paint flecks from the side of the aircraft being impressed on the plane's turbines (engines). Therefore a bomb had gone off, causing the crash.

It had occurred to me that it might have been the same plane, and I always wondered about it. But, of course, this haunted me a little bit, as the crew had been so memorable and likeable on that occasion.

I completed High School in 1987 and went with Dad in 1987 and 1989 on a trip to the West and beyond using Space Available in California.

Chapter 38

ET's Flying Bike and1987 Road Trip and The Pacific

In April 1987, I was still in the States, and Dad and I made the trip up from Tennessee to New Jersey along the infamous Route 81. We arrived at McGuire, and Dad managed to secure quarters, and we had a good sleep after a long trip North. We visited the local K-Mart near my sister's house in Flemington, NJ and on a whim, decided to buy a bike!-a 27" tyre racing bike in a big damn box.

We carted the bike in Dad's boat of a car to McGuire and decided to fly out to Goose Bay. Labrador has a USAF detachment; of course, Canadian Forces are primarily based there with an RAF contingent too. It was our best chance of catching a flight to England then. I remember it being 20 degrees cooler than NJ and giant mosquitoes; for some reason, that's all I remember, perhaps because of the unsmiling woman hotel clerks at the visiting officers' quarters. Probably the cold affected them, and the fact that it was a big mosquito town. I just needed to meet the right people. No good, we had to fly back to McGuire to try again; the outbound flight to Mildenhall had been cancelled, and we were back at McGuire with my bike having to be taken off and waiting for us at the terminal.

Time to go to Class VI and get some beverages. I sure didn't miss Goose Bay, though. Back in Flemington, we took Josie and the kids to the BX at McGuire to shop. Looking at the flight schedule to the UK, it could have been better. We decided to go to Dover AFB in Delaware to check out if any of the enormous C-5 transports were available to go to Europe. The terminal at Dover was small and cramped, unlike at the New Jersey Base. Outside on the lawn, a black sergeant was doing some Karate

Kid-type exercises and sat in the lotus position for a while; I guess he was getting desperate, too, minus a bike.

Back at my sister Josie's house, I went to the community pool and got some laps in. The female lifeguard was pretty and chatty, and we recuperated for a day or two. But it was back to McGuire, where The Sarge who had lugged my bike onto the carousel to Goose' was the same one and recognized us and laughed-guess he thought we were running a racing bike business to Suffolk, England or Goose Bay. Better luck this time, and the bike was on its way again to parts known this time, and we finally made it to England on a C-141 transport! We stayed in the West End of London with my bike box in tow, having got a ride by coach down to London Town by military transfer. Dad wanted information from the US Embassy, so we stayed the night. The night porter sure did shoot us a strange look with this massive box in the foyer. Later, we got a limousine ride to Victoria Coach Station, where Mum picked us up and drove us back to Uxbridge. Fortunately, she had an estate car which could accommodate it, the giant boxed bicycle was touring the world.

My Mother was looking at houses in the West Country to move out of the city, take our Grandmother, and provide her with an annexe, so she could be close. We made a few trips out to the country, and she decided on a large bungalow, which was directly opposite an Iron Age hill fort at a hamlet called Marshwood, just north of the seaside town of Lyme Regis in Dorset, where Uncle Albert was living in a vast place that was a former hotel with swimming pool. He and his son-in-law had purchased it at auction for a very reasonable price. It was a former hotel and had a helicopter port at some point, but the owner was in trouble, and the place was put up for sale.

It had beautiful views of Lyme Bay.

My Grandmother could also be close to the family in Lyme, and it served a dual purpose in 1987.

Lyme Regis is where the bastard son of Charles II, The Duke Of Monmouth, landed to usurp the throne of his Uncle, James ll in July 1685, who was trying to take the country back to Catholicism in Church and state. Having only a few followers and many country folks in his army, who had little army training, he lost decisively to the Royalist forces after attempting a surprise attack and being caught in a ditch at the Battle of Sedgemore in 1685. He was tried in London and executed at The Tower Of London; it was a botched execution which took three blows of the axe to remove his head by the executioner. No mercy was shown by Uncle James II. It is also the spot where the Hollywood film, The French Lieutenants Woman was filmed in 1981 and had a longing and forlorn Merryl Streep gazing out on top of the famous stone sea wall, The Cobb. The famous 'Jurrasic Coast' is here too. A World Heritage site, it is renowned for its many dinosaur bones in the local crumbling cliffs and mudstone. In fact, a Victorian lady called Mary Anning was an avid fossil collector who correctly identified an ichthyosaur skeleton here before studying paleontology and quite literally became 'a ground breaker'.

It had beautiful views of Lyme Bay. In 2009 when it was put up for sale, it garnered interest from none other than the actor Roger Moore, and he sent his 'man' along to check it out. The parking put him off; it was on a hillside and virtually sat on a typical English street with seaside bungalows, some larger than others, and it was tough to park your car and maintain privacy. It would have been hard for James Bond to bring in his helicopter at that point! Unfortunately, my mother lost out on the Marshwood property because of a bureaucrat back in London. Dad and I were to return to England in August to help her look for further homes. But we returned to the States a week later.

We drove out West first and had a memorable trip in May 1987 to Washington and west the north-westerly route from Knoxville, Tennessee, the site of the mountain cabin in the nearby Smokie Mountains where my father was living.

Dad had a dry sense of humour sometimes and would casually remark that when you saw a brightly lit billboard (often with a happy family smiling down at you with perceived divine wisdom) advertising a hotel room, say, The Holiday Inn advertising rooms' for $25.99 and 'Up' 'including free cable! Dad said it would always be the 'Up'.

We drove via St Louis and Missouri, signposted as the 'Gateway to the West'. Some attractive hills and terrain were on offer, but it did not quite match the serene compactness of The Smokies.

Dad did not stop to go up the St Louis Gateway Arch, and we only saw it from the interstate and stopped the night at Scott AFB to the East of the city.

We arrived late, and as no rooms were left, we were allowed to stay in the Officer's Lounge, which was quite accommodating.

I remember 'Jaws' was playing on the television, and I thought there was little danger as we were pretty far from any coast in the central USA!

We moved on through Nebraska and hit South Dakota.

South Dakota was a place you could imagine from the Old West. However, it was generally very sparsely populated at the time.

We stopped at Deadwood, the famous old west town which seemed to be in a gulch or miniature canyon as I pictured it. It was so named because of the 'dead wood' found in the gulch when the settlers arrived for the first time. It became famous when gold was found in the 1870s and the nearby Black Hills, a renowned episode in Frontier history. The discovery of gold was announced by non-other than George Armstrong Custer on an expedition to the Black Hills in 1874 but did him little good in the end as he perished with all his troops at the Battle Of Little Big Horn by combined Indian forces led by Crazy Horse and others. Deadwood had some notorious outlaws and old-west figures, including Wild Bill Hickok (who served as an outlaw and lawman, among other feats). But, unfortunately, he never left; he was killed there on August 2nd, 1876, and buried in the local cemetery. Also, Calamity Jane is buried there, but she died of natural causes at the start of the nineteenth Century. A Dora Dufran also ran a very famous brothel in town, and there were a few of these too. I could see an Omar Shariff type charismatic outlaw being held up here with his gang, sparring with the itinerant good guy and promising the greedy section of locals and perhaps some 'odd' Englishmen shares in a gold fortune found in a mystic canyon. Ultimately most of them are killed by the natives, with the help of an earthquake, before they can escape. Omar, a pretty lady and good guy, do escape, though. Hang on; this may be the plot of a great movie I once saw.

Gambling is allowed in town, and we partook. Well, Dad played Black Jack and won- a wily player. I did not win, however, as I played the slot machines, where mainly the element of skill and luck combined needed to win anything doesn't really exist, and it is all luck and one machine may be 'loose' for awhile to draw in the other 'fish'. So maybe there is a system, but I never found it and lost money. We moved from Deadwood to Wyoming at night and saw little of it. However, it is a very underpopulated and quite beautiful state. This is the site of 'Devil's Tower'-an ancient volcano which lies in the Northeastern quadrant of the State. The pop culture mind was thinking again in terms of the great scene in 'Close Encounters of the Third Kind' at the climax of the movie where the aliens are met with flashing lights and rhythmical music tones, and all sizes and shapes of UFOs appear, until the closing with the big mother ship. Unfortunately, it was at night and just to the north of us, so we missed out, I'm afraid, just passing through. The same can be said of Montana, which never seemed to end as we traversed the whole state length, partly at night, past Billings and on to Bozeman, where we stayed the night.

At the time, a promotion was going on with the Fast Food restaurant McDonald's, and they were offering a Scrabble Game with the chance to win a $100,000 top prize. You had to write a long word to win the top prize. Dad habitually stopped at McDonald's because he liked their cheap coffee! We did not always partake of the food, but when we did, we would be given a letter to try and win.

At the said establishment, somewhere in deepest, darkest Arkansaw off I40, I found the letter H strapped to a cheeseburger(I am sure it was the letter H). Still, as the window was open, somehow it blew out and casually ended up somewhere along this barbed wire fence line with a 'C' that had also escaped. I made a cursory look but figured they were a part of 10 million 'Hs' or 'Cs' and did not bother searching further.

This would haunt me as we went to various Mcds' across the continental United States and then in Hawaii and Alaska too. So I dutifully collected and stored all the little letters and the Scrabble board to do at a later date.

It was only when I returned to the Continental United States and sat on a bed at a hotel somewhere that I could nearly spell 'amburger' or could it have been 'heeseburger'. It only needed an 'H' or 'C' to pocket the hundred grand!. A sickening feeling dawned upon me and the conciliatory fact that I had won maybe 10 instant free cheeseburgers!

On returning to the Arkansaw location (hopefully, they all tend to look alike), I desperately hoped the barbed wire fence was the same one. We looked and sweated for about an hour in the uncut grass next to the wall of wire, sometimes getting nicked by it, and my paranoia kicked in. Had I really lost all that money? But, unfortunately, we didn't find the 'H' or 'C'- surprise surprise! Heck, it could have been Ronald McDonald I needed to spell, but I am sure I was just one letter short of a fortune; blast that cheerful clown to this day. What happened to him, by the way? When he went to star in the Steven King Horror 'It', he probably lost kid appeal and his reputation.

I felt dejected for a week. Was it an F anyway to win a six-inch Ronald McDonald doll-I really hope so. In any case, I'm still 80% confident I was one letter away from big money, and I'm sure the winning scrap of a letter was floating in an Arkansaw meadow somewhere and might be still!

We had a great trip to Alaska and then on to Korea and Hawaii, and I saw for the first time the wreck site of the USS Arizona battleship, which had been sunk by The Japanese at Pearl Harbour. It was left as a memorial and gravesite for the

dead sailors and has a platform sitting over the underwater superstructure for viewing. A very poignant and sad occasion.
Waikiki Beach was very nice but very crowded. However, we did have a large hotel next to the beach, and this made a change from staying on base.

Overall the locals were friendly, except for one who chastised a lady eating her sandwich on a bus. She was careful not to litter, and he looked in his mirror and ticked her off.
This was an older American lady who I had a chat with. She sat next to me across the Isle. She was happy to talk to me further, perhaps in a bar, but that may not have been the best idea.

What amazed me about the Pearl Harbour visit was the escape of tiny bubbles of engine oil, which would periodically rise to the surface even after all those years from the wreck.

The 'going by US Air Force trip experience' was as my brothers had experienced all those years before. However, it still only costs $10 on each leg of the journey!
Even though frequently you would have to wait around, it was quite a privilege to be able to do this. I don't know if any other countries military would offer the same thing.

From there, we went on to Yakota AFB in Japan, located in the Western part of Tokyo. I was amazed at how crowded Tokyo was, but it seemed well-ordered mostly and worked as a unit, even in the seeming chaos of the town. I remember workers near our hotel at about 2 am, very diligent and fixing something that needed to be done quickly. A little different to some of the practices in Europe, where they are a little more laid back regarding road construction. I remember a quote from Bob Hope when he was talking on a chat show in England about the 'roadworks' he had seen about London and the quip- "England would be a fabulous place once they get the place finished"! Also, the concept of raw fish did not sit well with me, which the Japanese eat a lot, being an island and all. However, I surprisingly enjoyed it, and Dad and I frequented the 'Sushi Bars'. It's usually raw fish (but it can be cooked) mixed with vinegar rice. We had the tuna and mackerel variety mainly wrapped in seaweed and prawns most of the time. I wonder if British-style fish and chips have caught on there yet, I have not been back for some time. From Japan, we flew to South Korea (Seoul) and only really stayed around the terminal area. I remember seeing the rice paddies on approach to the base, and the site of these stretching to the horizon was a very different landscape to how Tokyo was very densely packed in. Of course, outside Tokyo, there is more space and various examples of terrain. From Seoul, we flew back to Hawaii, another overnight stay, and on to Norton AFB in Southern California (The base is now closed and redeveloped). Dad wanted to avoid going downtown LA or hitting the beaches. He liked to remember it as it was when he was here in the 1940s and hitchhiked across the USA with his friend Fuchet. He had also been here in the 1970s with my brothers, and things were starting to change. More restrictions and 'bigger government' and things were less open and accessible, according to Dad. Having been back there since I tend to agree with that. It does have some interesting sights, sounds and incredible scenery, however.

We did toy with the idea of climbing Mount Gorgonio in the San Bernadino mountains or at least travelling part of the way up. After going to flight training near here many years before, Dad still had a soft spot for the area.

Recently, Captain Dean Paul Martin crashed here in his F-4 Phantom fighter jet after becoming embroiled in poor weather conditions/low clouds and losing his way. The flight leader had requested a higher altitude from the control tower because of the gloom and rain. There was too much commercial traffic up top, and they were diverted away. Martin made a left turn, and his trajectory set up a crash into solid granite. Captain Dean Paul Martin was the son of the famous singer and actor (and Rat Pack member) Dean Martin Senior. Dean Junior acted for a while before flight training and eventual transition to jet aircraft and The Air National Guard. I remember him in a 1979 film called 'Players' where he played an up-and-coming Tennis star trying to make it, and starred Ali MacGraw as the love interest. Dean was, in fact, a pro tennis player in real life and played on the circuit. I remember this film too because of a young, cynical John McEnroe playing a match with him and my interest in tennis being increased by this movie. Dad said Dean Martin Senior had never really gotten over his death, and this was a partial cause of his decline. A sad situation for a guy who was successful on his own merits and was relatively young.

I considered being a pro tennis player for a time but had started too late and was not concentrated enough to get where I wanted to go in the sport. I could have taught had I really practiced sufficiently and settled down. I am interested in old Hollywood and the 'ghosts of the past' perhaps. Oddly, many of the old estates, restaurants and streets etc, have disappeared or are disappearing. I want to visit them before they're gone, as many have. I cannot understand why people would let some old houses, such as Errol Flynn's and Rudolf Valentino's residences, be destroyed for development and greed or at the whim of the new buyer. Why not put a preservation order on these places? Obviously, they are not historical in the sense of a president/ king or great historical event, and it is only 'entertainment'. But the arrival of Europeans in the United States is relatively recent in terms of their historical significance, and Hollywood was a big part of the culture and its evolution. Funny enough and, in a sense, ironic, the opposite has happened in Britain as far as entertainment goes. Here are a few examples and just my opinion.

As a kid in the late 1970s', we visited Jamaica Inn on Dartmoor, made famous by the book by Daphne Du Maurier with tales of smugglers, heroes, damsels and mad aristocrats. It seemed very authentic and original. I was allowed in and sat and had a lemonade with Mum and brother Frank. Inside, I can remember an old man with what looked like a clay pipe seated by the fire and was struck, even at a young age, by how authentic the place was. Clay Pipe could be getting ready to go with his cohorts to wreck a ship on the coast-he could have been the one that was about to snuff out the lantern, for heaven's sake. On my return in the 1990s, the place did not just not the same; it felt like a theme park, with a gift shop, tourists and an extension. Still a fascinating place, but just not the same. A similar thing happened with Warwick Castle. We all visited in 1985 as a family. It was all very authentic and even had Elizabeth The Firsts riding saddle on display when she was young and an accomplished horsewoman even then. Best of all, it had ghosts, and we were led on tour with a voice recording (maybe a bit Hollywood!), but it was just enough to describe the Ghosts. Happily rich Sir Fulke Greville, who lived there from 1604, was stabbed by his much-trusted servant for some cash. He did not get anything in the will, however, and with that and remorse, cut open his own throat and left Sir Fulke to die in agony and entirely alone in the South Tower. His moans for help have reportedly been heard, and his spirit is seen near his portrait. We walked through this same tower with nieces and nephews, and it was enjoyable and spooky. I went back to Warwick in the 2000s with a girlfriend, and things seemed to have changed. It may be fun for the kids, but they now have jousting reenactments and rides and more hurdy-gurdy type stuff, plus a more extensive gift shop and higher prices. I like these things to a degree, but they seemed to lose their authenticity and significance somewhat...It all seemed to be, I don't know, just quieter in the past, and you had to use your imagination more. Even the London Dungeon in the 1980s just had the wax figures, some cheesy displays, of course, but a real sense of what the dark past may have been like and just a tiny gift shop. When I went back, it had a theme park ride through the place with more underpaid actors (I know the Feeling-I, have since become a voice actor) presiding as judges or Jack the Ripper-it was just not the same, and it was all geared for speed. There was less time to just 'stand and stare' to quote the poet. Get them in and get them out quickly to increase the 'buck'. I must say, however, though small, the Klink Gaeol Museum on the South bank is quieter and better at preserving things. The same can be said of some countryside locations, and I think that has to do with the influx of people and more bodies moving through. I like theme parks and attractions, don't get me wrong, but also reflection, quiet and authenticity is desirable. If you are in the West Country in England and you have the need to see a stone circle, I can recommend Avebury- a grand, aloof and larger version of Stonehenge...a bit like a brooding Mr Darcy. Whereas Stonehenge is the Mr Macawber of the show- fascinating, but a bit more showy and bawdy in the hope that 'something good will turn up'. Before the 1990s, you were actually able to walk on the stones, and it was tranquil. I can understand them stopping this due to the masses of people and the erosion caused, but with the A303 being expanded and roads, in general, busier, it's not the same.

There may have been busy periods in the summer in the past too, but now it is mad, with heavy queues of traffic and forlorn people with warm strawberries for sale at the side of the road. There may be a decent museum and information, but now you are 'bussed in' with hundreds of tourists like an airport(except without the trepidation of taking your clothes off virtually to board a flight). Upon visiting the Stones, however, even where you walk, you are carefully guided around the car park, with student security guards looking important. What's worse is that a mile away has been built an industrial estate with fast food and the dreaded Mcdonald's. This is just not England; more like a stop off the New Jersey Turnpike. I actually blame Mcdonald's for the downfall of England when it came over in the 1970s. A bit like a fast food version of William The Conqueror; doomsday. The Stones do remain fascinating, though, especially from a distance or with a meteorite flying over it in a postcard. I must say I enjoy McDonald's cheap coffee (as did Dad), but these SOBs also cheated me out of $100,000 with their flimsy, wind-blown playing pieces too!

Back to the US trip, we were now on a road trip back to Tennessee and turned north to I-40 (Interstate 40) and back through Barstow and decided to stop off at Lake Havasu. Lake Havasu is a reservoir formed by the Colorado River and Parker Dam. An excellent place for recreation and fishing, and I must say the beach looked inviting with actual golden sands and some beautiful people looking in beautiful boutiques the day we were there. It is most famous for 'London Bridge', which was purchased by an American entrepreneur in 1968 from the City Of London. The granite blocks were shipped over, and I can imagine at quite an expense. The story goes he thought he was getting 'Tower Bridge' and was duped. I fail to understand this, as I imagined he went and actually saw the bridge for himself before he bought it. I think it was a story, and you don't buy anything large and expensive before actually viewing it in person (unless you buy from eBay or Amazon).

Robert McCulloch, the businessman and entrepreneur and Robert Plumer (the real estate agent who found that the bridge was for sale) completed the purchase in 1968. The 10,276 granite blocks were cut and numbered and shipped through the Panama Canal, and unloaded at Long Beach. Later trucked out to Havasu 300 miles away, and hey presto, you have a giant three-dimensional painting by numbers to construct. Construction began on the 23rd of September 1968, and the foundation stone was laid by the Lord Mayor of London no less, Sir Gilbert Inglefield. It opened in 1971 to great fanfare, with a new canal dredged underneath to complete the River Thames look. The venture was not a white elephant, however, and proved financially successful from a town of a few hundred; it grew to thousands through the years and turned a profit-only in America!

The problem was we arrived late at night, and there were no hotel rooms vacant. We ended up sleeping at the edge of the bridge in Dad's massive gold Chrysler Newport, which was like a travelling boat. An extensive and very comfortable ride in most respects, but sometimes a little floaty on long road travels. It had that big 1970s Ricardo Montalban (Khan in Star Trek) promise and feel of Corinthian leather that a Greek god would request as mandatory if he had to travel on the interstate for long journeys. Ricardo Montalban had appeared in US car adverts some years previously. The drawback was sometimes you stuck to the seat in hot weather, and when you got out of the car, it sounded like your body was a damp velcro shoe being unfastened. At sunrise, I opened my sticky eyes to the strange silhouette of a British bridge in the middle of the desert.

Probably my grandparents and relatives had touched those stones as youngsters in a time long before, going to work or at play, happy or sad, and now it was here.

I got out before Dad was awake and walked the bridge, and it was unusual and exciting. At the time, there was a TV film with David Hasselhoff, with the premise that Jacks the Ripper's spirit or some such had time-warped to the bridge and was now murdering again /up to his wicked ways, quite a bit of hokum! It was the anniversary of the murders (100 Years in 1988) and the film had come out a couple of years earlier. I had seen this film and remembered it, as a light mist covered the bridge on this early morning in the middle of Arizona, and it was a little spooky, I must say to a young adult.

We had an eggs and bacon breakfast at a local diner, and still feeling a little worse for wear and tired, we walked over the bridge and under it along the edge of the water. Unfortunately, there was no boating or sunbathing for us, and we moved on to the next phase of I:40 with various stops in New Mexico, Texas and Oklahoma. We stopped at the 'Tinker Air Force Base in Oklahoma City, and part of it sits just next to I:40. I remember looking at flights bound for Tinker and Oklahoma on the departures board at Mildenhall AFB in Suffolk, England and thinking of a wild place with tumbleweed, desert and men in cowboy hats lassoing steers from horseback near the runway. There are places like that in mid-America, but the base is quite industrialized and sits next to strip malls and hamburger joints near the interstate. It hosts a variety of aircraft, from refuelling tankers to fighter jets and is a sprawling complex. Because of Dad's rank as a Colonel at the guard gate, they usually saluted him, and I also felt like a VIP! We went to the Terminal for kicks, and sure enough, there was a flight to Mildenhall, England, that very day. That was quite lucky, but we could not travel to the land of milkmaids and thatched cottages because we were headed for Tennessee. The average American might think of cows and thatched cottages in Mildenhall, and for the most part, in that instance, they would be right (except perhaps for the milkmaids)? We then headed to get something to eat at the local grill, a great meal of cheeseburgers, fries and onion rings, and we were hungry.

Dad met a 'fellow traveller' from the 1970s trips to South East Asia and beyond with my brothers. Another generally happy retired traveller with that spark of wanderlust in his eyes, with no particular place to go with his wife this time. She was off shopping in the BX store (Base Exchange) for clothes for the tropics or Alaska, I can't remember which! Her husband had seen many of these places in the war years of 1941-45 in the Pacific theatre of operations under very different circumstances. He was now on the move again in the regular clothes of a retiree. He and Dad had a good old chat about current events and the war years of long ago. I listened with interest as an outsider but could not relate to or imagine those times as they must have experienced them. As with many other family members, aunts and uncles, I wished I'd jotted more recollections down at the time. I can relay some of it through Dad's notes and good diary keeping. I did a few years later, but I needed details to tie certain events together. That is why I suggest people write a diary of events each day, as only specific details may be remembered the following day or a few days later, and the rest lost. Headline events are usually clearly remembered, but specific nuances and butterfly-floating thoughts are forgotten later.

After staying the night at Tinker AFB, we moved on the rest of the way through and arrived in Knoxville and the cabin in the early hours-a long drive but a great trip. Before the advent of the interstate, this would have taken days, but now it was just a day straight through to Eastern Tennessee and 'home'. The trouble with the interstate is you don't see the many small towns dotted throughout the States. Because of the advent of interstates, many of these places wither if they rely on traffic stopping for services like motels and restaurants or business access. Consequently, many 'dead or dying towns' are strewn about like time capsules. I would love to take a trip to the back roads and places of interest.

Chapter 39

Return to England, Moving and A Brush With Evil

We returned to England, and this time, brother Frank and Roland picked us up from Mildenhall, and we returned to London in early August. Upset that the Marshwood house had fallen through, Mum went on a whistle-stop tour of the West Country, as she had sold the house in Uxbridge and needed to move ASAP. We walked around Hungerford in Wiltshire after viewing a place in the area and had tea and a light lunch at a cafe in town. Dad and Frank remarked how they had moved through a spiderweb/cobweb in the doorway and had an odd feeling, and joked about being entrapped by a spider but just 'brushing it off'.The house was lovely and roomy but not quite to our liking, and we went home.

On the 18th of August, we again travelled through Hungerford, just on the outskirts this time, having left the M4 Motorway in the morning and visited a house for sale near Bradford-On-Avon in Wiltshire; this house was put on a short list of desirable possibilities. The others waited in the car, and afterwards, we all went on a relaxing walk around Bradford-On-Avon, a historic town. We returned to the A4 road past the Savernake Forest later in the day. A pretty area, but somehow it gave off bad vibes; I don't know why; perhaps it is the history imprinted on the place, but otherwise, it is just pretty woodland incorporating various species of trees, including some ancient oaks. It does have some 'notable people history' too, and King Henry VIII was beguiled by one of his 'lucky' wives, whose head didn't go to the chop in the form of Jane Seymour. John Seymour (her father) had invited Henry to stay at his manor, which incorporated the Savernake. All Henry had to do was get rid of Anne Boleyn, and they were married.

However, Jane was to die in childbirth after giving birth to the future boy King, Edward VI. This did not deter the fat, old king, and he married again. When I was taught history at my last British comprehensive school in England, I happened to be in only a few of Mr Tottenham's classes, my history teacher. He was one day talking about the Roman Emperors and was about to go on and give some lurid details about their exploits, but stopped himself short and smiled to himself. The other kids said he looked like a frog because of his somewhat bulbous eyes. Roland, Frank and Bob had been taught by him in the 1960s and had not got on with him too well. Only a year or less after my encounter with him, his boyfriend and himself had been found hanged together in The Savernake Forest from an oak tree. He and a Drama teacher at the school were having an affair, and I guess they were not ready for any scandal. We passed through the forest on this warm, late summer day and passed a petrol station that seemed to be taped off and windows broken. We had assumed it had been vandals or even a robbery and whizzed by onto Hungerford.

There appeared to be a lot of traffic, and Dad thought there may have been a 'fete'-a charity fundraiser or some such with entertainment; British churches often put these on, and families often attended. This was to be far from the truth. It was too late for a 'fete', but 'fate' had indeed occurred here somewhere. Maybe a funfair or county show? We stopped at the 'Tally Ho' pub just out of town and had a quick drink. The local patrons all seemed to be glum, sitting around, and many just staring. What was the matter with them? We later learned of what happened after returning home and my listening to the radio next to my bed. I told the family, but they didn't believe me and thought I was playing a distasteful, surreal joke. They turned on the TV, and we found out what had happened. Michael Ryan, a local to Hungerford, had gone on a shooting spree, eventually killing 16 people. He had started in the Savernake Forest and shot and killed the mother of two children on a picnic driving from the town of Reading after stalking her from the car park. They were found later, just wandering around in a daze. He went to the petrol station I mentioned, but after trying to shoot the cashier after purchasing petrol, his semi-automatic rifle jammed, and he drove back to Hungerford. Wandering around the town center and outskirts, he shot indiscriminately, and more death occurred before he held up in his old school and committed suicide. We had only been there a week before too, casually wandering around the ordinary English country town. The episode faded from our minds after a few months, but it is a scar the town carried for a long time and something really unimaginable in a sleepy English village.

Chapter 40

The Cabin

Dad's cabin in the foothills of the Smoky Mountains in Tennessee is an odd curiosity. He bought the property in 1981 from his Landlady, Mrs Hodge, a local 'mountain lady' with various antiques strewn about her house. When I went there as a child, I remember taking a double take as a civil war Gatling Gun was mounted on the porch. I was amazed. The Gatling Gun first saw service in 1962, during the American Civil War, and this was no replica. I think she offered to sell it to Dad, and why he didn't buy it, I don't know unless she was asking a lot. Today it probably would be worth $100,000 dollars. It was not cleaned, which may have been good if not done by someone who knows what they are doing, but I remember it in reasonable condition. I never saw it fire, and that could be a good thing!

Mrs Hodge was helping with Dad's Watermelon crop on the big hill (the cabin encompasses eight acres) when he remarked that some property down the road appeared left in a 'hodge podge' condition. A 'hodgepodge' is a generic term for a poorly done job, but she took offence. Perhaps that is why the deal on the Gatling Gun never went through; who knows!   According to Mrs Hodge and her grandparent's stories, the cabin was built by a crusty old prospector who paid for the land with a bag of gold. I have no reason to think this was not true, as Dad mentioned the guy's name which sounded like 'Fudge McFarlane', which sounds like a prospector's name. Very often, Dad would speak to Mrs Hodge and not understand a word she was saying. The same could be said of Mrs Hodge as she most times mumbled and did not understand a word of what he was saying. The same thing happened with the lawnmower repairman; they would both talk and not understand a word of what the other was saying or talk on top of each other to compound the effect, but would somehow manage to agree with each other. The Lawnmower Man would fix the mowers he bought for a song or found on the side of the road, roll them down his properties' embankment and paint a FOR SALE sign and stick it on a mower, and that was it-a excellent business model and cheap. Locals, tourists or Knoxvillians would come and buy!

Dad sometimes hesitated and smiled, and she just looked bewildered, and consequently, the prospector's first name may not have been Rudge? Perhaps a grizzled Scottsman, maybe the son of an immigrant, who had left Scotland because of being turfed off his land by the local gentry in what was to become known as the 'Clearances of The Highlands'. Raising sheep in the Highlands was more profitable than having pesky people living there, so most were moved to coastal areas or left the country as migrants. I spent some time at the cabin working and driving into Maryville and Knoxville, the central city of East Tennessee.

There are many descendants of Irish and Scottish living in the South and this area of Tennessee.

Cabin life was fascinating. We were working the eight acres of land, mainly clearing and cutting, as we didn't have any crops when I was there. We had a friendly 'Black snake' that wards off and kills venomous snakes. He lived on the top of the hill. Dad had heard something 'big' moving through the long grass before it was cut one day. He said it seemed it was a large fellow or lady, as it took a long time to pass! He just caught a quick sight of a black body as it stealthily moved away from the presence of humans.

I had an incident years later with snakes when hiking up in the Smokies along an old Indian trail. About halfway up this trail, I came upon two ladies standing on the path motionless, looking at something in horror next to the granite wall in scrub grass; on the opposite side of the pass was a drop-off down the mountain. It turns out it was a coiled rattlesnake, agitated and aggressive. The path was only about 4 feet wide, so they were afraid and didn't know what to do. I waited momentarily to see if he would slink away. This didn't happen, so in the end, I suggested I would carefully take them one by one around the drop-off, hoping the snake's bite radius was not long enough to catch us. I did this with each woman, and Mr or Mrs Rattlesnake remained coiled and agitated. I assumed we were too far away, and we were? They both thanked me profusely and were on their mobile phones to their husbands, talking about the Australian snake expert who had helped them out of a sticky situation. My UK and US accents combined confused them into thinking I was from the land down under.

After Dad passed away in 2000, I did more hiking all around the mountains and had yet another incident with a snake with a bad result, not for me, but for the snake. I had more fun walking along the Rich Mountain trail towards the Cades Cove area. Cades Cove is an 11-mile loop trail that can be driven, cycled or hiked along. It included many of the old cabins that were lived in during the pioneer days of the 1800s and beyond, including an old watermill. It is very picturesque in a bowl-like geographical setting with mountains all around. About halfway to Cades Cove, I came upon a big old rattlesnake that looked to me to be about 5 and a half feet long and thick-bodied. I went a reasonable distance around as this was a reasonably level surface area and had clearance. However, I heard a short distance behind the sound of horses. It was two people on horseback, a man and a woman. There I stayed for a moment as I wished to warn them of the snake that might spook the horses and maybe worse. The guy in jeans and a cowboy hat got off his horse, looked for something in the bushes, came out with an five-foot piece of two-inch or so diameter tree limb, and started beating the shit out of snake from a distance. Unhappy, I yelled and said, "Why don't you just ride around".The guy mumbled something from under his hat and continued doing what he was doing. Disgusted, I just walked off and chatted with some ladies who also disagreed with his actions' pointlessness. If it was a life or death situation, and it was either the snake or me, things would be different, but in this instance, there was no need for the battering.

On another occasion, I went past the Tuckaleechee caverns on the park's west side, looking for a more secluded area to hike. Proceeding up the steep drive in my old small gold hatchback Mercury car, which was taking a pounding, the campaign was twisting and turning and was quite steep, but we soldiered through. At the top, there could be found a levelled area, a posted trail to the left of me to Cades Cove, and a more obscure path to the right. I followed the more obscure trail and felt odd about the whole experience. On the way, I was accosted by a more hostile copperhead snake on the side of the path, which I gave a wide berth to as it hissed 'go away'. For some reason, I again felt uneasy and carried on for an hour before returning to the car and driving back. I thought I was being watched on this occasion for no apparent reason. There was evidence of old railroad activity and remains, which added to the feeling of slight desolation and fear. After reading a little about the area, I found a reference to a story that may go back to Cherokee legend about a woman who haunts the woods and dislikes men. Perhaps she was jilted at some point, or her husband was killed or even murdered in the past. Could the copperhead have contained her spirit? Probably not, as I try to keep a rational head. However, I do have an open mind about such things, but why the irrational fear?

When I returned to the Cabin, I went to bed but felt something on my leg. It turned out to be a tick, so I quickly got in the shower to 'heat' the little bastard up and not let him get any of my blood. How he knew I was going to be there at that particular moment in the woods of Tennessee to eventually live on me, I don't know? It is best to get the whole body out, as sometimes, if you just pull it out with your fingers, it leaves the head, and ticks carry Lyme disease. It came off in one piece after my shower.

There is a story about a bride jilted on her wedding day whilst staying at the Greenbrier Lodge in the tourist town of Gatlinburg, about 30 miles away, but that is a separate case.

The groom didn't show up at the wedding chapel, and at first, being stoic, she later got depressed and hanged herself at the hotel from an overhead wooden beam. A maudlin ghost of a girl is said to wander the hotel, now an upscale restaurant.

On another visit to the same trailhead, I followed the trail on the left side of the parking area, on the Rich Mountain Road, down to Cades Cove and completed most of the loop road, a series of switchbacks. I always looked back to see if anyone was following, as again, I felt I was being watched, but as it turns out, possibly by something more corporeal in nature. After having lunch at the Cove, I made the tiring climb back up the switchback road and through the wooded trail back to my car. Upon returning to the car, I saw a note under the window wiper. It was from a couple who were on vacation and stated that they were both walking on the same trail I was on and were approached by a giant black bear, so they decided it was high time to return to their vehicle and get going! This was a friendly warning note that I was appreciative of. I figured they had been walking the same trail I was on, but I had passed the spot earlier in the day and missed the bear. I got in the car relatively quickly and took off.

Though many black bears live in the Smoky Mountains, attacks are rare, and I felt relatively safe. Having said that, I have had some contact, though mainly fleeting. One day on the trail, I was startled by something scuttling up a small hill through the bushes. It turned out to be a cub returning to its mother in a relatively timely and disturbed fashion. Mama bear stood on her hind legs and started sniffing the air, and she had not seen me at this point, and wanting to keep it that way, I hurriedly moved off down the trail back towards the car. Although bear attacks are relatively rare I kept telling myself, there occurred the death of a Tennessee woman who was visiting the park in 2000 about two miles up the Little River Trail, which starts at a campsite called Elkmont. I traversed the trail in 1999 with Dad and decided to revisit the spot in 2005. We could have been a 'statistic' only a year later, but the lady in question was quite thin and smaller in frame compared to two relatively large guys. I located the spot near a fork with the Goshen Prong trail where two bears attacked and killed Glenda Bradley: an underweight female and a smaller bear, presumably a juvenile and cub. Her husband had been fishing at a nearby river whilst she had decided to go for a walk and was attacked because the bears were emaciated and hungry. Glenda was a seasoned hiker, but even knowledge and experience will only sometimes save you from the wild. After 2005, fatal bear attacks increased. Statistically, you are more likely to be killed by wasps or hornets than by a bear. However, I still have to be cautious and check over my shoulder when hiking in the mountains.

Life was pretty 'fun' at the cabin, but there was always a lot to do in clearing land and general upkeep. The nearby neighbours ran horses, and Dad would let the horses graze on the top field of the property after not raising crops for some years. This dual purpose was not mowing the grass every week and helping out the neighbour.

In 1996 Dad returned from a trip to England and, upon walking up the hill, found that someone had parked their trailer up on the land and encroached on the property. They would not move, and after a long legal battle, Dad agreed they could stay if they would purchase the land, but after lawyer's fees made nothing from the legal battle. The trouble was he had been away for a year, and they appeared to have some squatter's rights at the time. Being magnanimous, Dad let them stay for nothing in the end, and they took two-thirds of an acre. Later, after he passed away in 2000 and we returned there to work on the old cabin for some couple of months each year, we found that they now toted semi-machine guns and AK-47s, which proved interesting. I stayed at the cabin in the mid to late eighties and into the nineties.

On one occasion, my brother Robert and their wives/girlfriends had come down from New York for a few nights, and we all stayed in the property on the various couches and beds that could be found. It was wintertime, and we decided to make a fire, and all went out to grab some logs and kindling to start it with. Kirsty (Bob's British wife) placed the kindling down. A moment later, she retreated in horror, as a snake had slithered down the chimney and rushed onto the wood floor towards her, probably panicking at seeing so many people, having probably not dealt with humans before. It was not huge and probably a juvenile. Ultimately, we managed somehow to shew it out the door, and it was safely away. Dad had a World War II gas mask, which had not helped. He had put it on in the back bedroom to scare the visitors as they arrived. He rushed out and caught Kirsty first (the one who had found the snake), and she retreated in fright at this replay of Friday the 13th. We had a few evenings on Kingston Pike, Knoxville's main 'strip' for nightlife and bars. The 'Pike' had a bar-come restaurant called 'Desperados'. It was lively with traditional rock music or, on some occasions,' line dancing in the Country and Western fashion!

On another occasion, Dad, Brother Bob, and I had decided to drive down and have something to eat and a drink or two. At the end of the evening, they would always play the song; 'Bullshit', a fascinating and to-the-point country song that folks would dance along to. On this particular night, a lookalike contest was going on. The judges (mainly bar patrons) had to decide who looked the most like Merle Haggard, the Country and Western singer who was quite popular in country music circles and beyond. Dad had quite a resemblance to the then president and former actor, Ronald Reagan, so superseding the Merle Haggard contest, we decided to make it a general lookalike contest, and in the spirit of everybody already having had several alcoholic beverages and lax entry requirements, we decided to enter Dad as Ronald Reagan.

To great cheers of delight, Dad entered the circle, raising his hand and exclaiming 'One For the Gipper', a President Reagan nickname. This saying refers to the American Football player George Gipp, who was the star player of the Notre Dame team in the 1920s. He was in poor health, and on his death bed had asked the Team Coach Knute Rockney to tell the team that if they were really up against the ropes, think of him win -aka

'One For The Gipper'! In the event, Dad won the contest as Merle Haggard pretending to be Ronald Reagan and the $100 prize money; needless to say, the night was paid for.

Chapter 41

Florida Trips

In 1990 and from Tennessee we decided to go to Disney, Cape Canaveral and other sites. At the time, I considered looking for a job at Disney World, checking in with their personnel department, and applying as a 'cast member'. We took the long drive through Georgia and stayed at a motel, and arrived at The Cape very late in the day, and it was about to close. Dad decided to avoid driving to Patrick AFB to find Officer's quarters as it was pretty late. Two guys arriving at midnight at the Space Force Base to look for lodgings in a big Gold Chrysler Newport might be considered unusual. Usually, we had no problems in the past, but Dad didn't want to do it this time. Ultimately, because it was the Summer season, we could not find any hotel rooms at short notice, and we got tired of looking.

In the early morning hours, we decided to drive to the parking lot at The Cape and ended up there for the night! It was another 'London Bridge experience'. I opened my sticky eyes, and with that feeling of having slept in the car, a strange vista lay before me. In the pre-dawn light, I could make out the tops of spaceships and their support structures. We were the only ones in the car park besides Titan, Atlas and Apollo Rockets! I don't know what the security must have thought. I felt horrible. It was like the scene in National Lampoon's Vacation, where Clark Griswold arrives at Wally World to find it closed for the season. He is so mad that he punches the plastic Elk Wally and forces a hapless security guard (John Candy) to take him on all the rides. However, first one and then another car appeared, and the parking lot was full before you knew it. However, we managed to get into the Cape legitimately (unlike the Griswolds) and toured the base sticky and tired. Trying to take in a serious talking Neil Armstrong animatronic with hands waving about, a Mission Control mock-up and the facts of science proved to be a bit daunting on an hour's sleep or so sat upright! The bus tour of the Vehicle Assembly Building and launch pads proved exciting and a bit more relaxing.

Later, we got a room at Patrick AFB in the Officer's Quarters and rested! We spruced up a little, showered, got something to eat at the Officer's Club, and went to bed.

Patrick has quite a long history stretching back to World War II. With the advent of war with Japan and Germany in December 1941, PBY Catalina and Mariner Seaplanes, based at this facility, held anti-submarine patrols along the coast of Eastern Florida. These seaplanes had a role in the search for the infamous Flight 19, when five TBM Avenger torpedo bombers from the Naval Air Station Fort Lauderdale went missing whilst on a routine training mission on the 5th of December 1945. When the flight failed to return, a search and rescue mission was launched, which included two PBY Mariner Seaplanes from Banana River NAS (Banana River was taken over by the Air Force in 1948 and renamed Patrick). Not only did Flight 19 disappear, but one of these search aircraft too. The theory was that a stray spark might have ignited aviation fumes, which caused the aircraft to explode. More 'way out' ideas includes abduction by aliens or other factors associated with the Bermuda Triangle. A more straightforward explanation may be that Flight 19 may have become disorientated and run out of fuel due to a compass malfunction, thinking that East was West or some such scenario. But a compass malfunction on all of the aircraft? Referencing 'Close Encounters' again, their aircraft appeared in the Sonoran Desert, thousands of miles away, in pristine condition in 1977 in the fictional motion picture.

We went to Disney Parks from Patrick AFB, and I enquired about the job, but they were taking only a few people on as staff at this point. This was disappointing, so we headed to Epcot,' The World of Imagination, and the 'World Showcase'. The Showcase is set around a large lake, with various countries displayed in their own individual little section—Japanese

Dancers, 'German' men in Lederhosen and wenches carrying beer. In the British area, there included more wenches, but also a pub mock-up and a red telephone box. Also a very jolly policeman wandering around with the iconic helmet and not so iconic truncheon in the sense it could bash your head. I could do this, I thought to myself (be a cast member, not bash someones head in.)

We enjoyed the Mexico showcase because they sprayed a mist, which was cooling in the humid Florida heat. It was dark, and a volcano appeared to be spewing lava in the background with some semi-seditious market going on like a Pirates of The Caribbean scene. You were able, of course, to buy something at the market. It was an enjoyable distraction.

The Giant Epcot Golf Ball was good, if not a little creaky on the ride cars, with visions of the future of jet packs and flying cars. Some of the animatronics were a little creaky, too and jerky at the time. I am sure I spotted a gesticulating Neil Armstrong again or someone like him, but was forwarned and ready for him this time and not so tired. It must have been his day off because the language was less technical but fun, and more in the spirit of 'New Worlds To Come' and a 'Magical Future' vibe. The passage through history was the most colourful thing and quite detailed. We spent a good week or more in Florida and came back somewhat refreshed.

Chapter 42

Space A-England Bound
Giant Boot Laces and Fish and Chips

I was staying at the Cabin in the late eighties, and we decided to take a trip back to England in January 1989, so we drove up to my sister Josie's house in Doylestown, Pennsylvania, a friendly and quiet town but quite a distance from Philadelphia to call it the suburbs. We hoped to get a flight from the nearby McGuire air force base in New Jersey. We drove up I-81 again, the now well traversed route that passes through East Tennessee, Virginia, West Virginia, and Maryland into Pennsylvania.

There are always many peculiar or interesting place names along American roads. Whenever we drove on I-81, I was always curious about the reason behind the 'Hungry Mother State Park' name in Virginia. Apparently, a group of settlers was attacked by a group of American Indians along the New River, just south of the park, and only a handful survived, including a mother and her daughter who were taken prisoner but ultimately escaped and wandered through the wilderness alone eating berries to survive, but close to starvation. The little girl was found and rescued. The only words she could utter were 'hungry mother', and the little girl led the searchers back to Molly (her mother), but it was too late, and she collapsed and died at the foot of a mountain. Today it is known as 'Molly's Knob' and the nearby stream is called 'Hungry Mother Creek'. A sad story and quite possibly true. It is one of those places you would like to stop and visit but always need more time as you are always rushing through, onwards, towards another destination.

Something closer to home occurred on the Interstate near Marion, Virginia. A road traffic accident on the interstate took the life of a distant female relative of Dad and, ultimately myself. The two newlyweds were heading north as the husband had to return north to the Navy Base in Norfolk, Virginia, as he was serving in the military. Somehow he had hit the central median and toppled over, and both inside the car were killed. Some years before, she had expressed a desire to meet Dad 'Uncle Jim the pilot', as she had heard about his exploits and association with England. A very sad and unnecessary event.

We passed very close to the Gettysburg Civil War Battle site but again did not stop as we were hurrying to see the family and try to get out 'Space A' from McGuire or perhaps even the C-5 transport base in Dover, Delaware.

Gettysburg would be of further interest to the family as brother Roland became friends and later married the former wife of the director of the 1993 Motion Picture 'Gettysburg' and later followed up 'Gods and Generals'-Ronald Maxwell, which starred Martin Sheen and many other well-known stars. They still attend the various functions that centre around the film, usually at Gettysburg and have met some of the celebrities involved.

We arrived in Doylestown, which still hosted a 'Woolworths' store at the time where you could buy anything from tennis balls to coffee and a danish at the counter. A vision of America more akin to Walt Disney's 'Main Street USA', devoid of the big box stores and malls, which were outside and a fair distance away. There is a place for malls and massive shops, but they take away from the 'mom and pop' hardware stores, butchers, fruit and vegetable markets, and other local businesses. A case of too much convenience and people unwilling to source items out in individual businesses and make an effort to keep the little guy alive. Even the big stores are under pressure from the likes of Amazon and other online outlets that are taking over. Hopefully, there will be a return to community shopping, where the food, for instance, is usually of better quality.

We stayed at Mcguire AFB for the day. Dad and I walked around the base and strayed on the tarmac apron where a number of visiting F16 fighter jets were housed and were stopped by a couple of MPs (Military Police) to ask what we were doing. We wore civilian clothes, so perhaps we aroused suspicion and thought we might try to take the fighters out for a spin or had nefarious intentions. Of course, some officials are more eager than others, and when they saw Dad's ID and mine, they just waved us on, and we stuck to the roads around the base.

Dad visited the Class VI store to buy some Jim Beam whisky to take back to England. I believe it is called Class VI because alcohol is not considered an 'essential item' and therefore comes lower than items like clothing in Class II. The odd thing is that coming in just above 'Class V' is ammo, missiles, bullets, detonators, fuses and so on! I would have thought that as this was the military, these items would come close to the top class or at least a little higher up. It would be a good idea if we did not stock up on ammo today at Class V as we would be trying to get a flight out as a Category 4 and might cause some raised eyebrows at the security checkpoint!. These items, of course, were restricted materials. Dad purchased the booze, and we decided to return to Doylestown to see my sister and family and take a break to see the marine life at the Philadelphia Aquarium. After all, there was no air life going on, as we could still not get a flight out, and we were getting tired of the plastic seats in the terminal-you could only stay so long in the Officer's Club. Before this, we visited the commissary and purchased some goodies for ourselves and the family; these included a giant bag of popcorn and some extra large Little Debbie Oatmeal cakes with white goo inside; these things, I think, are pure sugar but went great with coffee if you were craving something sweet. We decided to try Dover AFB the next day. Still, the base was also crowded with active duty personnel, so we drove back to McGuire and stayed overnight as there was a flight going out to the Azores the next day and a connecting flight via C-141 to Mildenhall and good old Suffolk in England. We made the flight out okay and were again winging our way across the Atlantic.

The 'United States Forces Azores' is based at Lajes Field and is a transit center for Atlantic Operations. It could also be used as an evacuation point for Europeans and those from Africa. It is composed of nine volcanic Islands but does have picturesque sandy beaches and hot springs to enjoy, but we needed more time but didn't have it to explore properly. There was little open on the base as it was a Sunday, and we went over to the Bowling Alley to rustle up a cheeseburger, though we had cheese and crackers still from the McGuire shopping trip. Staying in a basic hotel off base the night, I had a small plastic coffee cup with me and placed it down on the table to visit the bathroom. When I came out 10 minutes later, a cockroach was at the bottom of the cup. Still can't quite figure out how it had climbed up the shiny surface and deposited itself at the bottom; it must have been attracted to the sugar residue in the cup. Safe to say, we sat at the table munching cheese and crackers with one eye open for any other local invaders and did not sleep well.

The next day we discovered that we were not flying on a C-141 but KC-135 refuelling tanker that would be refuelling a fighter halfway up to England in the Northern Atlantic. It was an exciting trip, and we were asked if we would like to view the operation. The crew member is known as the boom operator and sits at a small observation window at the rear. The umbilical cord is fed to a point in the middle of the aircraft, and said operator is careful not to spill any or resist the urge to tap it on the side to get the last drop as you might do with expensive gas for a car! There was a lot of equipment, and we had to lie down in a tight squeeze to watch the operation, which was fascinating. No hiccups or spilt fuel. We arrived in one piece at Mildenhall and bought candy bars and coffee at the vending machines upstairs in the terminal. Later we caught the train to Victoria and then a coach to Heathrow, where Mum would pick us up. At Heathrow, Dad picked up a gift basket and 'Heathrow Bear' for her; although separated, they were usually on good terms, especially as the years passed. Jean (Mum) had also worked at Heathrow in the Health Unit for some years, and we were going to go 'airside' to say hello, but there was no one around she knew. In response to our gifts, she bought us a meal near Uxbridge, and we went and chatted with Uncle Stan and family in Hillingdon before heading back to her house near Bath, where she was living at the time.

The Semington village was part of old England and the vibe it gave was the old world, trying to fuse with the modern. Watching a more senior fellow cycling near Christmas, with trouser clips and returning from the local town of Melksham to the village with a box of 'Dairy Milk chocolates' strapped to the back of the bike with bungee cords (probably for his wife) was refreshing.

I decided to dust off my old mountain bike and take a ride into the country. Dad said he would come along too, but his mode of transport was a fold-up small-wheeled city gents bike that I thought might not make it all the way. The bike looked like something John Steed (Patrick Macnee) would ride for a lark in the British espionage fantasy programme, The Avengers. The destination was the historic city of Bath which lay about 16 miles away if we followed the canal all the way from our village of Semington in Wiltshire. Bath lies in the county of Somerset (the northern edge). Dad said he would ride part of the way and see me off. We set out on our way.

We had to manoeuvre a pedestrian swing bridge to proceed over the canal to get to the opposite bank to the towpath, and it required both of us to do it like a pit crew from Jason and the Argonauts with ropes. This part of the canal wasn't paved, and Dad, on his city gents bike, was finding it hard going with the many ruts and was bouncing up and down. Even I was having difficulty with my mountain bike.

I had proceeded under a road bridge which dipped down and created a blind spot. If a furiously fast cyclist was coming the other way and you met under this bridge, you might have a collision. I was just ahead of Dad after passing under the bridge, and guess what? A furiously fast cyclist was coming the other way, and before I could say anything, he and Dad collided, and

Dad became unseated and crashed off. He was okay, with a few minor cuts and bruises, but the twit on the bike kept going.

Dad decided to return home after that, but seeing he was okay and him telling me to go on, I cycled on through some magnificent countryside. The towpath became paved after Bradford-On-Avon, and it was easier going and less ache in the posterior. Through a wooded valley, I noticed a mansion and, due to a local newspaper article, recognized it as belonging to Jane Seymour, the actress. I toyed with the idea of stopping by for tea, but I decided to pedal on as she was only an acquaintance from Sweetcroft days. Ironically, she used to pass our house walking or in her little MG sports car before becoming famous, and now I was passing on a bike with much less money than her.

Along the path were several very pretty little tea gardens that offered treats like tea and scones with strawberry jam. I did not partake, as I had sandwiches in the backpack. Most of these were closed anyway because it was winter. I crossed the mighty Dundas Aqueduct, which carries the Kennet and Avon Canal over the River Avon. It was designed by John Rennie between 1797 and 1801. It is made of Bath Stone and has ornate carvings in the rococo style. A colony of bats lives under the structure, and any work done has to be mindful of them. I would not like to come here at night and would have to be returning later on; I could imagine a black flowing cape greeting me halfway in the semi-darkness! I proceeded on and parked the bike on the edge of town and walked passed the many Georgian houses with their creamy complexions. Then went over the Poultney Bridge, which is quite beautiful and is one of only four in the world with shops that span its length on both sides. I imagine much like the medieval London Bridge, but this one is made of stone. It was designed in 1769 by Robert Adam. As this was a quick trip, I whistled past the Grand Cathedral and Roman Baths and sat down to have my coffee and packed lunch, which consisted of a scotch egg, slightly squashed with my exertions but still quite delicious for a hungry traveller.

On one occasion in the past (I had done a lot of cycling on this route), I lost control going over one of the bridges and smashed into some hedges at speed, almost going down an embankment to the railway track and having a visit with the fast trains to London. Not realising I had some deep cuts on my face and a scar (which remains on my nose today), I walked around Bath and went shopping. My visage must have looked like Frankenstein's monster on day release, as some shop assistants were a little wary. I could not find a bathroom with a mirror.

Back to the present, I bought some sausages from a shop displaying hundreds of sausages from different counties and towns. I decided on the Cumberland and Somerset variety and then returned to the canal, sausages and postcards bought on the bridge packed on my back. On the way back, I passed a guy of about the same age on a racing bike, and he decided he wanted to race and passed me in a frenetic fashion. About 100ft ahead of me, something flew out of his backpack, and in his need for speed, he decided not to return for it. It turns out it was his deodorant spray, and he decided to abandon the fragrance as it is more weight and he might lose an advantage over me. I did not try to catch up and returned very tired, hopefully smelling better than him. It was a 30-40 mile round trip, but I surprisingly made good time and made it home in under ninety minutes from where I had parked my bike next to the canal. Mum and Dad were waiting. Dad was okay with a couple of plasters, one on his head, but no lasting damage. Mum made a pleasant dinner, and we sat around chatting about the day's events-cycling can be a demanding sport!

We also chatted about an incident a few years before when Dad and brother Frank were at the local Wiltshire Spar Shop. Dad had a penchant for bargains and, on one occasion, was at the local shop. While picking up some milk, he spied a box advertising 'Giant Boot Laces'. As Dad had a problem with his right ankle after dropping into Germany on Guy Fawkes Day in 1944 unannounced and twisting said ankle, he often wore high-top basketball-type shoes, as they supported his foot better than always wearing dress shoes. The thing was, these laces were bright purple. Still, thinking they were a bargain in any case, Dad picked them up and at eye level started stretching them! Whilst being watched by the assistant with suspicion, who was becoming somewhat agitated. "Children have to eat those"! she exclaimed in a Wiltshire accent. It suddenly dawned upon Dad what was happening as Frank had also tried to tell him whilst starting to fall about laughing, much to the clerk's chagrin! He chucked the box down and bought '100 purple 7-inch liquorice boot laces' there and then on the spot. Dad was somewhat old school and wasn't used to the sometimes whimsical and odd ways of British sweet advertising. I was at home and surprised to see an entire box of purple sweets on the counter. It must be a surprise party. I had just come out of a dream and still thought I was possibly asleep in Willy Wonka's Chocolate Factory? Dad had trouble living this down for a while, but when the story was told in the company of Uncle Albert, Albert came up with his own incident about shoe shopping to alleviate Dad's embarrassment. Albert also had his own 'Fish and Chips' saga that went on for a while!

We took a trip to see Albert in the West Country (Lyme Regis) and went on a hunt for the first evening to find the perfect fish and chip shop in a small seaside resort called Beer, not too far away. Albert's son-in-law thought we were mad to go out at twilight to search for a fish and chip shop in the middle of nowhere that might or might not still be there. But these were war veterans, so we were not averse to some adventure in the English countryside along winding country lanes. On a couple of the arteries, you had to back up half a mile to give way to oncoming traffic; if it was your turn or the other driver was a brick and would not move back, as the road was about 8 feet wide. We found the little village with its pretty seaside villas and pleasing picturesque cliffs, but the fabled fish shop was closed, and we had to settle for sandwiches back home. Having seen no car traffic on the way back, I thought somehow we had gone through a time warp and were possibly in the 1690s. I wondered if I had any pens/pencils or paper to hand to write down my experiences or explain perhaps to a bemused local with words and diagrams to try to prove we were not witches.

Anyway, back in Lyme, Uncle Albert regaled us with a story about him and Aunt Peggy, his wife when they had gone on a shopping expedition to Exeter. Sometimes Albert gets a little distracted with Peg, and the last thing he did was put on his shoes, grab the car keys and bundle into the car in slight and light confusion. He was hunting for new shoes this time, so they decided to visit a shoe shop in town. It turned out that Albert had put on a very similar but slightly different shade of light brown brogue shoe at home on each foot. He sat down and slipped off his footwear while the shop assistant bought another pair of soft brown shoes, but one was the wrong size. She could only find the one, and he tried this on, but she said she would look for the other one in the shoe dungeon. Some other shoes of a similar size and colour also lay not too far away, and they got mixed up even further. He took it off and found that he had 3+ shoes of differing shades, and on return, the assistant wasn't sure if he had either lost a shoe, come in with only one, or stolen one of theirs. She was a little flustered and apologized to Albert that she could not find the match to the one he liked whilst they hunted for his lost shoe. Albert then realized what had happened after close examination in better light and tried to explain, but I'm not sure if he was believed. She smiled and waved as they left with a vague look in her eyes and perhaps thinking about looking for some other type of employment that didn't involve shoes. Albert also had spied on another fish and chip shop whilst in town, and we would try to visit this one a couple of years later after he committed it to memory. Unfortunately, it was a fair distance, so we padded it out with a visit to a donkey sanctuary with his daughter. Turns out it had closed, so we grabbed some pub food with about 100 students waiting to be served; the fish was pleasant enough, but this was strike two on the perfect fish and chip search.

On the subject of the fish and chips, on our trips to the base at Mildenhall, we would always try to stop at a shop in Baldock in Hertfordshire, as it was a tradition for the past 25 years.

Baldock is a reasonably pretty market town in a flat part of the country. The establishment changed hands a couple of times, and it was not quite as good as it was at the beginning of Space A travel adventures, but it was always a staple layover, leaving or returning the country from the base.

The thought of the fried goodness when you passed Baldock for the next visit was a draw. We always seemed to park next to a mass of local taxis; I never quite understood how there were so many places to go in this remote little town, but it makes me hungry even now when the name 'Baldock' is mentioned. You called always tell too if you were getting close to the town, as off the A1 it turns into the country again and then (at the time) a little roundabout at which you made a left turn and went past the Wolford Tights Factory, which displayed some shapely legs on advertisement hoardings in varying shades of ladies tights, which changed through the years.

Travelling to RAF /USAF Mildenhall always invited some adventure or other. On one occasion it even got so foggy, that Dad had to get out with a torch to lead the way down a dark country road, as it appeared the fog lights weren't working on our car we had at the time.

Chapter 43

West Country Spirits
and We Are The Men In Black

The village of Semington, near Bath, where the family lived, was again to play a part in the supernatural occurrences the family had had.

We all visited the 'Crop Circles' that became a big deal in the early 1990s in the County of Wiltshire. People are still arguing about what it all meant, and I believe that many were elaborate art forms or hoaxes, perhaps not all. There happened to be a meeting on the subject and a village hall near Bath, a sort of a 'UFO' conference for believers and people who 'sit on the fence'. In the 1960s, UFO sightings occurred near the town of Warminster (and the strange object became known as the Warminster Thing!)

The meeting was organised mainly by the local GWR Radio station, as one of their presenters was very interested in the subject and held discussions and invited 'experts' on his radio show. My brother Frank and I decided to dress up for the occasion, wearing dark blue two-piece suits, though I think mine was primarily black. We went to the hall, listened politely to the talk and passed the time of day with a few people after having a cup of tea and a sticky bun. It was all very English. A few days later, the discussion of Crop Circles etc, came up again on the radio and a meeting review of the talk in the hall. The presenter and a few people calling in had remarked on people with American accents wearing dark suits having attended the meeting. It added further to the mystery, were these The Men In Black or even CIA spying, trying to uncover what the Brits' were researching; I don't know? Doris from Devizes thought we must have been The Men In Black!

In 1995, Dad, myself and Mum were at the unlikely spot in the British supermarket Tesco car park, just outside the parochial little town of Trowbridge in Wiltshire, only a few miles away from the house. I liked the post office there as you could seem to send any size package or letter without the fuss of measuring it to the nearest quark, or making sure that it will fit through the size of a slot no bigger than the width of a Poundland sandwich as happens today. Who has a door slot that small in the world? I once sold some crutches on eBay, no questions asked, no measuring and at a reasonable price which made my day. The private computer corporate mind has taken over.

Anyway, back to the car park. We had just finished shopping and loading the car, and Mum, Dad, and my brother were staring at something darting between the clouds at high altitude that had caught their attention suddenly to look upwards. I must confess I had an eyesight problem then and couldn't see it myself. They said it appeared rounded, small and silver and moved in a controlled way, stopped suddenly and went back into the clouds. Unlike birds that don't usually move in such a rigid pattern, they can change direction suddenly, especially in flocks, but this was different, and this moved very fast. Then there were two and a moment later, three, moving in the same darting pattern between the clouds and the blue of a long-ago summer day. Drones were not a feature then; these things were high up -maybe 10,000 feet or more. I would have thought it an unexplained anomaly, but later, in news reports from Mexico and South America, hundreds of people reported the same thing. The early video was shown on the many early unexplained mystery programmes just starting to become famous as a genre. We shrugged our shoulders and left Tesco in a slight daze.

Come to think of it as I write this, I remember a British video of a crop circle in Wiltshire, England, and a small silver object moving about the fields in an odd pattern. Were they linked and making the crop circles? Who knows?

In 1992, Roland would be in England and visited the flight simulators in Bournemouth while getting some time in jet training. He stayed with Mum, and I was there too. A day later, going to see a friend near Bath, and on the A350 main road towards Trowbridge, there was a guy with a guitar and beard, dressed in hippie style, travelling attire, walking in the center of the highway, according to Roland. He looked back in the car mirror and said he 'lost sight of him'; it was dark, and he forgot about it and proceeded to Bath and saw him no more. In 1995, Roland again visited England and came to Semington again. This time, he borrowed my little sports car and made the same trip to Bath to meet up with a friend at the pub. On his way back, low and behold, the same thing happened. The man with the same guitar and disheveled looks was walking in the middle of the A350, virtually down the road's center line. When Roland got back to the house, he felt the guy was in trouble and might be hit by a car, so he thought about calling the police to make them aware of the fellow and maybe offer some assistance. It was not in Roland's nature at that point to think this might have a supernatural angle, though he had felt and seen some odd things in the past. It was only when I reminded him of the incident 4 years before that it twigged, and thinking about it said the guy was virtually in the same place! Some kind of replay of events that happened long before in the past, perhaps; had he been knocked down and killed and was still looking for somewhere to play his guitar or a long forgotten gig he was never to headline?

Chapter 44

Florida Trips and Hiking Adventures

I was working in London in 1999, but my contract ended. I was looking around for something to do, having recently acquired a History degree at Westminster University in London. I thought I might teach history at one point, but the thought of controlling a classroom of kids just put me off. I had never really liked school anyway. I enjoyed the more open and relaxed university environment later in life, and school was sometimes the 180-degree opposite of that; you just wanted to get out of there in the summer and all school holidays. Later, I became a freelance voice actor; this can be hazardous to your wallet when the work is slow, but also rewarding.

Things changed somewhat at the American School in London, but there was always the pier pressure-school wasn't always the best place to learn. The teachers were all very professional and erudite and embraced the Anglo American lifestyle. I had won a scholarship to go here, but the fees were still relatively high. Sometimes US and European companies would pay their employees' sons' or daughters' fees to attend. It was very international, with Japanese and Arab students as well. The School was very ornate, having been the seat of Lord Hillingdon for many years. It was, in effect, a Georgian mansion with Romanesque columns and ornate Rococo styling. A great atmosphere to learn, like a castle (and it now reminds me of Hogwarts in the Harry Potter series), especially if I had been older and wiser. Girls and tennis were more interesting to me.

I wanted to become a professional tennis player as mentioned, but I had started too late, I believe, and it never panned out. It would have been nice to teach as a pro in Florida and live the life. Anyway, my girlfriend and I at the time were wandering around London and happened upon a bookshop in the Strand that was having a sale. She picked up a bunch of postcards, including a few vast 8 x10" size movie stills from the X Files TV series, which was popular then. One particular example was the stars Gillian Anderson and David Duchovny walking in a fog. Fun to keep, I suppose, as I had seen a few episodes. Recently, I had been at the family house and noticed a prize draw and creative contest associated with Great Ormond Hospital in a glossy magazine: a two-week trip to Florida with £1000 pounds spending money. At university, I'd completed a minor in photography. The creative element of the contest required you to take pictures of London sites or people. The characters and landmarks photographed were to be used on British Airways in their flight Magazine, and money from the promotion was to be given to the Great Ormond Street Hospital as well there was also the separate element of the competition that was pure luck, and you just had to send a postcard! Well, I thought, I'll send the oversized 8 x10 postcard from the X Files off for a laugh to the draw, which was to be picked from amongst the photography entrants. Two weeks after sending it, I found out I'd won by a white envelope dropped on the floor! The trip included £1000 spending money and unrestricted access to all the Disney Parks. Then you would stay at a luxury hotel in St Petersburg (St Pete's Beach) the following week. The hotel was the Don Cesar, where F. Scott Fitzgerald had once stayed and written in one of the guest suites.

I took Mum, Frank and his girlfriend, the intention was to meet up with Dad, who would travel down to Florida with his friend, and this would be a family reunion; Mum had not seen Dad for three years. We stayed at the Floridian Hotel near the parks, which was pleasant. The staff I described as 'Gatsbys' all wore that style of dress from the 1920s', rounded caps (newsboy style) and knickerbocker trousers, even when emptying the rubbish bins. Maybe I could become a 'Gatsby' for awhile and bum around. The central court at the hotel was impressive, and upstairs you could ride to the parks directly from the hotel. The photography element was good, as I had appeared in a magazine in a semi-professional capacity, but it never really panned out further, except for selling a few stock photographs in the future and making a side income. The promotions lady said she would do some work for me on that score, but I heard no more and didn't push myself in the photography world.

We enjoyed the MGM Studio experience, and one particular ride where you are on some kind of space station and the calming female voice is directing you to space pods or whatever. Not unlike you are in the movie 2001: A Space Odyssey with the lady who walks a 360-degree course around the spaceship. Suddenly there is an alarm; the violent alien recently captured from a planet for research purposes and put in quarantine for some rogue experiments has escaped and is rampant aboard our vessel. You hear screams, and it all goes dark, then hearing something behind you, you feel drips and hot breathing on your neck, and another scream! Finally, the alien is recaptured, with goodness knows how many fatalities and the calming lady returns and directs you to your pod again. While waiting in line for the ride, a rather unattractive man was making out heavily with a very attractive blond lady, which became a little too much enjoyment on his part. Mum later said she should instead have taken her chances with the alien in his place. I thought it was part of the ride experience.

We visited all the parks gratis and later drove to St Petersburg to stay at the 'Don' and meet up with Dad. He would come with our 'Tennessee Aunt Gladys' (we also had an English Aunt Gladys), who was quite the character. She had a place next to Dad at the cabin and worked as the manager in the general store in Maryville for a while. She also had at her house a shotgun and said if she had known people were encroaching on the cabin land, she would have gone up there with said shotgun and run them off (as she put it)-I have no doubt she would have. Dad showed up with his friend (who Mum got on with ok, for peace's sake), but unfortunately, Gladys was not along on the trip. She wasn't talking to Ruby, (the friend dad had come with) as they had some kind of feud. One of her Glady's sons was a preacher and a nice guy. Another worked at the prestigious Maryville College as a Professor of History; he knew Shakespeare's works very well and was no slouch. Dad showed up with the big Chrysler Newport, not unlike the local Mafia boss arriving at the 'Don' Cesar, and we had a good time together. Dad was dressed in a suit and tipped the porter well; they may have thought it was Ronald Reagan out and about. One day we all went on an excursion from St Petes' on a party boat and had free beer for the duration whilst watching dolphins and relaxing, Mum and Dad enjoyed it, and I caught some good photographs of them both. We did some of the touristy stuff as you do. We all played miniature golf and had some tasty meals at the hotel.

Somebody suggested we drive to Cape Canaveral and take the tour, which we did, and this time, we did not have to sleep in the car park. I also caught up with my old friend, the animatronic of Neil Armstrong, or it may have been Buzz Aldrin this time?! He looked a little slower and tired.

It may get humid and hot in Florida, but you can't help but usually have a good time in the sun. If you had to take a regular job, it might not be all smiles, but it is like that everywhere, unless you are a party boat skipper? It all had to end, but I decided to travel back with Dad to Tennessee and perhaps do some hiking in the mountains. But I could tell Dad was not quite feeling himself, so we took it easy and stayed in a hotel on the drive back to Tennessee. I stayed at the cabin, and Dad stayed at Ruby's house.

At the time, the cabin did not have a flushing toilet, and there was only one of those portable affairs in which you have to put a 'corrosive' blue liquid into the bowl. The first order of the day was to go to a camping store and purchase the mesmerizingly beautiful blue liquid! All very different from the luxury at the Don Cesar 5-Star Resort. I enjoyed the simplicity of cabin life again, and being some distance from people on either side of the property. A lot of work needed to be done, but one had to overlook that and get on with it. Dad was a collector and had a lot of antiques, it was a little like the Indiana Jones warehouse, and you didn't know what to expect. He had many receivers and transceivers (On which, as a ham radio operator, you could also send out communications) and thousands of radio tubes. He even had a big old unit from the 1950s' in the bright red shed at the back of the cabin with a 'DANGER HIGH VOLTAGE' sign attached to it.

My Mother said he had the same thing in his shack outside with the Ham Radio set-up in the 1960s-DANGER HIGH VOLTAGE and a cage to contain it. She was always worried the kids would go out and try to play with it.

Later in the Spring, I started some hiking adventures and traversed the highest peaks, including Mount Leconte. I had heard stories of wildmen or even 'bigfoot/skunk ape' creatures in the mountains, but this stretches credulity. Even in it did exist, the far North West of the United States or the wastes of Canada would be the place for it. Fontana Lake and the large dam structure lie on the park's southern edges. A cousin of mine, Judy, had said her friends were fishing, and something spooked them with loud grunting noises one night near the lake. They knew what wild hogs and bears sounded like and were old hands at being in the wilderness. This was different from your average tourist spooked by something in the woods. Large, dark shapes have been seen on the park's southern edge and elsewhere. I even had an eerie feeling around the cabin on some nights. With all the uncertainty in the world and talk of parallel dimensions, I do not dismiss the possibilities of unknown bipeds and feral people in those strange yet beautiful mountains. As mentioned, the temperature is at least 20 degrees cooler, usually at the higher elevations, and even in May, there can be a thin layer of snow or snow in patches. LeConte has some cabins whereby you can stay. You have oil lamps if one has to 'visit the wilderness' at night and bunk beds- very rustic. Also, a central lodge area where you are served breakfast in the morning before your hike down to the trailhead the next day.

I walked up the Alum Cave trail, the easiest way up the mountain. Alum Bluffs are just an overhang of rock, whereby the softer rock is worn away, thus creating the 'cave' appearance. There are a few narrow ledges on the way up, and it is about a 10-mile round trip. Some lovely views from the top, of course. Dad had walked up here with British cousin Gary (Uncle Frank's son) when he stayed at the cabin in the early 1980s. On the way back (I had left early in the morning), I met a girl near the car park who asked me how far it was to the top. I advised her she would probably not return before dark and not to go, but she thanked me and carried on-"oh; I can make it", she said- good luck, thought I.

I heard stories of a group of college friends who had gone up into the mountains off-season and planned to stay overnight in one of the cabins. They were all settling down in the cabin, on their bunk beds (about six of them), just chatting and getting ready to sleep, when one of the group pricked up his ears. Faint at first but becoming louder, something on the outside approached. It paced around and made low growls. To them, it sounded like a biped and not a bear (bears would usually be hibernating). They all went quiet, and suddenly there was a significant cracking noise; all eyes turned to the main door, which was apparently literally bowing in under tremendous pressure. After a minute, it stopped and whatever it was moved away. They swore they were not drinking or taking any drugs. Needless to say, they packed up in the early morning and went back down the mountain in a hurry and out of the hills? I never encountered Bigfoot, but I don't doubt there may be people living wild off the trails. You venture off the track for half a mile, and perhaps the area hasn't had human footfall for 100 years or so?

When the family were on a road trip in the United States in the 1960s, they visited the scenic Kings Canyon National Park in California and stopped for a picnic amongst the giant sequoia trees in a lonely location; there were fewer visitors in those days, and they had the place to themselves. It was getting relatively late in the day, and they didn't want to be there at night. There were granite boulders, but the treeline was close, with a small lake just beyond. The canopy of trees enclosed them, apart from one gap, whereby you could see the mountains in the distance. They had just set up all the picnic gear when suddenly they heard a 'CRACK' somewhere in the trees a little farther away. Again, another crack of twigs under footfall (or maybe pawful).

Dad was spooked and quietly told everyone to move slowly back to the car while he and Mum packed the gear/picnic things before they ate! She was a little more fearless and slightly rebuked Dad for scaring the crap out of everyone. He was pretty serious, though. Mum thought it might be animals, but Dad was thinking in terms of a more malevolent human presence. As they drove out from the picnic grounds, four small faces in the back seat turned hesitantly and with trepidation out of the rear window to see if anything was trying to catch up with them and perhaps grab the car. It was time to get to the motel and grab something for diner elsewhere! One of the younger ones, Frank, would later say he was sure that something was 'looking at them' from behind the trees, hiding and occasionally peeping out. He felt it acted and looked like a female, but it was hard to get a look at because of its stealthy motions. He only mentioned this later, and his musings were generally thought of as only the imaginings of a child; but who knows. He detailed the account, which was unusual for a young boy. Perhaps a feral person who lived in nature?

In November 1999, sister Jane and her children came down to Tennessee from Massachusetts by Greyhound bus, and we picked them up in Knoxville. We had a fun time visiting Gatlinburg and the mountains, Cades Cove. Also, the 'Green Acres Flea Market near the airport where you can buy anything from a snake to lonely store mannequins that have been replaced because of changing fashions, or the store had gone out of business. I have bought everything there, from an M16 replica BB Gun to Swedish stamps.

Also, along the 321 Highway to the mountains, they sometimes had a 'flea market' at the old outdoor drive-in movie theatre. One day a vendor was selling everything for 25 Cents, and I picked up a luxury set of new sheets and pillowcases and a rocking chair and heaven knows what else; a bargain. Sweet treats at these places include Tennessee Banana Cream Pie and the famous Moon Pies (sold elsewhere) that consist of chocolate covering a biscuit with some sort of marshmallow interior, slightly different from the cream of Little Debbies- I was becoming a connoisseur! We all went to the cabin and had coffee and a Moon Pie. Jesse (nephew) had bought some fireworks, sold in massive warehouses off the side of the road the size of Walmart in certain counties in Tennessee.

Some counties and jurisdictions in the State do not allow them, but they were easier to buy than in Massachusetts and places north. It was a Sunday, and Jesse let a couple off in the front driveway. Dad came up with his usual observations and, off the cuff and said, "The neighbours might not like you letting them off today, especially as it's a Sunday, son; wait until you get back to Massachusettes, and you can blow them up there"- BANG, BANG and SPARKLE, BANG. We all were deciding what to do and said we were drinking too much coffee deciding what to do. Five minutes later, we decided to go out and eat somewhere. I said, "Let's have another coffee before we go," Dad perked up and said, "Well, sure, that's a good idea". Jesse let off some more fireworks outside while we sat on the couch sipping our coffee. Later that week, they needed a ride to the bus station, and Dad took them in the big old gold Chrysler Newport to the Greyhound Bus Depot. This was a quaint way to travel.

I came to Charleston, South Carolina, in 1982 from Mildenhall, England, with Dad, and we took a 'Trailways bus' to Tennessee from Charleston. Charleston was lovely, very different from East Anglia and Suffolk in character which had a different charm. But it was named after an English Monarch, Charles II-originally 'Charles Town' and founded by the English in 1670. It has a subtropical climate, and I remember the palm trees and angel oaks, big sprawling trees with twisting and fascinating branches on and near the base. Downtown, the beautiful southern Antebellum houses are located and mostly privately owned. It is not unlike Savannah in Georgia in style and atmosphere. The beaches are also sandy and picturesque.

The bus driver came over with the announcement- 'No smoking in the back of the bus, it's a federal law'! Somewhere near Columbia, South Carolina, the bus pulled up at the side of the road in town, and the Sheriff came aboard-he looked a little like Sheriff Buford T. Justice (Jackie Gleason) from Smoky and The Bandit, the comedy film starring Burt Reynolds. I thought someone may have been smoking at the back of the bus, but it turns out there was a fugitive aboard! "Come on Billy, you don't want to hold these nice people up on this, fine bright day, better come with me". Sheriff Justice was relaxed and didn't pull a gun to his credit (low-level crime?) A thin unkempt youth from the back of the bus meekly slouched towards the front and went with him without struggle. And that was it; we were on our way again to Knoxville. At the cabin, I enjoyed burning at the back of the property, hunting logs, and kindling for the fireplace later in early autumn. Dad even saved some of our toys from Sweetcroft Lane in England after it became derelict, and I think to be reminded of when we were all younger.
Casper, the friendly ghost from a 1970s board game, waved to the mountains as he sat on the shelf in the kitchen.

Squatters had entered the house at Sweetcroft Lane in London in 1981 after we had left and were still transporting belongings from the home. Not only had they lived in the place, but also had taken items, including my sister's Barbie dolls, which probably would be worth a fortune now and heaven knows what else. Maybe they needed a place to stay, but thievery was uncalled for. The local police were useless; as they say, they had 'rights'; what about our rights to our possessions? It was a good thing some things had been removed all ready. Some louts that came in for the park had even taken all the copper out from the kitchen, where Mum and Nan used to cook, and we would play board games. Even announcing themselves in spray paint as the 'Hillingdon Court Park Casuals'. Not a very nice ending for the old house.

11 Sweetcroft Lane would be demolished in 1983. Dad stayed there awhile to try and maintain it, but it was sold, and the proceeds split. We didn't get the actual value of what the

place was worth, and the developers made millions from the land. The local Hillingdon Council were of no help and wanted to condemn it because of the subsidence. Jobsworths (English slang for petty officials who like to hold to rules that sometimes defy common sense) had already harassed Dad for the beam at the back of the property, but at the time, thought he was either KGB or CIA, these local officials having small capacity in reality, like a 1970-80s version of Mr Bean in local politics, they held off trying to have it removed. The beam was disassembled, and Dad got a storage unit for the various sections and bits and pieces left at the house we had not taken, or the squatters had not pillaged. On the edge of the wilderness area that bordered the park, we knew a family of teachers, one a chemistry professor. They called Mum one day out of the blue at the new house and asked if she knew about the removal of the considerable maple, pine and oak trees at the back. One day they were there; the next, they had been chopped down for clearance for private housing development by the local council; so much for tree preservation when money talks. The end of an era.

Chapter 45

Changing Course

Uncle Stan's wife (Aunt Eileen) had died in later in 1999, and he and his sons were planning a trip to see Dave and Josie (sister) plus Dad in July 2000. The plan was to fly to Charlotte in North Carolina, see him in Tennessee, stay there for a few days and drive out to California on a road trip with the hire car they had. Then the bombshell came. We heard the news in early July. Dad had passed away in Tennessee very unexpectedly, so trip arrangements changed, of course, and we had to coordinate to fly out to Tennessee, and Mum had to make some arrangements for Dad's services. Stan had been good friends with Dad starting in the 1950s after he had met Mum. They had got on well, each enjoying the English pubs and get-togethers the family had with my other English relatives and their friends. The immediate family was spread out at this time in 2000, with half living in Europe and half based in the United States.

We all made it, some arriving on different days and staying at the various hotels in the area, then later at Darnell's house in the country; Darnell was a niece of Dad, and her family welcomed us to their home. It was too small at the cabin, and it also needed some work on the interior and exterior. Mum took over the proceedings from the friend Dad was living with outside of Knoxville, and the funeral was held in mid-July. It was solemn, but an honour guard of military personnel played TAPS and fired a salute overhead. Next, they presented Mum with the carefully rolled-up Stars and Stripes to conclude the service. We retired to Darnells', and she provided a nice meal and some of us were invited to stay there. The next day, we all met at the cabin, looked at pictures, and reminisced about the past, but we were still deciding what to do with the property. For the moment, we have decided to keep it and hopefully come and take turns to restore and look after it. None of us lived in Tennessee full-time. Stan and his family arrived a few days later and paid their respects. Stanley was reticent to go to the gravesite, I guess wanting to think of Dad the way he was, alive and full of life.

Stan and crew enjoyed Tennessee as best they could and took a liking to the country's way of life -very different to the environs of London and quite the culture shock. They decided to continue the road trip, and when everyone had departed, I was left by myself and decided whether to risk taking Dad's small Mercury car all the way across the country when I was not sure of its reliability in taking it on the trip. Well, I thought, why not? Dad always enjoyed adventures, so I decided to plow ahead. So with a model of a B-17 in the middle of the dash as a mascot, I drove on. Stan and family had left two days previously, and it would take about four days to get there, and I was unlikely to catch them up. I gave the car a quick service and hoped for the best for my trip out west. Near Memphis, which lies on the western fringe of Tennessee, I stopped at a Mcdonald's (for the coffee!). Before getting back on the interstate, I saw the split signs, one for Little Rock, Arkansaw and one for Knoxville back East, and after a moment of thought, decided to press on like the old pioneers; of course, they did not have McDonald's to save them back in the day.

I-40 is a well travelled interstate, and as you didn't veer off into the backcountry or desert along the way, you would be ok - or get a tow back to Tennessee in the event of trouble! The first night near Little Rock, Arkansaw, I decided to sleep it out at a rest stop to save on cash for the trip and expenses. Perhaps a foolish move in hindsight.

A couple of weeks later, in August, a girl looking to fulfil her dreams by driving to California in a VW camper van had stopped at a remote rest area off I-40 near Morrilton, Arkansaw. Kristine Laurite had travelled down from New Jersey and was a seasoned, free-spirited traveller searching for adventure. She had stopped to let out her dogs and get some exercise in the careless way you might, with thoughts of the road and the trivialities of where you might eat next in your mind. Three years earlier, a truck driver had been shot in this cab at the same stop, but she did not know of this. Two truckers noticed two dogs wandering around the next day, looking lost and confused. They called the police, and later that day, Kristine's naked body was found; she had been stabbed ferociously and repeatedly in the neck, raped and left near a small pond used for cattle a few hundred yards away.

After placing billboards along the side of the road and using forensic technology, they finally caught up with the guy, who, it turns out, was a serial murderer, but mysteriously died in prison.

The dogs were later adopted by Kristine's aunt, who had taken them to a local beauty parlour/hairdresser one day. Everything was fine until the aunt tilted her head back for her hair to be washed, and the dogs started barking frantically at this, perhaps something chilling in their memories being recalled? I had been one rest stop away from this place at roughly the same time. The perpetrator had not limited himself to women, also killing one man. The remote rest stop has now been sealed off and closed.

Passing Oklahoma City, where I had stopped with Dad in the years before at the Air Force Base, I stopped for the night, this time in a hotel room in Shamrock, Texas. It is famous for having Route 66 bisect it and a Blarney Stone, which you can apparently kiss, but I knew nothing about this. But there is also a Pioneer museum you can visit. I walked through a car park to a cafe where I ate an indifferent ham and cheese sandwich with coffee. It seemed a long way to walk anywhere this day in the heat. I have that bland sandwich, and the Route 66 crossroads stuck in my mind when I thought of Shamrock. Guess I just hit the wrong spots, which sometimes happens and alters one's perception of a place, either good or bad, or just indifferent as the cheese sandwich. I was making good time but did not catch up with Stan and family. There were many people in the car, including Eddie's son, Curtis, and it must have been a carload. It reminded me of the Wacky Races and the Bulletproof Bomb

#7 hanging out the windows and churning up dust, but they had a big old Buick Car, so there was sufficient room. My uncle had said to come with them, but it would have been tight in there. As it was, it was tight in the 'Mercury Capsule', like a NASA pioneer with the uncertainty of arriving at my destination intact. I traversed through the spectacular desert of New Mexico and Arizona to Flagstaff, Arizona. It has the highest elevation in the state and is often 20-30 degrees cooler than in the canyons and valleys of the central and southern part of the state, and Phoenix, where the boys had stayed with Dad in 1973 and buried the coins.

I recall in the Smoky Mountains, Mt LeConte is about 6600 ft in elevation. One July, I walked up the summit to the top, and I was surprised at how the weather had become about 20-30 degrees cooler than the 90 degrees below. It is always advisable to take some sort of jacket or poncho-it rains a lot up there, and the weather can change very quickly; I was wearing shorts when I reached the cabins at the summit of Leconte; heck, it was still 60 degrees!

I drove up the aptly named 'Mars Hill' in Flagstaff and quickly drove around, again in a hurry to view the Lowell observatory. It was founded in 1894, making it one of the earliest fixed-site telescopes in the United States, by the astronomer Percival Lowell and his family. From here, another astronomer, Clive Tombaugh, found and mapped the planet Pluto in 1930. A few other telescopes form part of the complex, dotted around the area. Declared a national monument in 1965, Time Magazine considered the site one of the world's '100 Most Important Places' in 2011. I stayed near Kingman, Arizona, in a big hotel with a plumbing problem and average rooms. There was dampness on the walls, but I looked around and saw no bugs, so I went to sleep and rested relatively well. I stopped at a local truck stop the following day that was actually quite pleasant, full of everything you probably didn't need and more; it was fascinating. I resisted the urge to buy a scorpion paperweight in some kind of a red resin deal and moved along. The coffee and sticky Danish pastry were tasty, though.

Actually, driving along here 5 years later with my sister Josie (the house of which in Pleasanton, California was my final destination), and stopping at the exact same truck stop to get fuel and let Josie's new little Dachshund dog stretch his paws, I remembered that same scorpion in resin; it might have even been the exact same one. I drove on and Made it to Needles, the border crossing and noticed the flashing lights of the checkpoint for fruit and vegetables being brought into California. I had two gigantic green watermelons for some reason, but this time was waved on with a smile. At least I did not have to get out and stand there and eat all my oranges like Dad had done years before. Perhaps he thought I was a fellow alien, bringing in more 'pods' so that the Earth people clones might mutate from these melons and make the takeover of human bodies on Earth easier; I did not know and hell, it was California so anything might happen. I was in California and had not caught up with Stanley and the Gang. The car was performing very well, and no accidents. Perhaps it was Dad's spirit riding with me and the mascot of his former plane sitting on the dashboard that helped, I like to think so.

On through past Bakersfield, I went. It was still scrub desert until mid-way when I even went through an area that grew roses and oranges. I-40 had ended, and I took route 99 instead of I-5, which was likely quicker. 99 travels through the central valley in California and was traversed in fiction by the Joad family in John Steinbeck's The Grapes of Wrath and includes a town named Delhi-no curries for me, though at this time. Many little towns and people are trying to run small businesses along the route to attract tourists. I didn't stop, trying to make it to Pleasanton by dark. I hit route 205 and then 580 and finally stopped at an IHOP (International House of Pancakes) to call the house, as I just had a rough idea of how to get there.

I called the house (no Google Maps), and Josie's husband, Dave, met me. The little car was working fine, and I had not pushed the engine on the trip or used the air conditioner too much. I remember Dad making the statement about watching the fuel tank needle actually move as he sat there watching it go towards empty if he had it on in the car too long. His car was the big gold Chrysler Newport, and I was in the small gold Mercury. He guided me to the house, and I met up with the gang there.

Stan and his family had made it a day before and had stopped at a few places on the way, including Meteor Crater. 50,000 years ago, a meteorite, approximately 150 feet wide and weighing many tons, had crashed into the desert about 20 miles from Winslow, Arizona (presumably then, no one was 'standing on the corner' as in the Eagle's song 'Take It Easy' as they would have had a shock, but apparently no humans were living in the area at that time). It sped at 26000 MPH, creating a crater 700 feet deep and 2.4 miles in circumference. Rocks the size of small houses were thrown out onto the rim, and wildlife was devastated for miles around too. Eddie (my cousin) had wondered why they hadn't put a medium-sized house at the bottom for scale. They do have a small research shack, but this was tiny. The absolute scale of the whole thing is incredible. The Apollo astronauts had trained here in the 1960s for the upcoming moon missions. In the 1960s, Dad and the family had visited the spot on their trip West to California, and my sister Jane had nearly fallen into the crater when she lost her footing on the trail. A quick-thinking family member watching her grabbed her before anything terrible happened.

They had stopped briefly at the Grand Canyon and then detoured to Las Vegas, which took them in a different direction to I-40 at that point. They saw the lights in Vegas and took a walk but decided not to gamble. Probably a good idea; it is not called 'Lost Wages' for nothing! Dad was a reasonable Black Jack or 21 (Ving et un in French) player. Well, he did not lose on the occasions I was with him, but he had his share of losing streaks in the past, so he said.

On my stay in Las Vegas with Dad in the later 80s, he remarked that if we got lucky and won some big money, we would not make it too far out of Vegas without being accosted by men in shiny suits and hidden holsters. Vegas then was still, I think, pretty much under Mob control, and it was only starting to get the ginormous hotels, and the start of 'family friendly' attractions and glitz, recreations of New York and Egypt were still a little way off. Being Dad, I wasn't sure whether he was fully serious, but it made me think. We wouldn't have to worry about winning a Jackpot; we had paid our dues, or at least I had!

Dave's son 'Davey', when he was older, became a decent poker player, won some high amounts at tournaments, and became a meteorologist after being fascinated with tornadoes all his life. When Josie and her family had lived in Flemington, NJ, a small one had ripped by only about 300 feet from their tiny isolated Bungalow, it came on so quickly they hardly had time to retreat to the basement. No sirens came on, and they watched it approach from a fence half a mile away.

At the time in 2000, I had a rather expensive 'mini Dv' camcorder with me and took some footage of the desert and canyons as I watched a couple and then two lone girls walk into the desert with backpacks. It was a scorching hot late July in Arizona as I watched both groups from the car park venture off before zooming in as they appeared to have gone miles into the distance. I sat there having my lunch in surprise yet trepidation; I hoped they knew what they were doing. People do regularly go missing all the time in the US, either getting lost or foul play. In the recent books by David Paulides, a former policeman who has written about 'missing people', he says some of these disappearances are unexplainable. Even search dogs, with their formidable smelling skills, can suddenly lose the scent and just stop. UFOs or bigfoot, hey, I was not too far from Roswell and the famous 1947 supposed UFO crash. I packed up my watermelon slice and cheese sandwich and moved on. I had a relaxing stay in California with the family in Pleasanton, pondering recent events. I could tell Uncle Stanley was a little down, not his usual ebullient self, and there was sadness in the air. He had known Dad for nearly 50 years. I had just wanted to leave Tennessee for a while perhaps relax a spell.

Somewhere, there is a picture of my Great, Great Uncle (Holder from England) standing outside a saloon he part-owned in San Francisco along Market Street. I would love to find this. Market Street was (and still is) the main thoroughfare through the shopping and commercial district in town. But instead of modern shops like Virgin Records or The Gap, there were in its place dusty streets, saloons and settlers looking to find their fortune; it sounded great.

We did the usual tourist-type stuff, taking a trip to Los Angeles along Route 101, which runs along the whole West Coast of the USA, usually hugging the coast, as it is a very scenic trip. Stan always asked where he could see 'David Muscletoff' performing his life-saving duties in red shorts. He was thinking of David Hasslehoff, of Baywatch and Knight Rider fame. Dave H. was not on Life Guard duties along the coast when we were there. Also heading the cast of 'Terror at London Bridge', the film about Jack The Ripper's spirit on a murdering spree in Lake Havasu. I think I caught sight of him there with Dad, or was it David Muscletoff in a lower-budget production? We stayed near the Beach in Santa Monica and went to the famous theme park at Universal; Dave, Josie, and their Daughter Maria were along with us and were good company. They asked my uncle to go on this one particular theme park ride dedicated to the 1982 Film 'ET'. I can remember Stan sitting on a bike that was part of the ET, The Extra-Terrestrial Dark Ride, an unusual site. Waiting for it to depart, he was saying, 'What the f' is all this', or words to that effect, but not really up to date with this type of movie genre, but just taking it in his stride.
I think he would have been happier with a fag (cigarette) and beer sitting at a table with umbrella.

Perhaps it was this grizzled, British, amusing war veteran sitting astride this bike of make-believe with a plastic head of ET stuck at the front and him mumbling (Stan, not ET). And the ironic juxtaposition of real long-life experience versus Hollywood and the ET soundtrack just tickled me. It would have been the same with Dad, and having them both, there would have been interesting.

The next day we went to the beach and had a day swimming. Dave and Josie went to secure another hotel room while they did the hard work for a few hours. It turns out they had proceeded down this long hill in the mountains, started to smell the brake pad odour, and saw a little smoke at the back. For a non-4x4, regular saloon cars can struggle in the mountains; the car was fine, though, and they became 'unlost' and found pleasant rooms. We had an easy life at Santa Monica, swimming and eating chips (or having a smoke for those who got 'em'). Careful to take the butts to the proper receptacle, and those who smoked par took of roll-ups. Californians were quite anti-smoking before it became the fashion to be.

I went swimming with everybody and had a singlet on because I felt cold like the men of the 1920s. I was trying to tell my niece Maria not to go out too far, as she kept edging away, though not to a great distance, rip tides and all that. I heard the call of a man in red shorts- ¬"Dude, why are you wearing a shirt", ignoring that I was trying to advise my niece to come back a little closer to shore. It may have been 'Son of Muscletoff' in training. Otherwise, it was a fun swim. We went to a nightclub the last night, met a pleasant girl, and exchanged telephone numbers. When the place closed, I had a few drinks at the hotel and called it a night. When we returned to Northern California, we hung around in Pleasanton and went to the condominium swimming pool for swims and the hot tub at night. The houses were attractive and plastered on the outside with red adobe brick. We chatted about the old times, and the subject of ghosts came up again. Josie had not mentioned much about it, but after a Mexican meal at a local restaurant, we returned, had a few drinks, and started chatting a little more.

It turns out they had experiences in this place, their townhouse in Pleasanton of a perhaps paranormal nature. On one occasion, the two cats the family had stopped at the foot of the stairs and just stared at something with their paws outstretched and seemed mesmerised by shapes on the mid-landing step. Josie thought they were probably just looking at an insect. My sister looked, couldn't see anything, and then went up the stairs and felt a 'spider web sensation', as if one were moving through a barrier, then came out the other side, but there was nothing to be seen. But dismissed it as a strange anomaly or cobwebs she couldn't see, and perhaps this was the case. A week later, their son Davey (The Meteorologist) went into his bedroom to find crispy pretzels spread over the floor when none was in the house and no one had come into the house with them to snack on. A week before, Dave (brother-in-law) had witnessed a boy move into his bedroom and thought it was either his son or a friend. He went in to say hello, as you might, and to his astonishment, there wasn't anybody there or even in the house. Dave Senior did not believe in ghosts and figured the kid may have gone out the window? I looked in the room, the drop was much too high.

The strange goings-on were corroborated In a bizarre event when the family were going away for the day, and some neighbours had agreed to come in, feed Chips, the family collie and take him for walks. Josie and Dave had left, and the neighbours had decided to move a big bag of dog food to the kitchen, as it would be easier to feed Chips there instead of in the garage. After lifting the heavy bag into the kitchen, she returned quickly to the garage to retrieve Chips, who she had left outside to clean off because taking him out was a muddy affair, and it had been raining for most of the day. Upon her return, she told Josie and Dave the bag had 'shifted' to the bottom of the stairs about 10 feet away from the entrance to the Kitchen, which was open plan. Apparently, she was a little unnerved by this (I don't doubt it), and I don't think she ever returned for pet duties after that and just wanted to leave. The family from England did not mention anything of 'Spirits', but usually having a few beers occasionally may have set one too happy and relaxed to encounter ghosts. The ghosts may have been reticent to come out with Stan and the boys about.

There are two further instances where the same thing happened on separate occasions. The family sat in the living room, relaxing and watching a movie. Suddenly, a sound like a bowling ball startled them out of their tranquil repose...BANG

BANG! It was from the above bedroom, and everybody had thought the bookcase had fallen over. They went upstairs, expecting to find a room full of displaced and scattered books. To their surprise, everything appeared normal and in its place.

On the second occasion, taking a break from working on the cabin one summer in the early 2000s, we had booked tickets to fly to San Francisco and spend a week with the family. We all went out to attend my niece's graduation ceremonies at her high school and have a meal out later, except my brother Frank, who had decided to stay after feeling a little off colour. He said he was sitting there reading an article about the recent death of President Ronald Reagan. He set the newspaper down and quickly thought that all the talk of ghosts and the paranormal was likely imagination. Then all of a sudden, BANG BANG BANG, the same noise, which he said sounded like an industrial wrecking ball, occurred in the same bedroom upstairs! He was a little reticent to go up there or even pass the stairs, so he spent the remainder of the time in the kitchen with a cigarette! He later joked that it may have been that the 'ghost' was reading his mind and wanted to make itself known to him, as it occurred the moment he was thinking about the subject.
Frank was relieved when someone picked him up, and we all went out to eat.

Mum had said she was unpacking her belongings and placed some new shoes near the bed. When she came back into the room- the, the shoes were now absolutely in the middle of the bed, equally- distant to the edges. We thought my niece Maria might have been playing around, but she swore she hadn't. It was as if something was playing or informing people of its presence.

Josie said that some years before, a boy had died when the car he was in spun out of control and hid at the edge of the stone canal system, which ran directly behind the property and actually entered the canal, its final resting place. Could this have something to do with the haunting?

Perhaps, from that ill-advised séance using an ouji board from years before at Sweetcroft, was something following one or all of us around? Josie also said that odd bones were dug up by the family dog, Chips, and an arrowhead was found in the communal gardens. Pleasanton has an extensive stone canal system, primarily used if in flood from mountain run-off. But I also don't discount earthquake activity, causing some strange events or even perceptions, and spookily cracks appeared in the condominium, though not to the same degree as Sweetcroft Lane back in England. But no one else in the area had ghosts as far as she knew, and she had a few friends she chatted to in the neighbourhood. California has its share of fault lines and possible seismic activity, found more here than in many other states.

Chapter 46

Beyond 2000

After Dad passed away in 2000, we decided to come over from the UK, perhaps once or twice a year, clean up the cabin, and have some remodeling work done. I could work away from home as a freelance voice actor and do a little work at the cabin or from the hotel room. The family had decided as a unit to keep the cabin and contribute as they could.

Mum, my brother and I came over in May 2001, and after sorting out all the state's legal requirements, we decided to start work. We requested the help of Dad's relatives and had a new roof put on, as the tin one was starting to deteriorate quite rapidly. Ellis was a cousin and roofer; with the help of his 'gang', the work was done quite rapidly and well. He later recounted his stories of Dad and was in awe at his trips overseas.

One day, on his visits back to Tennessee, he said Dad squinted his eyes and furrowed his brow as if he was trying to listen to something close or was in the process of getting mad, and I apparently had the same 'look'-perhaps like The Man With No Name-Clint Eastwood!

This tickled Mum.

Ellis was also recently in a race to become Sheriff of Blount County (In which we were sitting)and told my Mother he came in second. Mum didn't quite understand and politely said coming second in a race wasn't all that bad, and it was good for his health as she wanted to lose some weight too...she thought he was running a road race, like a marathon! Ellis was quite a stout guy at the time. Oh, English mannerisms, but the misunderstanding was cleared up...I think? We returned, and they all sat on the porch on a break one day. It looked like a scene out of Gettysburg, waiting at the old Fuller place to get their next set of orders whilst resting their bones. They finished it and did a good job. Also, a new floor was put in, and to finish it, we hired a floor buffer with various levels of grit to get a smooth finish. We then would lacquer it. The trouble was that the vibration was that of a pneumatic drill, and Frank felt it in his hands for about three months afterwards. I was lucky, as I was the porch man. We replaced some of the wood and white picket fencing around the outside, which took longer than I thought and involved much sanding and cutting on a workbench. I am not a carpenter, and I had to 'learn on the job' as it were, consulting books or the internet, which was not as informative with sites like YouTube in their infancy. Blood and sweat were spilt as it was sweltering and humid in the summer and early spring of East Tennessee.

I disliked the small black mosquitoes and gnats, which plagued us. You could not help sweating to some degree, and body heat would attract them more ferociously, and they appeared to mock you. Sanding wood takes more time than anything, let me tell you.

Mum designed and fitted shelving to go around the fireplace and put in a marble surround to the fireplace, and at that time was in her 60s. She was quite erudite and could turn her hand to many pursuits. It was too bad when she was young when she wanted to fly that the opportunities were not available in England in her youth. She was busy with six kids when she got to the States. In 2002 we returned and continued work, spending more time outside on the brush and weeds.

It was a lot of work, and the bugs were back. We bought and delivered a vast flat-pack set of boxes containing a metal shed which included about 3000 screws and bolts, many tiny. It took Frank and myself a few days to build, with oft-confusing instructions and sometimes relying on our own intuition to finish it. We were again harried by the biting gnats and pesky mosquitoes. We also tore down the remains of a back porch with mallets and sheer force. It was too rotted to save. The cabin sits mid-level on a large hill, and below is a creek which may contain water moccasins, and we were cautious not to get attacked. Much of the land had been untouched, and snakes had been seen locally. On our first trip, we hired a local couple to remove some rubbish and unwanted bits at the cabin. The husband said he had seen many snake skins around, whereby the snake sheds its skin periodically, as when the snake grows, its skin does not, and it has to clear itself of the unwanted layer. This process also gets rid of parasites. The gentleman and lady were both strong mountain people, but the man's wife was seemingly doing much of the heavy lifting. It was a bit like a Benny Hill scene. Dad also had a lot of radio equipment and old radio tubes stored. One of these old receiver radios I sold on eBay and had shipped to Ohio. The fellow was happy with the purchase and was quite surprised to open up the back and find a full snakeskin wrapped around innards, which he left as a positive comment!

I unearthed a red salamander with black spots at the creek one day. The Smoky Mountains are known as the 'Salamander Capital of the World', and 24 species live here. The little critters are lungless and breathe through blood vessels in the skin and linings in the mouth. After showing him to the family, I put him back under the leaf litter where I found him.

I remember my Aunt Gladys in Tennessee relaying a story about some people on vacation in the mountains and stopping at a gas station and finding it was closed; they decided to just get out and stretch their legs whilst the kids ran about and played. During their play, they found an old abandoned Coke machine. The boy, thinking there might be some still left in the mechanism (the money slot was gummed up), stuck a hand up the machine's innards and a moment later screamed out in pain! It turns out he was bitten severely by a family of Copperhead snakes who had made it their winter home. There is no reason to doubt this story, as it was reported in the newspaper.

I was cautious when poking around old wood piles that might house a family of snakes, even in wintertime, as they may be hibernating. They hibernated (and were thankfully gone, and only the skin remained) when I sold one of Dad's radio receivers. The purchaser got a mild shock as mentioned (and not from the tubes or electronics inside) when opening up the back. Hence, a scenario like this is very real.

It was also interesting to see the remains of the old outhouse that used to sit back in the yard. Dad, at one point in the 1980s, had lit some newspaper to put down the hole in fear of black widows or brown recluse spiders being present around the 'bowl'. It turned out to be a hot day, and the wood of the outhouse caught fire, and the shack burnt to the ground. Fortunately, Dad installed a garden hose, and the fire was put out eventually. In dry, hot weather, it is very easy for the underbrush, needles, dried small twigs, etc, to catch light and creep towards denser vegetation and leaves. One day the 'creep' occurred, and one had to quickly rake the scene. I see how fires in dry wooded areas start promptly and become uncontrollable in many instances. The cabin was shaping up after consecutive yearly visits. The local handyman in Walland installed fans and needed access to the loft. The loft had not been visited in years, and brother Roland had proceeded up there in plastic shopping bags on his head with two eye holes in fear of the many creepy crawlies that may be lurking about!

He was trying to find one of Dad's valuable radios, which we had trouble locating. It still not has been found. Christianity and church services are more well attended in Tennessee, the moral ethic much more observed, and the fellow who installed the fans was of the Baptist persuasion and the ones we encountered seemed pretty genuine. We found that the Baptist people helping us charged reasonable prices and were willing to 'step up to the plate' and, on the whole, were not the type of people to just pay lip service to the Christian ethic.

The work was hot and we carried on whilst there on this 'working holiday'.

Chapter 47

Ghosts Follow Us?

In 2003, following Dad's death and the various trips over, I had prepared the way for Frank, his girlfriend and our Mother, Jean, to stay. It was nearing my Mother's birthday, and in preparation, I had a cake made at the local Walmart store in Maryville. Usually, 'Mom' is the correct spelling for 'Mum' in the United States. I was fully expecting this to be the case when the lady came to use the icing for the lettering. In this instance, however, it was spelt in the English way, and I was pretty surprised. Had she heard an accent? Was it ESP?

The first unusual happening of the trip. I started hearing things before the family arrived and dozed on the couch one night. Rhythmical and instrumental, it was music! It sounded like 1940s radio tunes or the Glenn Miller Orchestra with trumpets and trombones playing. Very strange, who would be playing big band tunes in the neighbourhood? I had a vision of Glenn conducting with a big wand. There were indeed no radios playing or neighbours with their volumes turned up. It felt like it was in my ear. Was I just imagining it or putting random night sounds together. I tried to be rational and just brushed it off as an anomaly. It sounded as if it was in the back bedroom in the place where Dad used to have a small ham radio set up.

Dad had a beam set up on the hill at the back of the property. In the 1990s, however, whilst on a trip to England, opportunist metal cutters had come onto the property and cut up his radio tower. All that was left was a triangular section that looked like a launchpad (or sledge run) for the many V1 rockets that had hit London and Northern Europe from occupied France and Belgium! When the family came over, I did not tell them of the 'ghost radio' incident and again just brushed it off as possible imagination. My explanation to myself ranged from the metal fillings in my teeth causing some sort of antennae and projection effect tuning in to a local 'old-time' radio station to the granite rock surrounding the cabin having the same result or even storing the sounds.

We enjoyed a small party at the cabin on the night of 'Mum's' birthday (mystery cake eaten). We went to bed happy, some sleeping on couches because of the limited space or roll-out cots. The next night, my brother Frank and a friend mentioned the 'ghostly music' and wondered if anybody else had heard it- it turns out I was not alone. We then discussed it, and I reviewed the different scenarios, again. It turns out, however, that the friend had no metal in her teeth! Does the employment of good dentistry prove the existence of ghosts? We left it unsolved.

A year later, in 2004, at the cabin one night at about 1am, we heard a scratching at the door; this was the arrival of Polly- the Russian Blue stray who we took in as she appeared homeless. A beautiful and intelligent inquisitive cat, she took to us all, and a cat bed was bought for her sleeping pad. We took her to the vet and found out she had a form of cancer, but it was benign. This was winter time, and we went out at night collecting kindling, and firewood-it got cold in the cabin and was a necessity to light the fire and keep warm. We did have portable heaters, which caused it to be stuffy in the smallish space. Polly followed us everywhere and climbed trees to show off her prowess in our presence. We noticed that the cancer did not seem to inhibit her in any way. She tried to surprise the chipmunks that used to come to pop their heads out of the earth bank that formed the driveway, but they were usually too fast for her. A live-or-die version of whack-a-mole, but to our knowledge, she never caught one?

One night we had finished a winter barbecue on the porch, and most of us had gone in to get warm. Mum and Polly sat on the porch, and something caught the eye of the inquisitive cat. Mum followed her gaze, and she described a wind and fallen autumn leaves being kicked up by what can only be described as a 'black amorphous mass' that appeared darker than the night surrounding it. It seemed to emanate from the top of the hill, went through the pine trees, came ominously down to the drive (mid-way down the mountain), went further down the hill on the other side, and simply disappeared at the creek next to the road. The fact that Polly had followed it's track/path had convinced mum she was not dreaming or imagining it.

I came up with the explanation that it might be a 'mini tornado' or some such high wind event, but it was the wrong time of the year, and the night was still. Tornadoes usually occur in the Spring or early Summer. They are rarer in Tennessee than in the plains of the Midwest.'Tornado Alley', as it is known, is a place where humid and warm air from the region of the equator meets the cool and dry air from Canada.

I once went with Dad up for a hike in the local hills, and we observed several pine trees which had been twisted and shorn of their bark. We presumed a tornado had touched down briefly and returned to the sky (as my brother and dad had also seen), hopping over the hills in a short-lived dance of destruction. However, In a 20ft section of forest off the trail somewhere, natural and 'supernatural' entities might reside. I am sure science cannot explain everything as it's constantly evolving and of an anthropomorphic nature; we see everything from our own perspective and experience.

We spent Christmas at the cabin and decorated the huge pine tree next to the road with a large number of lights and ran a cable to the house, which disturbed a sleeping nest of the Cicada insects that make that iconical continual clicking noise most often heard in the summer in the United States and especially in the South. They spend up to 17 years underground in a larval or 'nymph' stage and emerge as a unit in one big flourish or synchronized event every 13-17 years. Their life span makes them the longest-lived insect as yet known! We hurriedly put the soil back over them to leave them in peace and wait for their hum next summer. I once had one land on me, and it stuck like glue with its sticky legs clinging to my shirt. They have huge eyes and wings and look reminiscent of something from the Jurassic period of Earth. Still, they were not biting insects and carefully removed him (or her) from my body. The winter of 2004 was often quite cold, and the temperatures in Tennessee can vary quite a bit, somewhat like the temperate climate of England-warm one day and cold and disturbed the next. In the mountains, of course, the temperature does decrease the higher the elevation, and there is usually a period of snow in the winter months. In the evenings, sometimes we would rent DVDs from Maryville as the TV reception could have been better, and we did not bother to put in cable or have a satellite dish.

In the late 1980s, Dad had a huge television set, which formed an integral part of the furniture with its large back for housing tubes. It was around Christmas time, but he could not get any sound from the set. I think it was still there. Mary Poppins was also playing on a local station, and he piped the soundtrack through a radio to the TV set. 'A Spoon Fall Of Sugar' sung by Julie Andrews reverberated through the valley.

However, with an attachable antenna to our tiny TV with DVD slot, we could sometimes tune into the local Knoxville TV stations, but often the signal would drop out. One night we watched the local news, and a segment came on about a man from East Tennessee who had gone out in the mountains by himself in frigid, below-freezing conditions and had fallen and broken his leg in the process. No one came to rescue him, and he had to spend the night with only his coat for comfort inside a tree hollow. A ranger found him by chance the next day and was airlifted out by helicopter. During the night, however, he had developed frostbite on his fingers. He had to have a couple of them amputated at the hospital. The news reporter quoted Mr 'Dimwitty' sure felt lucky he was found after going out for a short hike in the mountains in freezing conditions; he could have lost his life'.The television lost reception and went blank as the segment ended. We put on 'National Lampoon's Christmas Vacation' for some light entertainment to recover.

Overall, we all had a pleasant Christmas and went to Gatlinburg across the mountains for the New Year celebrations at a dinner and dance type affair. Gatlinburg has everything needed for the whim of the tourist and thrill seeker. Central to this is 'Dollywood' -a theme park owned by Dolly Parton, the famous country and western singer born in a shack but made good as a singer and later actress. It is done quite well, and the Christmas lights at Dollywood and the town are generally remarkably 'illuminating' and festive in season. One kind of parades through town looking at the various goodies on offer, from exotic doughnuts to earthquake rides with some clunky animatronics, an escaped gorilla for some reason in a box near a subway train and the requisite shaking of the ride car, or is it the set? The Ripley Believe it or Not is fun and randomly thought-provoking with the random shrunken head.

There is also 'Alcatraz East', which is a crime museum housing things like the serial killer Ted Bundy's Volkswagen Beetle to another serial killer's possessions, that of John Wayne Gacy, the former kid's clown performer and all-around creep. These include his paintings of clowns done whilst in prison and costumes, all very bizarre but ghoulishly fascinating. Further down the highway towards Sevierville and Knoxville is Pigeon Forge, home to bigger rides, go-kart tracks and cowboy boot shops. There are also the 'outlet stores' for discounted clothes and such, like in Knoxville and West Town Mall, which was generally more exclusive and employed classical piano players in the foyer.

The family left in January 2005 for the trip back to the UK, and I stayed at the cabin to work remotely and look after the place. It was a good idea to have someone stay there, as you could not expect the family in the local area to always be on guard. My brother Roland was in NJ, flying executive jets and teaching at a company called Flight Safety, and the girls were spread across the country. The rest were in Europe! I did not mind the isolation for the time being; there was also the cat Polly to consider, as she would have had to go to another home and was an orphan. Polly would want to go out in freezing temperatures and 'tap' when she tried to come back in, so I was awakened and, of course, let her back in every time...she took liberties but was as loyal as a dog.

The sound of the *phantom* radio that plays in your ear, periodically returned and is not solved to this day.

Chapter 48

Another Trip West

Five months later, my sister Josie came out for a visit, as her son Dave and daughter Maria were living in Oklahoma, and she was helping them with their second home. Maria was to give Josie a ride back to California on a road trip, but in the event she could not, it was decided I would take her back. I trusted the old Mercury again, but she was ageing. I had to leave Polly with the neighbours, and we proceeded on.

Somewhere just west of Memphis, it happened in good old Arkansaw. The car started to chug, steam and finally stop. Turns out the radiator had been struck by a stone from a passing truck which I heard go up under the car; I grimaced but thought we were ok. However, there was a small hole letting out all the water, allowing me only to travel a few miles down the road. I was lucky enough to make it to a truck stop and was about to call around for garages when an old local came around and asked what was wrong, I explained, and he said he could do it right then and there! I went with him to auto zone and bought the radiator, he fitted it, and we gave him a good tip. Amazingly, we were all fixed up and ready to proceed. He was a bit like an American version of Uncle Stan. There were 'ladies of the truck stop' hanging around and wondering what we were up to. Myself and the mechanic were a little oily and the worse for wear; They did not come over and ask us if we needed any help or could we lend them $50! We were off, and the car was fine the rest of the way. Along the route, we stopped at Santa Fe, New Mexico and had a coffee and salad in an adobe-style Mall; it was pleasant. Santa Fe has so much history, and I would have liked to stay and explore, but again time was an element, and we made our way back to I-40 and next stopped at Kingman, Arizona. Aboard was Josie's new Dachshund puppy, and we had to stop and give him some refreshments as well as ourselves. I spotted the truckstop I had stopped at 5 years before, and probably with Dad before that, and lo and behold found my scorpion in red resin! But this time, he had a mate next to him encased in some type of purple resin; we all need friends and 'purp' was his. Also, it was decided to stop at my old favourite, Lake Havusu and see Dad's and my old haunts and the bridge. It was about 110 degrees, and we had to carry Cody around with us, as the pavement was too hot for him to walk on. We did a quick tour of the bridge where I had had the experience with Dad years before and our car park sleeping quarters! We had something to eat, and we were off.

We finally got to I-5 (interstate 5) and saw something in the darkness about an hour after first joining the highway. It was a light that appeared along the side of the road, and I assumed it was a helicopter following the Interstate, perhaps a police helicopter that was monitoring traffic or similar. It made absolutely no noise, however, and it went across atop the traffic to my right, and I saw it make erratic manoeuvres in a field. It almost turned 360 degrees, and we concluded it was not a helicopter. It hopped about and appeared to have three white pulsating lights on either side of a wing-like structure. I wanted to stop, but Josie was nervous, so I kept going. It did this strange manoeuvre twice in a field, moving and changing direction quickly and seemingly acting like a gyrosphere in flight. I thought it was likely a test vehicle from Nasa's Ames Research facility in Oakland, California. Still, I was trying to understand why they were testing it near a busy road. We were close enough, between Coalinga and Los Banos. A drone?; but this was very early in the technology. Possibly it was of military origin out of control? We arrived safely in Pleasanton. Josie reported it, and we later discovered that I5 was a hotspot for UFOS. I have seen satellites and lights in the sky, but this was my only UFO sighting, and there were two of us.

Perhaps this and the other family experiences can be explained, but what's not to say the person next to you in the supermarket may be a ghost or alien, no one can be sure? At

least we had made it back without being abducted or breaking
down again.

Conclusion

I have written in these pages some of Dad and Mum's stories and my family's life experiences across both sides of the Atlantic. Sadly, we have had more time to reflect since this time without Mum and Dad. It has been an exciting ride, with people now living their own lives and hopefully having more adventures in the future. All I can say is live for the day, write some of your experiences down or record them on any medium to hand. All the paranormal events here are accurate and are open to interpretation. Research as much as you can (preferably keep your old history books, as Dad used to say, and learn history), and watch out when using Ouji Boards.

Epilogue

This concludes a condensed version of specific events and times in the life of the Fuller Family and, by extension, the Holder Family and friends and acquaintances. The first quarter concerns my Dad and his wartime experiences, as mentioned. I have included a snapshot of some of the main events and strange events in our evolving lives in the United States and England and the dichotomy of experience between the two involving people and places. Also included is some of the story of the ground and sea we inhabited and how that may have undoubtedly affected our lives and others. I have revisited old letters and newspaper reports and recollections by relatives and friends about the past. Dave Holder (nephew) and cousin Victoria Hoggart-Willis in England are still studying the genealogy records, hoping to unearth more. Dad's detailed writings and Mum's were written down word for word. Also, my recollections and chats with them and my uncles, aunts and cousins have been recorded here. Dad died in July 2000 and Mum in 2017, and we miss them for their kindness and wisdom and just being there as good friends, always willing to help out and provide shelter in good and bad times. Also, the many uncles, aunts, cousins, and friends have left the stage, but we had them around to interact with happily for a while somewhere in time.

References

1: The life of William Allen Fuller Geni.com

2: The Anvil To The Pulpit Tom Sexton Published 1906

3: Faribault County Register, Blue Earth, Minnesota February 25th 1958

4: British Executions Journal-Albert Pierepoint. Period in Office 1932-1956

5: The International Journal of Maritime History

6: The Air Force Times, April 16th 1958

7: San Antonio Express, February 10th 1960

8: Middlesex Advertiser and Gazette, May 30th 1968

9: Wally Herbert, Polar World Magazine

10: Alice Springs History: Encyclopedia Britannica

11: Guam Geography and History: Encyclopedia Britannica

12: Uxbridge Post (England January 26th 1977)

13: Unsolved Disappearances in The Great Smoky Mountains, Juanitta Baldwin and Ester Grubb

14: Bear Attacks: Smoky Mountain News

15: Arrow Air Incident; Simply Flying Magazine

16: Murder of Kristine Laurite, Medium.com

The End?